Third Edition
Solutions

Intermediate

Student's Book

Tim Falla   Paul A Davies

OXFORD
UNIVERSITY PRESS

Unit	A Vocabulary	B Grammar	C Vocabulary	D Grammar
I Introduction	**p4 Holidays** Tourist and visitor attractions (*aquarium, castle*, etc.) Holiday activities (*lie on the beach, hire a kayak*, etc.) **Grammar:** Past simple **Speaking:** Describing holidays	**p5 Present tense contrast** Dynamic and state verbs **Vocabulary:** Social activities (*meet friends in town*, etc.)	**p6 Adjectives** Adjectives describing feelings (*anxious, ashamed*, etc.) Adjectives describing personality (*flexible, honest*, etc.) -*ed* and -*ing* adjectives Negative prefixes (*un-, dis-, in-*, etc.) **Speaking:** Describing personality	**p7 Articles, *will* and *going to*** **Speaking:** Talking about plans for the future

Unit	A Vocabulary	B Grammar	C Listening	D Grammar
1 Generations	**p8 Ages and stages** Stages of life (*be an adult, be a centenarian*, etc.) Life events (*be born, be brought up*, etc.) **Speaking:** Talking about your family and background **Recycle:** Past simple 🎧 Teens talking about their families and backgrounds	**p10 Past tense contrast** Past simple, past continuous and past perfect	**p11 Family tensions** **Strategy:** Listening for tone of voice **Vocabulary:** Attitude adjectives (*accusing*, etc.) **Speaking:** What causes family arguments? 🎧 Teens talking about family tensions and arguments	**p12 *used to*** Contrast with *be / get used to*

p18 Exam Skills Trainer 1 • **Reading:** Multiple matching • **Listening:** Multiple choice • **Use of English:** Multiple-choice cloze • **Speaking:** Role-play • **Writing:** A message

2 Leisure time	**p20 Love it or hate it** Activities and sports (*use social media, bake cakes*, etc.) *do, play* and *go* (*do ballet, play basketball, go cycling*, etc.) **Speaking:** Sports and leisure quiz **Recycle:** Present simple and adverbs of frequency 🎧 Teens talk about things they hate	**p22 Present perfect and past simple contrast** **Speaking:** Talking about experiences	**p23 Eating out** **Strategy:** Identifying the context of a dialogue **Vocabulary:** Food dishes (*curry, pie, pudding*, etc.) **Vocabulary:** Phrases to describe experiences (*a bit special*, etc.) 🎧 Two teens talk about eating out	**p24 Present perfect simple and continuous** Use of English
3 The human body	**p30 Parts of the body** Parts of the body (*ankle, bottom, brain*, etc.) Treatments (*antibiotics, bandage*, etc.) Accidents and injuries (*bang your head, break a bone*, etc.) **Speaking:** Human body quiz **Speaking:** Role-play: at the doctor's **Recycle:** Present perfect and past simple 🎧 At the doctor's	**p32 Speculating and predicting** *will, may, might, could* First conditional **Speaking:** Making predictions about your future	**p33 The body's limits** **Strategy:** Listening for numbers, dates and measurements **Vocabulary:** Large numbers, fractions, percentages, ratios, etc. 🎧 The limits of human survival	**p34 Future continuous and future perfect** **Vocabulary:** Future time expressions (*in 100 years time*, etc.) **Key phrases:** Asking for and offering a response (*What's your view?*, etc.)

p40 Exam Skills Trainer 2 • **Reading:** Missing sentences • **Listening:** Multiple matching • **Use of English:** Open cloze • **Speaking:** Picture comparison and discussion

4 Home	**p42 Describing houses and homes** Types of home (*bungalow, thatched cottage*, etc.) Parts of a house and garden (*attic, balcony*, etc.) Describing houses and rooms (*beautifully restored*, etc.) **Key phrases:** Describing where you live (*It's a flat*, etc.) **Recycle:** *some, any, much, many* 🎧 An estate agent shows someone round a house 🎧 Teens describe their homes	**p44 Comparison** Comparative and superlative adjectives and adverbs, double comparatives Use of English	**p45 Young and homeless** **Strategy:** Recognising paraphrases of simple verbs in a recording **Strategy:** Register and context **Speaking:** Discussing homelessness 🎧 People talking about aspects of homelessness	**p46 Imaginary situations** Second conditional *I wish … , If only …*
5 Technology	**p52 Computing** Digital activities (*download music*, etc.) Computing verbs (*comment, forward*, etc.) Computing: useful collocations (*empty the trash*, etc.) **Speaking:** Technology quiz **Speaking:** Instructions for digital technology **Recycle:** Imperatives 🎧 Calling a helpline	**p54 Quantifiers** *every one of* and *none of* Use of English	**p55 Navigation nightmare** **Strategy:** Distinguishing fact from opinion **Vocabulary:** Gadgets (*camcorder, digital radio*, etc.) **Key phrases:** Expressing opinions (*I believe that …*, etc.) 🎧 A dialogue about an amusing satnav mistake 🎧 Problems with gadgets	**p56 Modals in the past** Modal verbs Use of English

p62 Exam Skills Trainer 3 • **Reading:** Multiple choice • **Listening:** True or false • **Use of English:** Key word transformations • **Speaking:** Picture comparison and discussion

6 High flyers	**p64 Describing character** Describing character: nouns (*ambition, cheerfulness*, etc.) Describing character: adjectives (*ambitious, cheerful*, etc.) Personal qualities (*show lots of initiative*, etc.) **Recycle:** Comparison 🎧 People discussing qualities needed for jobs	**p66 Defining relative clauses** Omitting object pronouns Use of English	**p67 Nellie Bly** **Strategy:** Listening for linking words and phrases Use of English **Speaking:** Discussing Nellie Bly's achievements 🎧 Nellie Bly's round-the-world trip	**p68 Non-defining relative clauses** Use of English
7 Artists	**p74 Talking about the arts** Art forms (*ballet, cartoon*, etc.) Artists (*actor, composer*, etc.) Artistic activities (*act, carve*, etc.) Cultural activities (*went to a rock concert, read a novel*, etc.) **Recycle:** Articles 🎧 People talking about cultural events	**p76 The passive**	**p77 Poetry in motion** **Strategy:** Listening for implications and subtext **Speaking:** Discussing poetry 🎧 *The Lost Generation* 🎧 People talking about poetry	**p78 *have something done*** Reflexive pronouns

p84 Exam Skills Trainer 4 • **Reading:** True or false • **Listening:** Multiple choice • **Use of English:** Multiple-choice cloze • **Speaking:** Role-play • **Writing:** A book review

8 Messages	**p86 On the phone** **Key phrases:** Collocations: using a mobile phone (*listen to your voicemail, lose the signal*, etc.) **Key phrases:** Phrasal verbs: phoning (*get through, speak up*, etc.) **Speaking:** Talking about mobile phones **Recycle:** Phrasal verbs 🎧 Phone conversations	**p88 Reported speech** Pronouns, possessive adjectives and references to time and place in reported speech	**p89 Global network** **Strategy:** Listening for gist **Strategy:** Answering multiple-choice questions **Vocabulary:** Phrasal verbs (*work out, set off*, etc.) **Speaking:** Talking about problems and solutions 🎧 A radio programme about communication	**p90 Reported questions** 🎧 An extract from a film
9 Journeys	**p96 Travel and transport** Forms of transport (*aircraft, cable car*, etc.) Travel: places (*airport, buffet car*, etc.) **Speaking:** Discussing forms of transport **Speaking:** Travel role-plays **Recycle:** The passive 🎧 Dialogues about transport	**p98 Third conditional** Contracting *have* in spoken third conditional sentences	**p99 Travel solutions** **Strategy:** Identifying names and proper nouns **Strategy:** Identifying register **Vocabulary:** Travel collocations (*board a plane*, etc.) 🎧 Travel problems	**p100 Participle clauses**

p106 Exam Skills Trainer 5 • **Reading:** Multiple choice • **Listening:** Summary completion • **Use of English:** Word formation • **Speaking:** Photo comparison and discussion
p108 B2 Exam Skills Trainer 1 • **Reading:** Multiple matching • **Listening:** Multiple choice • **Use of English:** Word formation
p110 B2 Exam Skills Trainer 2 • **Reading:** Missing sentences • **Listening:** Multiple matching • **Use of English:** Multiple-choice cloze • **Speaking:** Interview

Culture Bank p112

1 Ethnic minorities in the UK 2 Tinseltown 3 British sporting events 4 Royal palaces
5 Benjamin Franklin 6 British public schools 7 Charles Dickens 8 Helen Keller 9 Victorian explorers

Vocabulary Builder p121   Grammar Builder and Reference p126
Extra speaking tasks p144
🎧 Listening

Word Skills	F Reading	G Speaking	H Writing
13 Phrasal verbs (1) Three-part phrasal verbs (*look up to, catch up with*, etc.) Dictionary work	**p14 Adolescence** How to handle your parents **Strategy:** Gapped-sentence tasks **Vocabulary:** Related nouns and adjectives **Key phrases:** Presenting your ideas	**p16 Role-play** **Strategy:** Preparing to speak **Vocabulary:** Exchange programmes **Grammar:** *should* and *ought to* for advice 🎧 Advice for an exchange student	**p17 A message** **Strategy:** Completing all parts of the task **Key phrases:** Polite requests
25 Compound nouns and adjectives Vocabulary: Sports venues: compound nouns Vocabulary: Compound adjectives 🎧 Students talk about school facilities	**p26 Field games** GPS challenge **Strategy:** Multiple-choice questions **Vocabulary:** Prepositions (*all along, beside*, etc.) **Vocabulary:** Adjectives (*addictive, boring*, etc.) **Key phrases:** Explaining preference	**p28 Stimulus-based discussion** **Strategy:** Using a range of phrases to express opinions **Vocabulary:** Adventure activities (*abseiling, bodyboarding*, etc.) **Key phrases:** Making and justifying a choice and rejecting other options (*I quite fancy*, etc.) **Key phrases:** Coming to an agreement 🎧 Choosing a leisure activity	**p29 A blog post** **Strategy:** Keeping within the word limit **Vocabulary:** School clubs (*art club, astronomy club*, etc.)
35 Word families Related nouns, adjectives and adverbs Vocabulary: Adjectives to describe feelings (*afraid, anxious*, etc.) Use of English	**p36 Body clock** Night and day **Strategy:** Matching questions with texts and paragraphs **Vocabulary:** Homonyms	**p38 Photo description** **Strategy:** Giving your description a structure **Key phrases:** Identifying people in photos (*the man in the red shirt, the girl with a ponytail*, etc.) **Key phrases:** Speculating about photos (*It looks like ...* , etc.) 🎧 Caring for your appearance	**p39 An opinion essay** **Strategy:** Structuring your essay and using appropriate language **Key phrases:** Introducing opinions, additional points, proposals and solutions, and conclusions
Writing: An opinion essay			
47 do, make, take Dictionary work Use of English	**p48 Alternative living** Alternative homes **Strategy:** Finding evidence in the text for your answers **Vocabulary:** Homes: compound nouns (*front door, housing estate*, etc.)	**p50 Photo comparison and discussion** **Strategy:** Developing your statements **Strategy:** Making time to think as you speak **Vocabulary:** In the house (*bedside table, bookcase*, etc.) **Key phrases:** Phrases for gaining time (*Let me see*, etc.) 🎧 The pros and cons of different types of accommodation	**p51 An email** **Strategy:** Appropriate language for informal emails and letters **Key phrases:** Beginning and ending a letter or email **Grammar:** *would rather, had better*
57 Adjective + preposition Dictionary work Use of English	**p58 Clever machines** Testing intelligence **Strategy:** Answering multiple-choice questions **Vocabulary:** Verb-noun collocations (*break a code*, etc.)	**p60 Photo comparison** **Strategy:** Using key phrases to compare and contrast photos **Vocabulary:** School subjects (*art, drama*, etc.) 🎧 Photo descriptions	**p61 An internet forum post** **Strategy:** Answering all the elements in a writing task **Grammar:** Concession clauses
Writing: An internet forum post			
69 Phrasal verbs (2) Separable and inseparable phrasal verbs (*work out, look after*, etc.) Dictionary work	**p70 #GIRLBOSS** Rags to riches **Strategy:** Answering gapped-sentence tasks **Vocabulary:** Verb + preposition combinations	**p72 Guided conversation** **Strategy:** Completing the task / Moving the conversation on **Grammar:** Indirect questions **Key phrases:** Indirect questions (*Could you tell me ... ?*, etc.) 🎧 A job interview with a hotel manager	**p73 A for and against essay** **Strategy:** Using rhetorical questions **Grammar:** Preparatory *it*
79 Indefinite pronouns Indefinite pronouns in offers and requests Vocabulary: Musical genres (*blues, classical*, etc.) Vocabulary: Aspects of music (*beat, chorus*, etc.)	**p80 Graffiti's softer side** Granny graffiti **Strategy:** Answering multiple-choice questions **Vocabulary:** In the street (*statue, stop sign*, etc.) **Key phrases:** Arguing your point (*In my opinion, As I see it*, etc.)	**p82 Photo comparison and role-play** **Strategy:** Using a variety of expressions **Strategy:** Phrases for introducing negative preferences **Key phrases:** Talking about likes and dislikes **Vocabulary:** Cultural events and shows 🎧 Choosing a show or cultural event 🎧 Talking about cultural events	**p83 Article: a book review** **Strategy:** Choosing a title for an article **Strategy:** Structuring your article **Key phrases:** Describing stories (*There are lots of twists and turns, It's a real page-turner*, etc.)
91 Verb patterns: reporting verbs Vocabulary: Reporting verbs (*admit, persuade*, etc.)	**p92 A novel idea** A different type of phone book **Strategy:** Answering gapped-sentence tasks **Vocabulary:** Reading matter (*biographies*, etc.) **Vocabulary:** Digital formats (*blogs, e-books*, etc.) **Vocabulary:** Compound nouns (*leisure time*, etc.)	**p94 Photo description** **Strategy:** Engaging with the person you are speaking to **Key phrases:** Speculating (*It could be (that) ...* , etc.) 🎧 Talking about emergency phone calls	**p95 A narrative** **Strategy:** Using adverbs and tenses **Key phrases:** Narrative time expressions (*a while back*, etc.) **Grammar:** Verbs with two objects
01 Verb patterns *stop, remember*, etc.	**p102 Miscalculations** Disastrous mistakes! **Strategy:** Matching more than one text with a question **Vocabulary:** Units of measurement	**p104 Guided conversation** **Strategy:** Using your preparation time **Strategy:** Interacting appropriately **Vocabulary:** Holiday activities and accommodation 🎧 Planning a holiday	**p105 A formal letter** **Strategy:** Starting and finishing a formal letter **Strategy:** Using paragraphs **Vocabulary:** Formal words and phrases

Writing: A formal letter of complaint
Speaking: Picture-based long turn / Topic discussion • Writing: An opinion essay
Writing: A report

I Introduction

IA Vocabulary

Holidays

I can talk about what I did in the school holidays.

1 SPEAKING Work in pairs. Look at the photo and ask and answer the questions.

1. Do you know where it is?
2. Have you been there? If so, did you have a good time?
3. If you haven't been there, would you like to go? Why? / Why not?

2 🎧1.02 Read and listen to the dialogue. Who had a more enjoyable holiday: Dave or Anna?

Dave	Hi, Anna. Did you have a good holiday?
Anna	Yes, it was great, thanks.
Dave	What did you get up to?
Anna	I went on a city break with my family.
Dave	Abroad?
Anna	No, we went to London.
Dave	Cool. Did you have a good time?
Anna	Yes, we visited the Tower of London and lots of museums. We went on a boat trip too.
Dave	Did you go on the London Eye?
Anna	No, it was too expensive. How was your holiday?
Dave	Not bad. But I didn't do much. We didn't go away. I hung out with my friends. We went to a music festival and we visited a theme park a couple of times.
Anna	Sounds fun.
Dave	Yes, it was OK. Just a shame the holidays weren't longer!

3 VOCABULARY Look at the list of tourist attractions below. Then underline three more in the dialogue in exercise 2. How many more can you think of?

Tourist and visitor attractions aquarium castle cathedral church harbour market monument mosque museum national park old town opera house palace park restaurant ruins shopping district square statue theatre tower wildlife park

➡ **Vocabulary Builder** Describing visitor attractions: page 121

4 SPEAKING Work in pairs. Ask and answer about the tourist attractions in exercise 3.

> Do you like visiting museums?

> Yes, I do. / No, I don't.

> Why? / Why not?

5 VOCABULARY Complete the holiday activities with the words below.

the beach   beach volleyball   a bike
a bike ride   cards   an excursion   kayaking
a castle   mountain biking   a theme park

Holiday activities
visit a museum / ¹_____ / a cathedral / ²_____
go shopping / swimming / cycling / ³_____ / abseiling / ⁴_____
go for a walk / for ⁵_____ / on ⁶_____ / on a boat trip
hire ⁷_____ / a kayak / a car / a boat
play table tennis / ⁸_____ / ⁹_____ / board games
lie on ¹⁰_____   eat out   buy souvenirs   sunbathe

6 Find three of the holiday activities from exercise 5 in the dialogue in exercise 2.

> **LEARN THIS!** Past simple
>
> The past simple of regular verbs ends in *-ed*.
>
> We use *did / didn't* for the negative and interrogative forms of all verbs except *be*. We do not use *did / didn't* with modal verbs (*can, must,* etc.).
>
> *I didn't go away in the summer.*
>
> *Did you visit your cousins? Yes, I did. / No, I didn't.*

7 Read the Learn this! box. In the dialogue in exercise 2, underline examples of the following past simple forms:

1. regular affirmative
2. irregular affirmative
3. negative
4. interrogative

➡ **Grammar Builder I.1** page 126

8 SPEAKING Work in pairs. Ask and answer about the holiday activities in exercise 5. Find three that you both did in the school holidays, and three that neither of you did. Give extra information in your answers where possible.

> Did you go mountain biking?

> No, I didn't. Did you?

> Yes, I did. I went mountain biking with my family near Bristol.

9 SPEAKING Work in pairs. Ask and answer about your summer holidays.

1. What was the most enjoyable thing you did during the school holidays? Why?
2. What was the least enjoyable thing you did? Why?

1B Grammar
Present tense contrast
I can use different tenses to talk about the present and future.

1 SPEAKING Work in pairs. Find out a) when and where your partner usually does his / her homework and b) what type of homework he / she likes most and least.

2 🎧1.03 Read and listen to the dialogue. Why is Sue annoyed with Dan at the end?

Sue   You aren't wearing your sports kit. P.E. starts in ten minutes.
Dan   I haven't got my sports kit today.
Sue   You're always forgetting things!
Dan   Well, I don't like P.E., so I'm not feeling too sad about it.
Sue   Sport is important. It makes you fit. What are you doing instead?
Dan   Mr Harley is giving me some extra maths homework to do in the library.
Sue   That's a shame. Mr Harley always gives us really difficult homework.
Dan   I don't mind. I need to do some extra work. We have exams next week.
Sue   I know. That's why we're revising together on Saturday. We arranged it last week.
Dan   I don't remember that! Sorry! I'm going away on Saturday.
Sue   Like I said … you're always forgetting things!
Dan   Let's revise when I get back on Sunday afternoon.
Sue   Sorry, I can't. My parents are decorating the house at the moment and I have to help.

3 Look at the dialogue again. Which verbs are in the present simple? Which are in the present continuous? How many negative and interrogative forms are there?

4 Read the Learn this! box. Complete the rules (a–g) with the correct tenses: *present simple* or *present continuous*. Use the highlighted examples from the dialogue to help you.

> **LEARN THIS!** Present simple and continuous
> We use:
> **a** the _____ for habits and routines.
> **b** the _____ for something happening now or about now.
> **c** the _____ for describing annoying behaviour (with *always*).
> **d** the _____ for a permanent situation or fact.
> **e** the _____ for timetables and schedules (e.g. school timetables).
> **f** the _____ for future arrangements.
> **g** the _____ in future time clauses (starting with *when, as soon as, after, if*, etc.).

5 Compare sentence a with sentence b. How is the speaker's attitude different?

   a You always go shopping with Cathy at the weekend.
   b You're always going shopping with Cathy at the weekend.

> **LEARN THIS!** Dynamic and state verbs
> Dynamic verbs describe actions and can be used in the simple or continuous form. State verbs describe states or situations and are not usually used in continuous tenses. Common state verbs include:
> *believe belong hate know like love mean mind need prefer remember understand want*
> Some verbs can be used as either state or dynamic verbs, depending on their meaning.
> Dynamic: *What are you thinking about?* (= mental activity)
> State: *What do you think of this film?* (= opinion)

6 Read the Learn this! box. Find five state verbs in the dialogue in exercise 2. How do you know they are state verbs?

   ➡ **Grammar Builder 1.2** page 126

7 Complete the sentences with the present simple or present continuous form of the verbs in brackets.

  1 I _____ (meet) Jack in town later. _____ (you / want) to come?
  2 We usually _____ (walk) to school, but tomorrow we _____ (go) by bus.
  3 I _____ (love) theme parks, but the tickets _____ (cost) a lot.
  4 My friends _____ (not want) to play tennis because it _____ (rain).
  5 _____ (you / enjoy) this film? Or _____ (you / prefer) comedies?
  6 I _____ (not believe) Ben's story. He _____ (always / invent) things.
  7 Why _____ (you / laugh)? I _____ (not understand) the joke.
  8 I _____ (catch) the train to London as soon as it _____ (arrive).

8 SPEAKING Work in pairs. Find out what your partner a) usually does at weekends and b) is doing this weekend. Use the words below or your own activities.

Social activities   go for a bike ride   go for a walk   go out for lunch   go shopping   go skateboarding   go to a café with friends   go to a friend's house   listen to music   meet friends in town   play basketball   play table tennis   play video games   watch TV / a DVD / a film

> What do you usually do at weekends?

> I usually meet friends in town.

> What about this weekend?

> On Saturday, I'm …
> On Sunday, I'm …

IC Vocabulary
Adjectives
I can form and use a variety of adjectives correctly.

1 SPEAKING In pairs, describe the photo. Would you like to appear on stage in a theatre production? Why? / Why not?

2 🎧 **1.04** Read and listen to the dialogue. Why does Mason change from feeling anxious to feeling terrified?

Ruby	So this is your first school show, Mason. Are you excited about it?
Mason	Yes, I am. But I'm anxious too. There's going to be a big audience!
Ruby	Don't worry. They're friendly!
Mason	I hope so. Where's Alex? He isn't here yet.
Ruby	That's strange. He's usually very punctual.
Mason	Maybe he's too frightened to come.
Ruby	Alex? No, it can't be that. He's a really confident person.
Miss Hart	Hello, Mason. I had a message from Alex. He's ill and can't perform tonight. He's very upset about it. Can you sing his song in the second half?
Mason	I know the song well, so maybe …
Miss Hart	Thanks, Mason. That's brave of you. Don't worry, you'll be great.
Ruby	You've got your own song now. How exciting!
Mason	I know. But I'm terrified!

3 VOCABULARY Look at the adjectives below. Underline five of them in the dialogue in exercise 2.

Adjectives describing feelings anxious ashamed bored confused cross delighted disappointed embarrassed envious excited frightened proud relieved shocked suspicious terrified upset

4 SPEAKING Work in pairs. Ask and answer the questions.

1 How do you think performers in a school show usually feel before a performance?
2 How might they feel afterwards?
3 Do you mind speaking in public? Why? / Why not?

5 🎧 **1.05** Listen to the speakers. How is each person feeling? Choose from the adjectives in exercise 3.

6 SPEAKING Choose four adjectives from exercise 3. Then find out when your partner last felt that way.

> When did you last feel cross?

> I felt cross when my sister broke my hairdryer.

7 VOCABULARY Work in pairs. Look at the list of personality adjectives below. Then underline four more in the dialogue in exercise 2. How many other personality adjectives do you know?

Adjectives describing personality   flexible hard-working honest kind loyal organised outgoing patient reliable sensitive shy

LOOK OUT!

Adjectives ending in *-ed* usually describe a feeling, while similar adjectives ending in *-ing* describe something or somebody that causes the feeling.

This game is tiring. I'm tired.

It's an exciting competition. They're feeling excited.

8 Read the **Look out!** box. Complete the sentences with an *-ed* or *-ing* adjective formed from the verbs in brackets.

1 The show wasn't great, but parts of it were very _____ (amuse).
2 The singing and dancing were _____ (amaze).
3 A few actors forgot their lines and looked quite _____ (embarrass).
4 The final scenes were actually quite _____ (move).
5 I was _____ (surprise) that it was over two hours long.
6 I was a bit _____ (bore) by the end of it.
7 My brother is really _____ (annoy). He's always going into my bedroom without permission.

LEARN THIS! Adjectives: negative prefixes

Adjectives beginning with *un-*, *dis-*, or *im- / in- / il- / ir-* have a negative meaning.

unenthusiastic disorganised impatient

9 Read the **Learn this!** box. Which adjectives from exercise 7 can have a negative prefix? Use a dictionary to help you.

➡ **Vocabulary Builder** Adjective endings: page 121

10 SPEAKING Work in pairs. Describe yourself to your partner using adjectives from exercise 7 (with or without negative prefixes). Include the modifying adverbs *a bit*, *quite* or *very* if necessary.

> I think I'm quite hard-working, but I'm a bit disorganised.

> I'm very loyal, but I'm a bit impatient.

Grammar

Articles, *will* and *going to*

I can use articles and talk about plans and predictions.

1 SPEAKING Look at the photo in pairs. Is this an activity you enjoy? Why? / Why not?

2 In pairs, read the dialogue and decide whether each gap should be *a / an*, *the* or – (no article). Write your answers.

Leah What are you up to at ¹____ weekend, Toby?

Toby I'm going to go for ²____ bike ride on Saturday. Do you fancy coming too?

Leah I can't, I'm afraid. I'm going to help my dad with some gardening. We're going to do some work for a neighbour.

Toby That doesn't sound like ³____ best way to spend your weekend. Gardening is ⁴____ hard work! And according to the forecast, ⁵____ weather isn't going to be good.

Leah I know. But ⁶____ neighbour is going to pay us for it. And my dad's ⁷____ gardener, so he's got all the right tools.

Toby Really? I'll come and help you. I mean, if that's OK with you and your dad …

Leah Sure. We'll share ⁸____ money with you: £10 ⁹____ hour. But what about ¹⁰____ bike ride?

Toby I'll go on Sunday instead. The weather will probably be better then. Do you want to come?

Leah Yes, please. I love ¹¹____ bike rides. But let's go in ¹²____ afternoon. I'll be exhausted when I wake up!

3 🎧 **1.06** Listen and check your answers. When are Toby and Leah going to do the activity in the photo?

4 Study the use of articles in the dialogue. Complete the Learn this! box with *a / an*, *the* or – (no article).

> **LEARN THIS!** Articles
> **a** We use ¹____ when we mention something for the first time and ²____ when we mention it again.
> **b** We use ³____ when it is clear what we are talking about, when there is only one of something, and in superlatives.
> **c** We use ⁴____ to say what someone's job is.
> **d** We use ⁵____ when we make generalisations.
> **e** We use ⁶____ to mean 'per' or 'in each'.
> **f** There are set phrases which do not follow a rule.
> go to school   at ⁷____ weekend   watch TV
> go to the cinema   in ⁸____ morning / afternoon
> on Monday   listen to the radio

5 Complete the sentences with *a / an*, *the* or – (no article). Use rules a–f in the Learn this! box to explain your answers.

1 My mum is ____ violin teacher. In fact, she's ____ only violin teacher in our town.
2 If you like ____ tennis, there's ____ sports centre next to ____ town hall. You can hire courts for £5 ____ hour.
3 I love ____ Chinese food and there's ____ great Chinese restaurant near my house.
4 ____ student in my class is having ____ party on ____ Saturday. I can't go to ____ party because I'm going to ____ theatre.
5 My brother, who is ____ accountant with one of ____ largest companies in London, earns £100 ____ hour.
6 If you're hungry, there's ____ sandwich in ____ fridge.

➡ **Grammar Builder I.3** page 127

> **LEARN THIS!** *will* and *going to*
> **a** For predictions, we use:
> 1 *going to* when it is based on what we can see or hear.
> 2 *will* when it is based on what we know or is a guess.
> **b** For plans, we use:
> 1 *going to* when we have already decided what to do.
> 2 *will* when we are deciding what to do as we speak.
> **c** For offers and promises, we use *will*.

6 Read the Learn this! box. Then underline an example of each of the uses of *will* and *going to* in the dialogue in exercise 2.

7 Complete the sentences with the correct form of *will* or *going to* and the verbs in brackets. Write which rule in the Learn this! box you are following.

1 That train _____ (not stop) here – it's going too fast. ___
2 'We _____ (spend) the weekend in Paris.' 'Lucky you. You _____ (have) a great time!' ___ ___
3 'Help! I _____ (drop) one of these boxes.' 'Don't worry. I _____ (take) one for you.' ___ ___
4 I _____ (go) into town this afternoon. But I _____ (not be) late home, I promise. ___ ___
5 '_____ (you / invite) Max to your party?' 'Yes, but he _____ (not come). He never goes to parties.' ___ ___

➡ **Grammar Builder I.4** page 127

8 Write sentences about these plans and predictions. Use *will* and *going to*. Use the list of social activities in exercise 8 on page 5 to help you.

1 two things you plan to do this evening
   I'm going to watch TV this evening. I'm also …
2 two things you definitely aren't going to do this evening
3 two things you think you will do next summer
4 two things you don't think you will do next summer

9 SPEAKING Work in pairs. Take turns to tell your partner about your plans from exercise 8. Are any of them the same?

1

Generations

Unit map

● Vocabulary
Stages of life
Life events
Attitude (adjectives)
Noun and adjective endings
Exchange programmes

● Word Skills
Phrasal verbs (1)

● Grammar
Past tense contrast
used to

● Listening Family tensions

● Reading Adolescence

● Speaking Role-play

● Writing A message

● Culture 1
Ethnic minorities in the UK

● Vocabulary Builder page 121

● Grammar Builder and Reference page 128

1A Vocabulary

Ages and stages

I can talk about the different stages of people's lives.

1 SPEAKING Work in pairs. Can you answer this famous riddle from Sophocles' play *Oedipus the King*? Explain your answer.

'What creature walks on four legs in the morning, two legs in the afternoon, and three in the evening?'

2 🎧 1.07 VOCABULARY Number the stages of life in the order that people reach them. Then listen and check.

Stages of life   be an adult   be a centenarian   be an infant   be a toddler
be a young child   be elderly   be in your teens   be in your twenties   be middle-aged

3 Match some of the phrases in exercise 2 with the pictures below of the woman at different stages of her life.

In picture A, she's an infant.

4 VOCABULARY Check the meaning of the life events below. At what age are they most likely to happen, do you think? Put them in groups A–E. Compare your answers with your partner. Do you agree?

Life events   be born   be brought up (by)   become a grandparent
buy a house or flat   emigrate   fall in love   get divorced   get engaged
get married   get your first job   go to university   grow up   have a change of career
inherit (money, a house, etc.)   learn to drive   leave home   leave school
move (house)   pass away   retire   settle down   split up   start a business
start a family   start school

A Before you are 20 _____
B From 20 to 40 _____
C From 40 to 60 _____
D Over 60 _____
E At any age _____

A   B   C

5 🎧 **1.08** Listen to four people talking about their backgrounds and their families. Circle the correct answers (a–c).

1 Bilal's dad
   a was born in the UK.
   b is going to have a change of career.
   c wants to study law.
2 Sandra's family
   a have owned a number of farms.
   b sold the first farm and bought a bigger one.
   c have owned the same farm for many years.
3 Charlotte's mum
   a brought up her daughter in France.
   b isn't married.
   c has been married twice.
4 Callum's parents
   a inherited and ran a successful family business.
   b didn't have a good education.
   c left Britain many years ago.

> **RECYCLE!** Past simple
>
> Remember that there are no rules for the affirmative forms of irregular verbs (e.g. *go – went*), and that the spelling changes with some regular verbs (e.g. *stop – stopped, carry – carried*).
>
> We form the past simple negative with *didn't* and the interrogative with *did*. (The verbs *be* and *can* are exceptions.)

➡ **Vocabulary Builder** Noun plural forms: page 121

6 🎧 **1.08** Read the Recycle! box. Complete the sentences with the past simple form of the verbs below. Then listen again and check.

be   buy   emigrate   fall   get   get   grow up
leave   move   not go   not leave   not retire   start

1 My grandparents _____ from Pakistan in the 1960s.
2 She _____ home until last summer, when she _____ married.
3 I _____ in the village where my family has lived for generations.
4 They managed to save quite a bit of money and eventually _____ a small farmhouse with some land.
5 They _____ in love, _____ engaged after a week and were married a month later.
6 I _____ brought up by my mum after she _____ back to the UK.
7 They _____ school at sixteen and _____ to university.
8 They _____ a successful business and _____ until they were in their seventies.

7 **SPEAKING** In pairs, ask and answer about your family and your ancestors. Give extra information where you can.

1 How long has your family lived in your home town?
2 Did any of them emigrate from another country? From where? When? Why?
3 Did any of them move from another part of your country? From where? When? Why?
4 Did any of your ancestors or members of your family emigrate to another country? Where to? When? Why?
5 Are you related to anyone famous? If so, who?

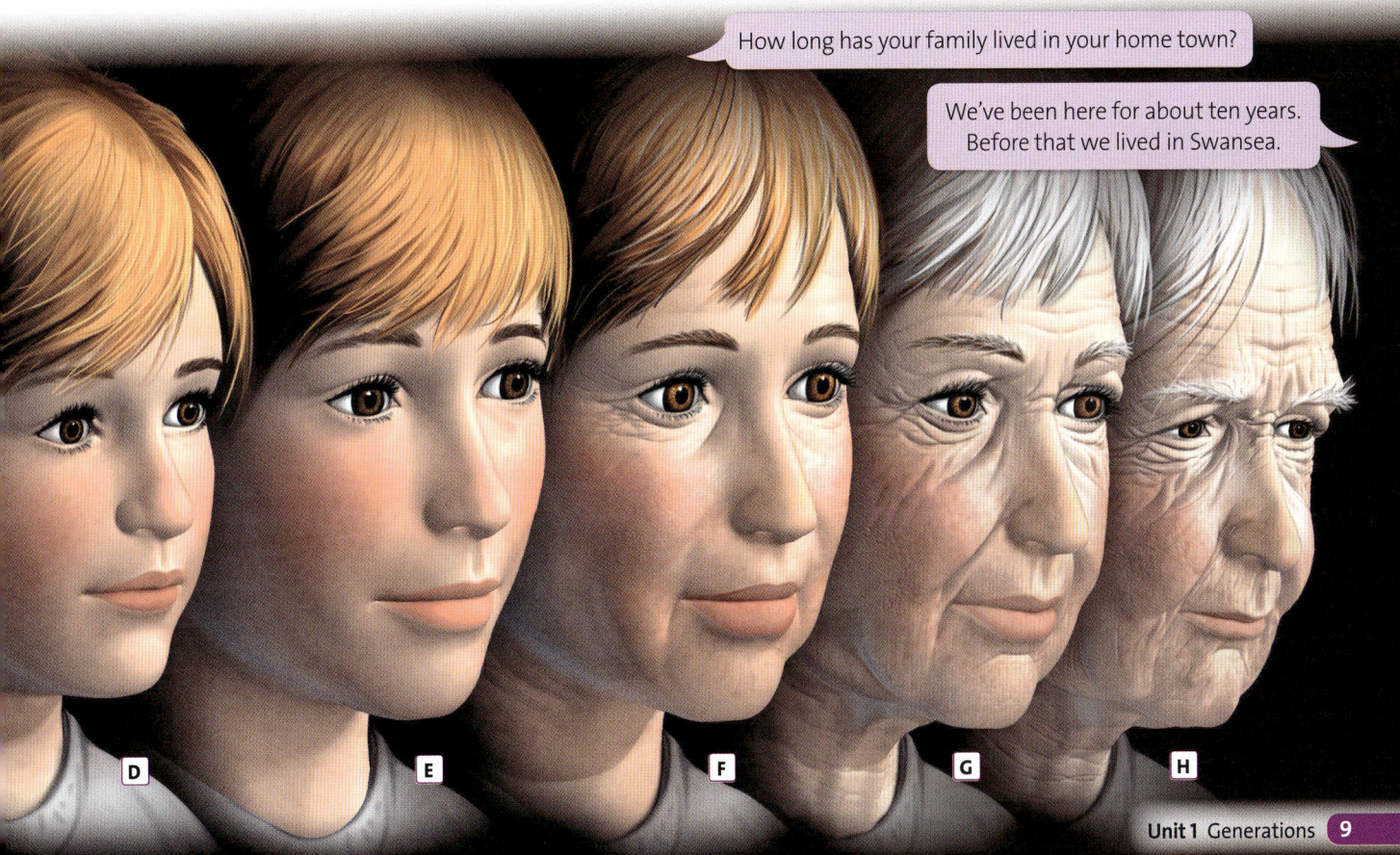

How long has your family lived in your home town?

We've been here for about ten years. Before that we lived in Swansea.

D   E   F   G   H

Past tense contrast
I can talk about the past using a variety of past tenses.

1 Look at the photo. How old do you think the woman is? Why do you think she is famous?

2 Read the text and check your ideas.

In 1875, the US army was still fighting Native Americans, and Alexander Bell was working on a new invention – the telephone. That was the year that Jeanne Calment, the person with the longest lifespan ever, was born in Arles, France. Her parents ran a shop in the town and she worked there when she was a teenager. While she was serving in the shop in 1888, she met Vincent van Gogh, who had come in to buy pencils. She thought he was 'dirty, ugly and badly dressed'!

In 1896, at the age of 21, she married Fernand Calment and then gave birth to a daughter, Yvonne. Fernand was very wealthy so Jeanne never needed to work. She lived in Arles for the rest of her life, dying on 5 August 1997 at the age of 122.

People of that age often have an enormous family with generations of grandchildren. But Jeanne didn't have any living descendants. Yvonne had had a son, but both she and her son had died many years earlier. So how did Jeanne manage to live so long? The French have their own theories, noting that she ate more than two pounds of chocolate a week and rode a bicycle until she was 100!

3 Complete the Learn this! box with the tenses below. Then underline an example of each of the rules (a–d) in the text in exercise 2.

past continuous   past perfect   past simple

LEARN THIS! Past tenses

a We use the ¹_____ for a sequence of events that happened one after another.
In 1989, my parents met, fell in love and got married.

b We use the ²_____ to describe a scene in the past. The events were in progress at the same time.
It was raining and people were rushing home from work.

c We use the ³_____ for a single event that interrupted a longer event in the past. We use the ⁴_____ for the longer event.
My parents got engaged while they were living in Wales.

d We use the ⁵_____ for an event that happened before another event in the past.
He had started a business before he left school.

4 Complete this sentence in three different ways using the three tenses in the Learn this! box. Use the verb *learn*. How does the meaning change?

When Tom left school, he _____ / _____ / _____ to drive.

5 Complete the sentences with the correct past simple, past continuous or past perfect form of the verbs in brackets.

1 We _____ (move) house a lot while I _____ (grow up).
2 After Joe _____ (learn) to drive, he _____ (buy) a car.
3 George _____ (leave) school, _____ (go) to university and _____ (study) engineering.
4 Where _____ you _____ (live) when you _____ (get) your first job?
5 My parents _____ (get) engaged in 1990. They _____ (fall) in love two years before, while they _____ (work) in London.
6 Kim _____ (want) a change of career so she _____ (emigrate) to Australia.

➤ **Grammar Builder 1.1** page 128

6 Complete the text with the past simple, past continuous or past perfect form of the verbs below.

be   be   become   die   get   leave   live
meet   not stop   retire   say   work   write

Japan is the country with the most centenarians: over 50,000. It is also where Jiroemon Kimura, the man with the longest lifespan ever, ¹_____ born in 1897, the year that Bram Stoker ²_____ *Dracula*. Kimura ³_____ school at fourteen and ⁴_____ a job in a post office. While he ⁵_____ there, he ⁶_____ his future wife Yae. He ⁷_____ a postal worker for 45 years when he ⁸_____ in 1962. But he ⁹_____ working! He ¹⁰_____ a farmer! In an interview just before he ¹¹_____ at the age of 116, he said he wasn't sure why he ¹²_____ so long. 'Maybe it's thanks to the sun,' he ¹³_____ . 'I'm always looking up to the sky!'

7 Choose a real or invented person from a previous generation (e.g. a parent, grandparent). Make notes about their life using the headings below to help you.

Born when / where?   Education?   Jobs?   Married?
Family?   Moved?   Other interesting facts?

8 **SPEAKING** Tell the class about the person in exercise 7. Look again at the vocabulary in lesson 1A. Use the prompts below to help you, and your own ideas.

* She was born …
* At the age of … she left school and got a job as …
* After she had left home, she …
* While she was living in … , she …
* She got married in …

Family tensions

I can identify the attitude and intention of a speaker.

1 SPEAKING Look at the photo. What do you think this app does? Why might some people need it?

2 SPEAKING Read the text and check your answer to exercise 1. Do you think the app would increase or decrease the number of arguments in your family? Why?

Kid's smartphone or tablet

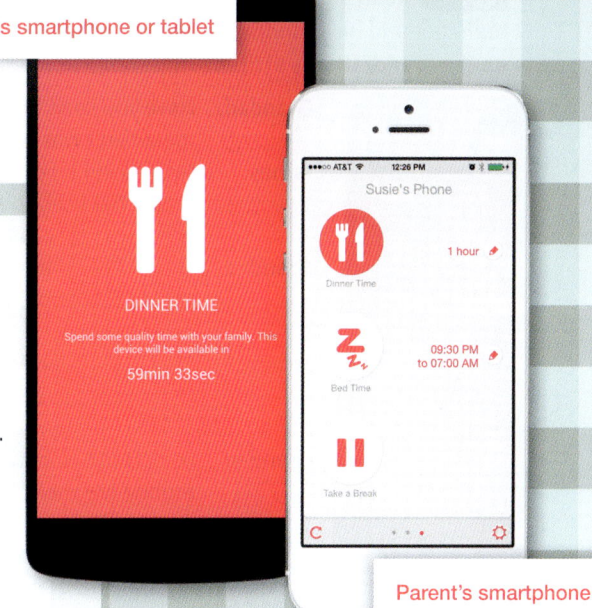

Parent's smartphone

Tablets for dinner?

An evening meal for all the family was once part of everyday life in British homes, but this tradition has almost disappeared. Some people blame technology: children and teenagers are so addicted to their phones and tablets that they do not want to stop playing with them, even at mealtimes. This causes a lot of arguments in families. But now, parents can get a free app called DinnerTime, which locks their children's devices at certain times of the day and night. During those times, the children are unable to access messages, games, or the internet. In theory, this means that parents and children can spend more time together, eating and chatting. But will it lead to happier families or more family arguments?

3 VOCABULARY In pairs, check the meaning of the adjectives below. Which describe a positive attitude? Which describe a negative attitude?

Attitude (adjectives) accusing aggressive arrogant bitter calm complimentary enthusiastic grateful miserable nostalgic optimistic pessimistic sarcastic sympathetic urgent

> **Listening Strategy**
> Sometimes, the words alone do not fully express the speaker's intention. You need to pay attention to the tone of voice as well. For example, an urgent tone of voice suggests that the speaker is giving a warning.

4 🎧 1.09 Read the Listening Strategy. Then listen and underline the adjective which best matches the speaker's attitude. Use their tone of voice to help you.

1 arrogant / pessimistic / confident
2 aggressive / miserable / sarcastic
3 calm / complimentary / optimistic
4 accusing / enthusiastic / sympathetic
5 grateful / optimistic / sympathetic
6 aggressive / bitter / urgent

5 🎧 1.10 SPEAKING Listen and compare two different ways of saying the sentences. Then, in pairs, say a sentence in one of the two ways. Can your partner guess the adjective?

1 'Thanks, Andy. That's really helpful.' (first grateful, then sarcastic)
2 'Our train leaves in ten minutes.' (first calm, then urgent)
3 'You and your sister always argued during dinner.' (first nostalgic, then accusing)
4 'You need to stop and think about what's happened.' (first sympathetic, then aggressive)
5 'I think we'll win one or two of our matches.' (first optimistic, then pessimistic)

6 🎧 1.11 Listen to four speakers. In pairs, try to agree which speaker sounds:

a urgent ___   c enthusiastic ___
b calm ___   d arrogant ___

7 🎧 1.11 Listen again. Match sentences A–E with speakers 1–4. Use the tone of voice to help you. There is one extra sentence.

A The speaker is giving advice about winning family arguments. ___
B We learn how a bad argument had a positive result for the speaker. ___
C The speaker is advertising a course for families who want to argue less. ___
D The speaker is persuading somebody to attend a family reunion. ___
E The speaker describes how a relative lost his job because of a family argument. ___

8 SPEAKING Work in pairs. Decide which of these topics is most likely to cause arguments in your family and why. Are there any others you can think of?

doing chores
doing schoolwork
staying out late
sharing a family computer
what to watch on TV
when to watch TV
too much time spent on social media and games
what to eat

9 SPEAKING Compare your ideas with the class. Find the topic which causes the most family arguments.

used to

I can talk about things that were different in the past.

1 🎧 **1.12** Read and listen to the dialogue between a teenager and his grandfather. Which adjective best sums up the grandfather's attitude: miserable or nostalgic?

Grandad	Have you seen this photo of me when I was your age?
James	No, I haven't. Let me see. Wow! You used to have great hair!
Grandad	I know. I used to spend ages getting it just right. It's much quicker now.
James	Your clothes look cool too. Did you use to spend a lot of money on them?
Grandad	I didn't use to have much money. My mother made some of them. And I used to share clothes with my brother.
James	I used to do that too. But he doesn't let me borrow them now!

LEARN THIS!

a We use *used to* when we want to talk about things which were true in the past, but are not true now.

I used to read my sister's magazines. (I don't read them now.)

b Pay attention to the spelling of the negative and interrogative forms.

My sister didn't use to like it.
Did she use to get angry? Yes, she did.

2 Read the Learn this! box. Underline an affirmative, a negative and an interrogative example of *used to* in the dialogue in exercise 1.

3 Complete the dialogue with the correct form of *used to* and the verbs below.

be   do   go   live   not have   not pay   wait

Mum	I ¹_____ opposite the Palace Cinema when I was ten.
Alice	²_____ you _____ there often?
Mum	Yes. But we ³_____ . It wasn't our fault – we ⁴_____ any money for tickets.
Alice	So how did you get in?
Mum	We ⁵_____ outside the fire exit and run in when somebody opened it!
Alice	I can't believe you ⁶_____ that! You're always telling me how important it is to be honest!
Mum	Well, yes. I ⁷_____ very naughty, but I grew out of it.

4 🎧 **1.13** Listen and check your answers to exercise 3. How is *used to* pronounced?

➡ **Grammar Builder 1.2** page 129

5 Complete these sentences with the correct form of *used to / didn't use to* and the verbs in brackets.

1 They _____ (live) abroad, but they moved back to this country last year.
2 She _____ (be) a student, but she finished her university course in June.
3 She _____ (eat) meat, but now she has chicken sometimes.
4 I _____ (like) cats, but I prefer dogs now.
5 I _____ (enjoy) TV, but now I find most of the programmes boring or annoying.
6 We _____ (spend) a lot of time together, but now we hardly ever see each other.
7 He _____ (speak) a foreign language, but he started going to Spanish lessons last year.
8 My grandad _____ (have) a lot of money, but he's quite rich now.

LOOK OUT!

! Do not confuse *used to* with the phrase *be / get used to* (doing) something.

I used to ride my bike to school. (used to)
These glasses feel strange, but I'll get used to them. (get used to)
She hates losing. She isn't used to it! (be used to)

6 🎧 **1.14** Read the Look out! box. Listen and decide if the sentences contain *be / get used to*, *used to* or both.

1   be used to

7 Think about what you used to be like at the age of five. Read the phrases and write true sentences about yourself with *used to* or *didn't use to*.

1 be afraid of the dark
   I used to be / didn't use to be afraid of the dark.
2 drink milk before bed
3 play with dolls
4 listen to stories at bedtime
5 draw pictures at school every day
6 watch a lot of cartoons
7 have piano lessons
8 walk to school on my own

8 **SPEAKING** Work in pairs. Find out what your partner was like at the age of five. Ask and answer using the ideas in exercise 7. How similar or different were you?

> Did you use to be afraid of the dark?

> Yes, I did. / No, I didn't.

9 **SPEAKING** Find out more about your partner's childhood. Use the correct form of *used to*. What did he or she use to …

have for breakfast?   watch on TV?   wear to school?
enjoy playing?   do at weekends?   *your ideas*

1E Word Skills

Phrasal verbs (1)
I can use three-part phrasal verbs.

1 Read the article about a film. Explain in your own words what is unusual about the main character.

I USED TO BE *older...*

The Curious Case of Benjamin Button certainly lives up to its title. It is a very unusual film about a man who lives his life backwards: he is born as an old man and dies as a baby.

The story begins in 1918 when a woman gives birth to a baby with the appearance of an elderly man. The mother dies and the father walks out on the baby, who is called Benjamin. Two workers at a nursing home, Queenie and Tizzy, decide to look after Benjamin, who fits in with the elderly residents at the home because he looks so old. But as the years pass, Benjamin becomes physically younger.

At the age of twelve, he meets a young girl called Daisy and gets on with her very well despite having the appearance of an old man, but later they lose touch when Benjamin signs up for a job on a boat.

Years later, he catches up with Daisy again in Paris. In their forties, they finally look the same age for the first time – and fall in love. They almost marry and settle down together, but they never go through with it. One reason is that Daisy could never put up with Benjamin's strange condition.

In the end, they run out of time: Daisy is becoming an old woman and Benjamin is becoming a child. He finally dies in Daisy's arms as a baby.

2 Match the highlighted phrasal verbs in the text with their definitions below.

1 to have a (good / bad) relationship with _____
2 to abandon or leave _____
3 to complete something _____
4 to match or equal _____
5 to use all of your supply of something _____
6 to agree to do something (e.g. work) _____
7 to succeed in finding or reaching somebody _____
8 to look and act like part of a group _____
9 to tolerate or be patient about something _____

3 Circle the correct words to complete the Learn this! box. Use the examples in the text in exercise 1 to help you.

> **LEARN THIS!**
> **a** A three-part phrasal verb has ¹**one** / **two** verb(s) and ²**one** / **two** particle(s).
> **b** Three-part phrasal verbs are ³**transitive** / **intransitive** (they have a direct object).
> **c** The object always goes ⁴**after** / **before** / **between** the two particles.
> **d** In questions, the three parts of the phrasal verb usually stay together.
> *What kind of course did you sign up for?*

> **Dictionary tip**
> Some three-part phrasal verbs have a different meaning from similar two-part verbs. When you look up a phrasal verb in a dictionary, find the correct part of the entry.

4 **DICTIONARY WORK** Read the Dictionary tip. Then find these phrasal verbs in a dictionary and check the difference in meaning between the two- and three-part phrasal verbs.

look up / look up to   get away / get away with
make up / make up for   get up / get up to
go in / go in for   go back / go back on

5 Complete the sentences with two- or three-part phrasal verbs from exercise 4.

1 We sent her a present to _____ the disappointment of missing the music festival.
2 I like football, but I don't _____ extreme sports.
3 We _____ his name on the internet to check his story was true.
4 You said you would take us on holiday this summer – you can't _____ your promise!
5 Did you _____ anything exciting while your parents were away?
6 Did you _____ that story or is it true?

➡ **Vocabulary Builder** Phrasal verbs: page 121

6 Use three-part phrasal verbs from exercises 2 or 4 to replace the underlined words.

1 Which famous people do you <u>admire</u>? _____
2 Which sports or games do you <u>enjoy</u>? _____
3 What did you <u>do</u> last weekend? _____
4 What kind of behaviour is the most difficult to <u>tolerate</u>? _____
5 What kind of people do you find it easiest to <u>be friendly with</u>? _____

7 **SPEAKING** Work in pairs. Ask and answer your questions from exercise 6. Add suitable follow-up questions.

> Which famous people do you look up to? Why?

> I look up to ... because ...

Adolescence

I can understand a text about how teenagers can get on better with their parents.

1 SPEAKING Do you sometimes argue with your parents? What do you argue about, and why? Use the ideas below to help you.

bedtime
clothes
going out with friends
homework
housework
staying up late
using computers or tablets

2 Read the text quickly, ignoring the gaps. Choose the best summary of the text: a, b or c.

a Parents may find it difficult to understand their adolescent children, but it is a parent's duty to communicate properly with them and avoid arguments.

b Although teenagers develop new ideas, values and beliefs during adolescence, that is no excuse for bad behaviour. They should listen to their parents.

c Teenagers experience big physical and emotional changes during adolescence. It's important to communicate with your parents and try to understand their point of view.

HOW TO HANDLE
your parents

 **1.15**

Parents get a lot of advice on how to handle their adolescent children, but what about some advice for teenagers on how to deal with their parents?
5 Psychologist Raymond Freedman offers some tips …

What is adolescence? It starts when you are aged between about ten and thirteen and is a period of rapid physical change
10 which transforms you from a pre-teen child, dependent on your parents, to the independent young adult that you become in your early twenties. **1___** Here are some of the most common social and emotional changes
15 that happen during adolescence.

FREEDOM You may not want to spend as much time with your parents as you used to. You want more freedom to choose who you see and when. You may feel that your friends are as important to you as your family.

PRIVACY You used to be most happy in the company of your
20 parents. **2___** You need your own space and some privacy.

INTERESTS You have new interests and they might include activities that your parents do not understand or think are a waste of time, such as playing computer games or chatting on the internet.

DECISIONS In the past, your parents made most decisions for you
25 and told you what to do. **3___** You may resent them telling you to go to bed, tidy your bedroom, or come home by ten o'clock.

OPINIONS When you were younger, you didn't have many strong opinions. **4___** Adolescents are often idealistic and feel impatient and at odds with the adult world. You may feel that you have all the answers, while
30 many adults don't have any!

3 Read the Reading Strategy. Then read the sentences below and the highlighted words in the text. Say which sentence links to which highlighted word and underline the part of the sentence which helped you to decide.

A They may not say so, but they are probably feeling a sense of loss and may even feel rejected by you.

B Your parents will expect you to behave responsibly.

C But now you want to decide things for yourself and don't want to be told what to do all the time.

D As your body changes, you also begin to think and feel differently.

E Despite this, you should always listen carefully.

F Now you are beginning to see the world differently, developing your own views and your own sense of right and wrong.

G Now you probably want to spend more time on your own.

4 Use your answers to exercise 3 to match sentences A–G with gaps 1–5 in the text. There are two extra sentences.

5 VOCABULARY Complete the stems to make a noun and an adjective. Use a dictionary to help you. Either the noun or the adjective is in the text. (Sometimes you do not need to add anything.)

1 *adolescence, adolescent*

Noun and adjective endings

1 adolesc_____	5 priv_____	9 safe_____
2 depend_____	6 ideal_____	10 irritat_____
3 free_____	7 impati_____	11 critic_____
4 emot_____	8 concern_____	12 distrust_____

6 SPEAKING Work in pairs or small groups. Discuss points 1 and 2. Use the phrases below to help you.

1 Look at the five social and emotional changes that the writer describes in the text (freedom, privacy, interests, decisions and opinions). Discuss them one by one. Which ones affect teenagers most, do you think? Give examples.

2 Look at the advice offered by the writer in the last but one paragraph. Is it good advice on the whole, do you think? Which is the best piece of advice? Give reasons.

Presenting your ideas

I agree that …   I don't agree that …
It's (not) true to say that …   In my experience, …
Personally, I believe that …   I'm not sure about that.
For example, …   For instance, …

7 SPEAKING Share your ideas and opinions from exercise 6 with the class.

All these changes are perfectly normal, but it is important to remember that they will affect your relationship with your parents and that they may be a source of conflict and arguments. So what can you do
35 to make life easier and make sure that you stay on good terms with your parents?

Firstly, your parents will feel much better if you let them know that you still love and value them. Remember that they have lost forever the little child you once were. ⁵___
40 Secondly, try to agree rules and boundaries. You may feel these are unnecessary, but your parents' main concern is often just to keep you safe. Once you have agreed what is and isn't acceptable behaviour, try to stick to it. It may feel like a nuisance to remember to phone them and let
45 them know where you are, but make the effort anyway. Thirdly, try to understand why they might be irritated by your behaviour. Do your parents get cross if you spend three hours chatting with friends on social media and leave your homework till the last minute? That's probably
50 because they want you to do well at school.

Finally, it's all about communication! Keep talking to your parents, tell them about what you did today, let them know where you are going, and ask for advice if you need it. The more disconnected they feel, the more
55 critical, distrustful and controlling they tend to become. Who wants parents like that?

Role-play

I can role-play a conversation about an exchange programme.

1 SPEAKING In pairs, look at the advert below. In your opinion, what would be the best and worst things about spending a year with a family abroad? Use the prompts below and your own ideas.

Exchange programmes eating different food gaining confidence going to a different school making new friends missing family / friends / home speaking a foreign language visiting different places watching foreign TV programmes

Study abroad

Home from home

Speaking Strategy

Use your preparation time well. Read the task carefully. Then think of one thing to say about each topic. If you have more time, think of more ideas.

Imagine the following situation: you recently spent a term as an exchange student in England. You are having a video call with a student from Japan who is preparing to take part in the same scheme and you are giving him / her some advice. Discuss the following points:

- getting to know your exchange student
- useful things to take with you
- going to school in England
- advice about staying with an English family

2 Read the Speaking Strategy and the task above. Then match one or two of the ideas below with each topic.

carrying a dictionary doing hobbies together eating in the canteen helping with housework keeping your room tidy wearing a uniform

3 🎧 **1.16** Listen to a student doing the task from exercise 2. Does she discuss all the topics? Which ideas from the exercise does she mention?

LEARN THIS! Advice

- We use *should* and *ought to* to give advice.
  You should / ought to take a dictionary.

- The negative forms are *shouldn't* and *ought not to*. However, we often use *I don't think you should ...* instead.
  I don't think you should carry too much money.

- We use *Should I ... ?* or *Do you think I should / ought to ... ?* to ask for advice.
  Should I send a thank-you letter?
  Do you think I ought to visit London?

4 Read the Learn this! box. Then complete sentences 1–5 using the words in brackets. Do not change the words, but add extra words if necessary.

1 You _____ (ought / find out) about his hobbies.
2 I _____ (think / should / send) him an email.
3 '_____ (think / should / take) some food from home with me?'
  'No, I _____ (think / you / should / do) that.'
4 You _____ (ought / take) a present for the parents.
5 What _____ (should / buy) for them?

5 🎧 **1.16** Listen again. Check your answers to exercise 4.

6 SPEAKING Work in pairs. Student A is an English student who is going to stay with Student B's family next month. Ask for and give advice about these topics.

1 suitable presents for the family you're staying with
2 how to stay safe when you're out
3 suitable clothing for the season
4 the best deals for calling and texting
5 how to improve your language skills quickly

What do you think I should buy for your parents?

I think you should get ...

7 Read the task below. In pairs, think of one or two ideas for each topic. Make notes, using questions 1–4 to help you.

Imagine the following situation: you spent three weeks with a host family when you did a language course in England last summer. You are having a video call with a student from Japan who is planning to do the same thing this summer and you are giving him / her some advice. Discuss the following points:

- preparing for the visit
- what you can learn by studying in England
- staying in touch with people back home
- staying safe abroad

1 What should he / she take to England?
2 What things could he / she learn, apart from the language?
3 How did you keep in contact with your family and friends while in England?
4 Should he / she go out alone at night in England? What else should or shouldn't he / she do?

8 SPEAKING Work in pairs. Do the task in exercise 7 using your notes to help you.

I'm going to stay with a host family in England this summer. You did that last year, didn't you?

Yes, I did.

I'd really like some advice about ...

1H Writing

A message

I can write a message in response to an advertisement.

1 SPEAKING Work in pairs. What is a penfriend? Think of three reasons why somebody might want a penfriend in a different country.

Find a penfriend

Hi! My name is Adam. I'm sixteen years old and I live in Newcastle in the UK. I'm looking for a penfriend from any country in the world. Send me a message and tell me about yourself and your family. Also, could you please tell me why you are looking for a penfriend? Thanks – and I hope to hear from you soon!

Click here to reply to Adam

2 Read the advertisement from a website for international penfriends above. What information does Adam ask for?

3 Read the task and the message below. Does Dominik provide all of the information that Adam asks for? What does Dominik ask for more information about?

You have seen this advertisement on a website for international penfriends. Write a message in reply and provide the information Adam asks for. Include a request for information in your message.

Find a penfriend

Hi! My name's Dominik and I'm from the Czech Republic. I'm fifteen years old and live in Prague with my parents and my younger sister. I'm into football, and my sister's mad about horses.

I'd like to have an English penfriend because I'm studying English at school and would like to visit England one day. Would you mind telling me more about Newcastle? I know it's got a famous football team, but that's all! Do you enjoy living there?

4 KEY PHRASES Look at the polite requests below. Which one does Adam use in his advertisement? Which one does Dominik use in his message?

Polite requests

Would it be possible for you to … ?
Could you please … ?   Would you mind if … ?
Would you mind (+ -*ing* form)?   I wonder if …

5 SPEAKING Work in pairs. Request the following information from your partner. Use different phrases from exercise 4 and verbs like *tell, explain, describe*, etc.

- his / her date of birth
- his / her earliest memory
- his / her ideal day out
- his / her taste in music

I wonder if you could tell me your date of birth?

Yes, of course. It's …

Writing Strategy

Make sure that you a) include all of the points in the task and b) develop each point, that is, add some extra information or detail. Try not to write just one sentence for each point.

6 Read the Writing Strategy. Then look at the message in exercise 3 again. Does Dominik develop the points or does he just write a single sentence for each one?

7 Match sentences 1–5 with sentences a–e. Think of other ways that extra detail or information could be added to sentences 1–5.

1 I go to Harford Community College. ___
2 I've got two brothers. ___
3 We moved to a house outside town last month. ___
4 My name's Jack and I'm seventeen years old. ___
5 Would you mind if I visited you in August? ___

a I live in Brighton with my parents and my sister.
b I'm doing my A-levels.
c We needed more space.
d I'd really like to meet you and your family.
e One is older than me and one is younger.

8 You are going to do the task in exercise 3. Plan your message, using the prompts below to help you. Think about how you can add extra details.

- Describe yourself and your family.
- Explain your reason for wanting a penfriend.
- Request information from Adam.

9 Write your message using your plan from exercise 8.

CHECK YOUR WORK

 Have you …

- referred to and developed each point in the task?
- used a phrase from exercise 4 to request information?
- checked the spelling and grammar?

Exam Skills Trainer

Reading

1 Read the strategy above. Then read the paragraph below and headings A–D. Choose the heading which best matches the paragraph.

The older generation seem to have chosen to forget so much about their past. It is obvious to a teenager that their parents must have made some mistakes in their youth, disagreed with their parents, listened to the 'wrong' music, or made the 'wrong' friends. But it is rare to find a parent who admits to it.

A Parents expect too much perfection from teens.
B Teens are unable to see a parent's point of view.
C Parents frustrate teens by denying their past.
D Teens should admit their mistakes to their parents.

2 Read the text about staying young. Match the headings (A–G) with the paragraphs (1–5). There are two extra headings.

1 ___ As people grow older, they often think back to the days of their youth. They remember the great friends of those days, great times together, and how bright the future looked. Of course, not everything was perfect – but it can look that way as we get older. And this can make people feel pessimistic and bitter.

2 ___ It doesn't need to be that way. There are many secrets to staying young in spirit well into old age. Why put up with feeling miserable when you can be enthusiastic instead? Here are some tips to keep you young at heart as you grow older.

3 ___ Relationships are extremely important. Family gives you comfort and support, and catching up with old friends can help older people to feel young. Making new friends is important too – but make sure they are optimistic, enthusiastic people.

4 ___ Bad things happen to all of us. We split up with a boyfriend or girlfriend, and later we may have to do a boring job for years. But don't think too much about negative things. Deal with them, and get on with your life.

5 ___ Always keep special things around you, like family photos or favourite possessions – and be grateful that you can enjoy them. Thank your loved ones daily for sharing your life too. When you see the pleasure on their faces, you will never feel old – even in your eighties!

A The importance of people in your life
B Ageing can be a positive experience
C You can choose to stay young
D Appreciate the things and people in your life
E Looking back can make old people feel bad
F Getting over the negatives and moving on
G Even pessimists can have friends

Listening

3 Read the strategy above. Then read the short extract and the question below it. Choose the correct answer (A–C). What makes the other options incorrect?

🎧 I used to think my childhood was great because both my parents were in the army and we were travelling around all the time. It was fantastic to see so many cool places, but now I realise that I missed out on getting to know my family back home in America.

The speaker says that the way she grew up …
A brought her closer to friends and family.
B was fantastic in every way.
C caused problems that she did not see at the time.

4 🎧 **1.17** You will hear six short extracts. There is one question for each extract. Choose the best answer (A–C).

1 What does Cara say about the incident that happened when she was two?
A She remembers it clearly.
B It still affects her today.
C She blames her parents for it.

2 What point does the speaker make?
A That young people are not reliable friends.
B That making friends is easier for young people than for adults.
C That young people end friendships more quickly than adults.

3 Who is the speaker?
A a hairdresser
B a customer at a hairdresser's
C a fashion reporter

4 How does the woman explain why she likes audio books?
A Her father records them.
B They bring back a good feeling.
C They helped her learn to read.

5 What does the woman say about the sport she liked at school?
A Her children are better at it than she was.
B She was never very good at it.
C She has stopped playing it.

6 Where is the speaker?
A in a classroom
B at a job training centre
C in a library

Exam Skills Trainer

Use of English

5 Read the strategy above. Then choose the correct option (A–C) to complete the text.

People's interests change and develop *over* time and they often like different activities ¹___ different stages of their lives. Children and teenagers, for example, often enjoy doing activities that they find exciting, like rollerblading or skateboarding. When people settle down and start ²___ family, they may prefer relaxing activities, such as reading magazines or listening to music. Many people who ³___ playing computer games as children later lose interest. But what about those who ⁴___ stop playing them? What ⁵___ some people stick with certain activities throughout their lives? Perhaps ⁶___ people simply choose not to grow up. But it's more likely that if a child ⁷___ an activity which helps them to relax in difficult times, they will carry on doing it. All of us have different ways of relaxing, and playing computer games can be ⁸___ as good as meeting friends or playing sports for some people.

1 A in	B at	C while
2 A –	B a	C the
3 A have started	B started	C start
4 A since	B ever	C never
5 A makes	B does	C brings
6 A some	B more	C much
7 A is finding	B finds	C find
8 A exactly	B like	C just

Speaking

6 Read the strategy above. Then read the task below. Think of one or two ideas for each topic. Make notes.

Your local sports centre has several different sport clubs for students. Your friend is trying to decide which sport club to join. Help him / her to choose a sport and give him / her some advice on the following:
- Why it is a good sport for him / her.
- How often he / she should do the sport.
- What clothes and equipment he / she needs.

7 Complete the sentences using the words below. There are two extra words you don't need.

about   advice   better   don't   idea   ought   should   to

1 You _____ to start playing football.
2 What do you think I _____ do?
3 I _____ think you should play ice hockey.
4 I'd really like some _____ on what sport to play.
5 Do you think I ought _____ buy some new trainers?
6 Thinking _____ the equipment, it would be better to borrow a racket.

8 Work in pairs. Imagine the following situation. Your friend from another town is coming to stay with your family for two weeks over the summer holidays. Give him / her some advice. Discuss the following points:
- What he / she should pack for the visit.
- Activities you could do together.
- Advice on staying with your family.
- What sports he / she can do in your town.

Swap roles and repeat the Speaking activity.

Writing

9 Read the strategy above. Then read sentences 1–3 below. Choose the option (A–C) that is the *least* suitable style for a message.

1 _____ left my mobile in your bag.
   A Sorry, but I
   B I am writing to tell you that I
   C I'm afraid I accidentally
2 _____ my mum calls me on it.
   A I'd like to get it back soon as
   B I need it back soon because
   C I'd be grateful to get it back soon since
3 _____ collect it, please?
   A When can I
   B Could you kindly let me know when I can
   C When is a good time to

10 Imagine the following situation. You were visiting a friend at the weekend and you left a book at their house. Write a message to him / her where you ask him / her to return the book to you. Include the following information:
- What kind of book it is.
- Why the book is important to you.
- Where in his / her house you left it.
- Where and when you want to meet him / her.

2
Leisure time

Unit map

● **Vocabulary**
Activities and sports
Food dishes
Sports venues
Prepositions of place
Adventure activities
School clubs

● **Word Skills**
Compound nouns and adjectives

● **Grammar**
Present perfect and past simple contrast
Present perfect simple and continuous

● **Listening** Eating out

● **Reading** Field games

● **Speaking**
Stimulus-based discussion

● **Writing** A blog post

● **Culture 2** Tinseltown

● **Vocabulary Builder** page 122

● **Grammar Builder and Reference** page 129

2A Vocabulary

Love it or hate it
I can talk about likes and dislikes and leisure activities.

1 **SPEAKING** Work in pairs. Ask about your partner's hobbies. Find two things that he or she a) usually does at the weekend and b) occasionally does at the weekend.

2 **VOCABULARY** Check the meaning of the activities and sports below. How many can you find in photos A–F?

Activities and sports bake cakes collect figures, cards, stamps, etc. draw hang out with friends make clothes read books read magazines text your friends use social media video blog watch videos online
do, play or go ballet ballroom dancing basketball BMXing board games bowling camping cards chess cycling drama gymnastics horse riding ice hockey ice skating martial arts a musical instrument photography rollerblading running shopping skateboarding table tennis volleyball weights

LEARN THIS! *do, play* and *go*

a We normally use *do* with individual sports and activities not ending in *-ing*.

b We normally use *play* with team sports, ball sports, games and musical instruments.

c We normally use *go* with sports and activities ending in *-ing*.

3 Read the Learn this! box. Which verbs do we use with the blue activities and sports in exercise 2: *do*, *play* or *go*?

4 Put the activities and sports in exercise 2 into groups A–G. You can put some of them into more than one group. How many more activities can you add?

A games
B music
C computer-based activities
D home-based activities
E outdoor leisure activities
F activities and sports you usually do on your own
G sports you do with another person or in a team

5 SPEAKING Which of the activities and sports in exercise 2 …

a have you tried and enjoyed?
b have you tried but didn't enjoy?
c would you like to try? Why?
d would you prefer not to try? Why?

6 🎧 **1.18** Listen to five people talking about why they hate certain things. What sports or activities do they talk about?

RECYCLE! Present simple and adverbs of frequency

We use the present simple for habits and routines.

Adverbs of frequency (*always, usually, often, sometimes, hardly ever, never*) come before the main verb but after the verb *be*.

7 🎧 **1.18** Read the Recycle! box. Then listen again. Complete the sentences with the present simple form of the verbs below and an adverb of frequency.

be   buy   go   play   use

a Speaker 1 _____ camping with his parents.
b Speaker 2 thinks that horror films _____ unrealistic and unconvincing.
c Speaker 3 _____ social media.
d Speaker 4 _____ things online.
e Speaker 5 _____ the guitar at school.

8 SPEAKING Work in pairs. Do you agree with the opinions of the speakers in exercise 7? Why? / Why not?

> I disagree with Speaker 1. I think camping is great because sleeping in a tent is fun.

9 Complete the quiz below with words from exercise 2.

10 SPEAKING Work in pairs or small groups. Do the quiz. Then check your answers at the bottom of the page.

SPORT *and* LEISURE QUIZ

1 In which sport are there 10–12 players in a team, with five of them playing at any one time?
  a b_____
  b i_____ h_____
  c v_____

2 How many pieces are there on a c_____ board at the beginning of the game?
  a 28   b 32   c 36

3 How many c_____ are there in a traditional pack?
  a 32   b 42   c 52

4 Which s_____ m_____ app allows users to post six-second video clips?
  a Vine   b Snapchat   c Pinterest

5 How long is a b_____ alley?
  a 12.3 m   b 18.3 m   c 24.3 m

6 Can you identify these collectible f_____?

7 The name of which m_____ a_____ means 'empty hand'?
  a karate   b judo   c aikido

8 Which of these is not a b_____ dance?
  a tango   b waltz   c ballet

9 Which famous b_____ g_____ , invented in 1933, involves buying streets and building houses and hotels?
  a Monopoly   b Cluedo   c Risk

10 Which of these m_____ i_____ has four strings?
  a violin   b guitar   c harp

1a 2b 3c 4a 5c 6 Spider-Man, Hulk, Captain America 7a 8c 9a 10a

Present perfect and past simple contrast
I can use the past simple and present perfect tenses correctly.

1 Look at the photo and the title of the article below. What is the man's hobby, do you think?

2 Read the article and check your ideas. Do you collect anything? If so, what?

Mike Fountaine has the world's largest collection of McDonald's memorabilia. The sixty-year-old McDonald's employee has spent almost fifty years collecting everything to do with the fast-food restaurant. He has already filled nine rooms of his house with 75,000 objects, including toys, badges, cups and uniforms!

Mike has been at McDonald's since 1968. His first job was cooking Big Macs. A year later he began collecting badges, and he hasn't stopped since! A few years ago, Mike opened his own McDonald's restaurant. He has decorated it with memorabilia. 'People say it's the most beautiful McDonald's restaurant they've ever seen,' says Mike proudly.

3 Find all the examples of the past simple and the present perfect in the article. Complete the rules in the Learn this! box below with *present perfect* or *past simple*. Then underline an example of each rule in the text in exercise 2.

> **LEARN THIS!** Present perfect and past simple
>
> **a** We use ¹_____ to talk about a specific occasion in the past.
>
> **b** We use ²_____ to talk about an event during a period of time that is still continuing.
>
> **c** We use ³_____ to say how long a situation has existed, often with *for*, *since*, or *how long*.
>
> **d** We use ⁴_____ to talk about an event that has a strong connection with the present, often with *just*, *already*, or *yet*.
>
> **e** We use ⁵_____ to talk about an experience at an unspecified time in the past, often with *ever* or *never*.

4 Complete the lists with the orange time phrases from the article in exercise 2. Which tense is used with 'finished' time phrases and which with 'unfinished' time phrases?

1 Time phrases with the past simple: yesterday, ...
2 Time phrases with the present perfect: already, ...

5 The verb *go* has two past participles: *been* and *gone*. Explain the difference in meaning between these two sentences.

1 Jake's been swimming.
2 Jake's gone swimming.

➥ **Grammar Builder 2.1** page 129

Jian Yang is in his thirties and collects dolls. So far, he ¹_____ (spent) twenty years and over £250,000 on his collection, which includes 6,000 Barbie dolls. The young man from Singapore ²_____ (start) collecting Barbie dolls when he ³_____ (be) just thirteen. The first doll he ⁴_____ (buy) was the 'Great Shape' model in a gym outfit and leg warmers. Jian buys dolls when he travels for work and ⁵_____ (purchase) 65 dolls on his last trip to New York. A while ago, a girlfriend ⁶_____ (walk out) on him because of his hobby. Apparently, she ⁷_____ (feel) threatened by his collection. Jian ⁸_____ (find) that worrying, but now he accepts it. Another problem is space: he ⁹_____ already almost _____ (fill) his house. So ¹⁰_____ he ever _____ (think) about stopping? No. If he runs out of space, he says, he'll buy the house next door!

6 Complete the text above with the present perfect or past simple form of the verbs in brackets.

7 Read the Look out! box. Complete the example with the correct tense of the verb *go*. (Remember that *go* has two past participles.)

> **LOOK OUT!**
> We often use the present perfect to ask or talk about an experience and then the past simple to give specific information about it.
>
> '¹_____ you ever _____ bowling?' 'Yes, I ²_____ bowling last week.'

8 SPEAKING Work in pairs. Ask and answer about the experiences below. Give more details using the past simple.

- go abroad
- go ice skating
- do martial arts
- have a Chinese meal
- play Monopoly
- see or meet a famous person
- visit the USA
- download music from the internet
- speak English in a dream
- break a bone
- ride a horse
- find any money

> Have you ever been abroad?   Yes, I have.

> Where did you go?   I went to the USA.

> When was that?   I went last summer.

A

B

C

D

2C Listening

Eating out

I can identify the context of a dialogue.

1 VOCABULARY Match each photo (A–D) with a type of dish from the list below. Which dishes do you like or dislike?

Food dishes curry pie pudding risotto salad sandwich soup stew stir-fry

A _____ B _____ C _____ D _____

2 SPEAKING Work in pairs. Do the food quiz. Then check your answers at the bottom of the page.

1 Which food from exercise 1 is Britain's favourite dish?

2 Match the dishes (a–f) with the countries (1–6) they come from originally.

1 France	**a** lasagne
2 Italy	**b** cola
3 Japan	**c** chocolate mousse
4 Mexico	**d** tacos
5 Spain	**e** paella
6 USA	**f** miso soup

3 Complete the sentences about special diets with the words below.

eggs fruit milk pork wheat

a If you follow a gluten-free diet, you can't eat _____ .

b Muslims don't eat _____ .

c If you're lactose intolerant, you avoid _____ .

d Vegans don't eat _____ , but most vegetarians do.

e _____ is a good snack if you're following a low-fat diet.

4 Which of these foods contains the most calories? 100 grams of:

a steak **b** avocado **c** peanuts **d** chocolate

➡ **Vocabulary Builder** Diets: page 122

Listening Strategy

In a listening task, you sometimes need to identify the context of a conversation. The context is implied, not stated, so you have to listen for clues. The information you need may be:

a When the conversation is taking place.

b Where it is taking place.

c Why the conversation is taking place.

d Who is speaking.

3 🎧 1.19 Read the Listening Strategy. Then listen to two extracts and answer the questions.

Extract 1

1 Why is the man talking to the waiter?

2 What time of day is the dialogue taking place?

Extract 2

3 Who is speaking?

4 Where is the speaker?

4 🎧 1.19 Listen again. Which words and phrases helped you to decide on the answers in exercise 3?

5 🎧 1.20 Listen to a dialogue between two teenagers. For each question, write the correct speaker: Matthew (M) or Scarlett (S). Make a note of the words that helped you to decide on the answers.

Which person ...

1 is in the city centre? ___

2 recently finished some exams? ___

3 is not confident about finding the restaurant alone? ___

4 is likely to be late? ___

5 wants a new phone? ___

6 Put the phrases below into the correct group (A, B or C).

a bit special a real let-down fine nothing special not up to standard out of this world pretty average

A good _____

B OK _____

C bad _____

7 🎧 1.20 Listen again. Match the phrases in exercise 6 with the different restaurants mentioned: Italian, French, Mexican and Chinese.

8 SPEAKING Discuss these questions in pairs. Try to use phrases from exercise 6 in your answers.

1 Tell your partner about the last time you were in a restaurant. How good were the food and service?

2 Which local restaurants would you recommend to a foreign visitor and why?

3 Do you enjoy eating fast food? Why? / Why not?

4 What are your favourite dishes to eat a) at home and b) in a restaurant?

4 c

3 a wheat b pork c milk d eggs e fruit

2 1c 2a 3f 4d 5e 6b

1 curry

Present perfect simple and continuous

I can use the present perfect simple and continuous correctly.

1 **SPEAKING** Ask and answer the questions in pairs.

1 How often do you watch films? How do you watch them: at the cinema, on DVD, on live TV, or online?

2 Are some types of film better to watch at the cinema than on TV? Why? Give examples.

2 🎧 **1.21** Read and listen to the dialogue. Who do you think is more enthusiastic about seeing the film: Jack or Ellie? Find evidence for your opinion.

Ellie	At last! I've been waiting for ages. Where have you been? What have you been doing?
Jack	My bus didn't come. I've been trying to phone you since 7.30 …
Ellie	You're 25 minutes late! The film has started.
Jack	Sorry. Do you still want to see it?
Ellie	Yes, I do. I've been looking forward to it for weeks. It stars my favourite actor. And I've already bought the tickets!
Jack	Let's go inside then.
Ellie	OK. But why is your hair wet? It hasn't been raining.
Jack	That's sweat. I've been running for 25 minutes! And I haven't eaten. Can we see the film later?

3 Read the Learn this! box and complete the rules. Use the dialogue in exercise 2 to help you. How many examples of this tense are there in the dialogue?

> **LEARN THIS!** Present perfect continuous
>
> **a** We form the present perfect continuous with *have* / ¹_____ + ²_____ + -*ing* form.
>
> **b** We use the present perfect continuous:
>
> **1** for an action that began in the past and is still in progress.
> You ³_____ working much this term. Why not?
> We often use *for* or ⁴_____ to say how long the action has been in progress.
> *How long have they been living in France?*
> *They ⁵_____ living in Paris ⁶_____ ten years.*
>
> **2** for an action that has recently been in progress and which explains the current situation.
> *I'm hot because I ⁷_____ running.*

4 Write questions about Ellie and Jack from exercise 2. Use the present perfect continuous.

1 How long / Ellie / wait?
2 How long / Jack / try to phone Ellie?
3 How long / Ellie / look forward to the film?
4 Why / Ellie / look forward to the film?
5 How long / Jack / run?
6 Why / Jack / run?

5 **SPEAKING** In pairs, ask and answer your questions from exercise 4. Find the answers in the dialogue in exercise 2.

> How long has Ellie been waiting?

> Ellie has been waiting for ages.

> **LEARN THIS!** Present perfect simple
>
> We use the present perfect simple, not continuous:
>
> **a** for completed actions.
> *I've set up a Twitter account. Will you follow me?*
>
> **b** when we say how often something has happened.
> *Our team has won three times this season.*
>
> **c** with verbs that are not used in continuous tenses.
> *I've owed him £50 since the summer.*

6 Read the Learn this! box. Underline an example of the present perfect simple for a completed action in exercise 2.

➡ Grammar Builder 2.2 page 130

7 **USE OF ENGLISH** Complete the sentences using the correct form of the words in brackets. Do not change the order of the words. You can add up to three other words.

1 I'm not sure what's happening in this film because I _____ (only / watch / it) for a few minutes.
2 How long _____ (Alex / be / member) of the film club?
3 I can't go to the cinema because _____ (I / finish / my homework) yet.
4 Those two girls in the front row _____ (talk / each other) since the film started!
5 My parents were watching a science fiction film, but they _____ (turn / off / TV) now.
6 How long _____ (they / make / movies) in Hollywood?

8 **SPEAKING** Work in pairs. Take turns to be A and B.

A Tell your partner that he or she looks:

exhausted guilty hot relieved sleepy upset worried

B Explain why you look that way. Use the present perfect simple and continuous.

> You look exhausted.

> I've been getting up very early for the past few days.

Compound nouns and adjectives
I can use compounds correctly.

A

B

C

1 SPEAKING Look at the photos. What do they have in common? Which is the most spectacular, in your opinion?

2 VOCABULARY Match the nouns below with the photos in exercise 1. Some nouns go with more than one photo.

Compound nouns flood lights football pitch main road mountain range safety net sea shore swimming pool tennis court tennis player tower block

3 🎧 1.22 Listen and repeat the compound nouns from exercise 2. Which word is stressed: the first or second?

> **LEARN THIS!** Compound nouns
>
> **a** Compound nouns are nouns formed from two words.
>   **1** noun + noun (*bathroom, safety barrier*)
>   **2** *-ing* form + noun (*dining room, recording studio*)
>   **3** adjective + noun (*wet room, whiteboard*)
> **b** We usually write compound nouns as two words, but sometimes as one word (*whiteboard*) or with a hyphen (*make-up*). Check in a dictionary.
> **c** The stress is usually on the first word.

4 Read the Learn this! box. Then look at the compound nouns in exercise 2. Underline at least one example of each type (1, 2 and 3). Which type has the most examples?

5 Work in pairs. Match the words in A and B to form sports venues, using a dictionary to help you. Find three more sports venues in exercise 2.

A athletics basketball bowling boxing climbing dance golf ice weights
B alley course court ring rink room studio track wall

> **LEARN THIS!** Compound adjectives
>
> **a** Compound adjectives are adjectives formed from two words.
>   *well-known half-eaten record-breaking wind-powered*
> **b** We usually write compound adjectives with a hyphen.
> **c** Sometimes, compound adjectives have more than two words (*state-of-the-art*).

6 VOCABULARY Work in pairs. Read the Learn this! box. Decide which sports venues from exercises 2 and 5 you are likely to describe with these compound adjectives.

Compound adjectives 25-metre 400-metre air-conditioned brightly lit eight-lane eighteen-hole full-sized open-air solar-heated soundproof well-equipped

7 🎧 1.23 Listen to four students arguing in favour of a new facility for their school. Match the facilities below (a–e) with the speakers (1–4). There is one extra facility.

a a state-of-the-art recording studio ___
b a well-equipped art and design studio ___
c a high-speed Wi-Fi network ___
d a 300-seat theatre ___
e an all-weather football pitch ___

8 SPEAKING Which facility from exercise 7 would you like most for your school? Why? Can the whole class agree on one choice?

Field games

I can understand a text about an outdoor game.

1 SPEAKING Look at the blog and the photos. What kind of game do you think the people are playing? What do you think happens?

2 Read the blog post quickly and check your ideas from exercise 1.

> **Reading Strategy**
>
> Multiple-choice questions may test:
> - factual information (detailed or general).
> - the writer's opinion.
> - the writer's intention.
>
> You can sometimes (but not always) tell what a question is testing by reading the first part without the options (a–d).

3 Read the Reading Strategy and the questions in exercise 4. Then answer the following questions.

1 Which questions in exercise 4 ask about …
   a the writer's intention?
   b the writer's opinion?
   c factual information?
2 How did you decide on the answers to question 1?
3 Which question in exercise 4 is about the whole blog post?

4 Read the blog post again. Choose the correct options (a–d).

1 To take part in geocaching you need
   a a mobile phone with GPS.
   b a mobile phone with GPS and a toy or gift.
   c a mobile phone, a toy or gift and a logbook.
   d nothing – just yourself!
2 The activity of geocaching
   a began in the 19th century, but only became popular after 2000.
   b was originally only popular in one region of England, but now has fans all over the world.
   c was called 'letterboxing' when it was first invented.
   d has similarities with a 19th-century game.
3 When you find a gift in a geocache, you
   a make a note of the gift on the website.
   b can borrow the gift, but have to return it.
   c are allowed to take the gift if you replace it with something else.
   d take a photo of the gift as proof that you have found it.
4 The writer thinks that the most enjoyable kind of geocaching is when
   a you have to find a public webcam.
   b you have to find a series of geocaches.
   c you have to find a geocache and then hide it in a different place.
   d you simply have to find one geocache.

5 The writer believes the 'Fumble after Dark' event
   a is less fun than geocaching with a couple of friends.
   b would be a very enjoyable event to attend.
   c is only suitable for adventurous people.
   d needs to attract more people.
6 The writer has written the blog mainly to
   a suggest that people try geocaching.
   b explain the differences between letterboxing and geocaching.
   c publicise a geocaching event in Sweden.
   d warn the reader that geocaching is addictive.

5 VOCABULARY Match the prepositions below with definitions 1–5. Underline them in paragraphs 1, 2 and 3 of the blog.

Prepositions across   all along   all over   below   beside   by

1 lower than _____
2 at many points on something long _____
3 in many parts of a place _____ , _____
4 next to _____
5 near; at the side of _____

> ➺ **Vocabulary Builder** Prepositions of place: page 122

6 SPEAKING Work in pairs. Would you like to play this game? Why? / Why not? Use the adjectives, verbs and phrases below to help you.

Adjectives addictive   boring   difficult   exciting   exhausting   healthy   time-consuming

Explaining preference
I'd find it …   It sounds really …
I'd like to play it because …
It appeals / doesn't appeal to me because …
I'm (not) really into …   I'd rather …   I can't stand …
I don't mind … , but …

7 SPEAKING Share your opinions with the class.

GPS CHALLENGE

🎧 1.24 **CLAUDIA'S BLOG**

Dear Friends,

Sorry I haven't blogged for a while. I've been a bit busy lately. You'll find out why … But first of all, have you ever heard of geocaching? It's a kind of treasure-hunting game that
5 uses a GPS device – usually your smartphone – to find small containers called geocaches. These are hidden all over the world – but usually people start with geocaches that are close to their home. The great thing about geocaching is that it leads you to some beautiful and amazing places that you probably
10 didn't know about. I can definitely recommend it – it's healthy and it's fun. Although I should warn you that it's also seriously addictive!

So how does it work, exactly? Well, the first step is to go to the geocaching website or download the geocaching app onto
15 your phone. Then you choose a geocache and you start looking. People have been hiding geocaches for more than ten years, so there are literally millions of them around the world. There are sure to be some near your home, wherever you live. (There are geocaches across all seven continents, including Antarctica!)
20 Some are very hard to find. They may be hidden beside a river, up a tree, or even below the ground.

Geocaching is quite a new game: it began around the year 2000. However, similar games did exist in the past. For example, in the middle of the 19th century, a game called 'letterboxing'
25 became popular in the south of England. People who enjoyed walking in the countryside began to hide boxes all along the route. These boxes contained postcards addressed to themselves. When other walkers found a box, they collected the cards and posted them. This often took many weeks, because
30 the boxes were often hidden in remote places, not by the paths.

In geocaching, the boxes don't contain postcards. They contain a logbook, where the person who finds it can write their name and the date. (They also record the find on the website.) As well as the logbook, geocaches often contain a toy or gift. You are welcome to take this, provided you replace it with something 35 you have brought with you.

The basic game just involves finding a geocache and recording it online and in the logbook. However, there are lots of variations. For example, there are multi-cache challenges, where each cache contains the co-ordinates for the next cache, until you reach the 40 final cache containing the logbook. There are also 'travelling caches', where each person who finds the cache then hides it in a different location and updates the information on the website. And there are 'webcam caches'. When you do these, you don't find a physical container or logbook; you find a public webcam 45 and then capture an image of yourself on the webcam as proof that you have been successful. I've tried all of these types, and personally, I've enjoyed the multi-cache challenges the most.

Geocaching is an activity you can do alone or, like me, with a couple of friends. But there are also geocaching events where 50 you can get together with hundreds of other fans of the game. For example, the 'Fumble after Dark' event is held every November in Sweden and sounds like great fun. About a thousand geocachers get together for a day of talks and presentations about geocaching. And then they head outside into 55 the darkness for some night-time adventures! I've been enjoying my geocaching experiences so much that I'm seriously thinking about going to 'Fumble after Dark' next year. So why don't you get into geocaching too, and I might see you there!

Bye for now!! 60

Claudia

Stimulus-based discussion

I can discuss ideas for a day out and justify my opinions.

1 **SPEAKING** Look at the photos. Match the activities with four of the adventure sports below.

Adventure activities abseiling bodyboarding bungee jumping climbing hang-gliding hiking karting kayaking mountain biking parkour snowboarding surfing

2 **SPEAKING** Work in pairs. Ask and answer the questions. Give reasons for your opinions.

1 Which of the activities in the photos looks ...
   a most fun?
   b most challenging?
   c most dangerous?

2 Have you ever tried any of the adventure activities in exercise 1? If so, did you enjoy them? If not, would you like to try them?

3 🎧**1.25** Read the task below. Then listen to two students doing the task. Which activities do they consider? Which one do they agree on?

> You and a friend are planning a day out doing an adventure activity. Discuss with your friend what you are going to do. Give reasons for your opinions. Agree on an activity.

Speaking Strategy

When you have to reach an agreement, be sure to use a range of phrases for expressing preferences, raising objections and coming to an agreement.

4 🎧**1.25** **KEY PHRASES** Read the Speaking Strategy and the phrases below. Check that you understand them all. Then listen again. Which of the phrases did the students use?

Expressing preferences
I quite fancy ...
I think ... would be (fun).
I'm quite keen on ...
I like the idea of ...
I think ... is a better option than ...

Raising objections
Sorry, but I don't really fancy ...
Don't you think it (would be expensive)?
The problem with ... is that ...
Sorry, but I don't think that's a very good idea.
I'm not keen on ... because ...
I don't think ... would be as (interesting) as ...
I'd rather (go climbing) than (karting).

Coming to an agreement
We need to make a decision.
Overall, ... would be better.
Can we agree on ... , then?
OK, I agree.
That's settled then.

5 Work in pairs. Prepare to do the task in exercise 3.

- Choose three activities each that you would like to do using the list in exercise 1 or your own ideas. Make sure you and your partner choose different activities.
- Make notes about:
   a why you want to do the activities you have chosen.
   b why you do not want to do the activities your partner has chosen.

6 **SPEAKING** Work in pairs. Do the task in exercise 3 using your notes and the phrases in exercise 4 to help you.

A blog post

I can write a blog post expressing an opinion.

1 SPEAKING Match the photos with two clubs from the list below. Which clubs from the list would you like to belong to? Give reasons.

School clubs art club astronomy club baking club ballroom dancing club computer club debating society drama society film club fitness club handball club photography club school choir school orchestra science club

2 Read the task and the blog post below. Which clubs from exercise 1 are mentioned? Which other clubs that are not in exercise 1 are mentioned?

> Your school recently organised an open day for parents and students to find out about extra-curricular activities. Write a blog post about it for the school website.
> * Where and when did the event take place?
> * Who attended the event?
> * What happened at the event?
> * Give your personal opinion of the event and say what effects the event has had.

One Saturday last month, the school organised an open day for students and parents to learn about all the school clubs. The event took place in the playground and also in the school hall.

More than two hundred people came to the school to find out about the activities the school can offer. Most of them were parents of primary school children who are going to start at the school in September, at the beginning of the next school year. Some students who are already at the school were there too, as well as most of the teachers.

More than twenty different school clubs had stalls in the playground. Students and teachers at the stalls explained to the visitors what goes on at the clubs. In the school hall, there were karate displays from the martial arts club and a short performance by the choir.

In my view, the day was a great success. Everyone seemed to have a very good time. Since the open day, lots of people have been asking for information about clubs. As well as that, the school has received suggestions for new clubs, including ballroom dancing and ice skating!

3 Answer the questions about the blog post.

What phrase does the writer use to …
a say when a past event took place? _____
b introduce a personal opinion? _____
c introduce an additional point? _____

> **Writing Strategy**
> Where there is a word limit for the writing task, make sure you keep within it. If you went over the limit, decide which words you can delete. For example, there may be unnecessary adjectives or examples. When you have cut the words, make sure that a) the text still makes sense and b) all four points in the task are still covered.

4 SPEAKING Read the Writing Strategy. In pairs, look through the blog post in exercise 2 and suggest twelve words you could delete. Then compare ideas with another pair.

5 Read the task below. Then prepare a plan for your blog post by answering the questions.

> You recently went to a show performed by a number of different clubs at school. Write a blog post about it.
> * Where and when did the show take place?
> * Who attended the event and how did they react?
> * Give your personal opinion of the event.
> * Suggest two improvements for next year.

Paragraph 1
* When and where did it take place?
* Which clubs took part? (Use clubs from exercise 1 or your own ideas.)

Paragraph 2
* Who attended the show?
* How did the audience react?

Paragraph 3
* What did you think of the show?

Paragraph 4
* What would make the show better? A different time / venue? Longer / Shorter? Different acts? Anything else?

6 SPEAKING Work in pairs. Compare your notes from exercise 5 and suggest at least one improvement for your partner's plan.

> You could mention what music the orchestra played.

> Why don't you say how long the show lasted?

7 Write a blog post using the task and plan from exercise 5. Include phrases from exercise 3 if appropriate.

> **CHECK YOUR WORK**
> Have you …
> * followed your writing plan?
> * kept your writing clear and concise, deleting extra words if necessary?
> * included appropriate phrases from exercise 3?
> * checked the spelling and grammar?

3

The human body

Unit map

● **Vocabulary**
Parts of the body
Treatments
Accidents and injuries
Adjectives to describe feelings
Homonyms

● **Word Skills**
Word families

● **Grammar**
Speculating and predicting
Future continuous and future
  perfect

● **Listening** The body's limits

● **Reading** Body clock

● **Speaking** Photo description

● **Writing** An opinion essay

● **Culture 3**
British sporting events

● **Vocabulary Builder** page 122

● **Grammar Builder and**
  Reference page 131

3A Vocabulary

Parts of the body
I can identify parts of the body and talk about injuries.

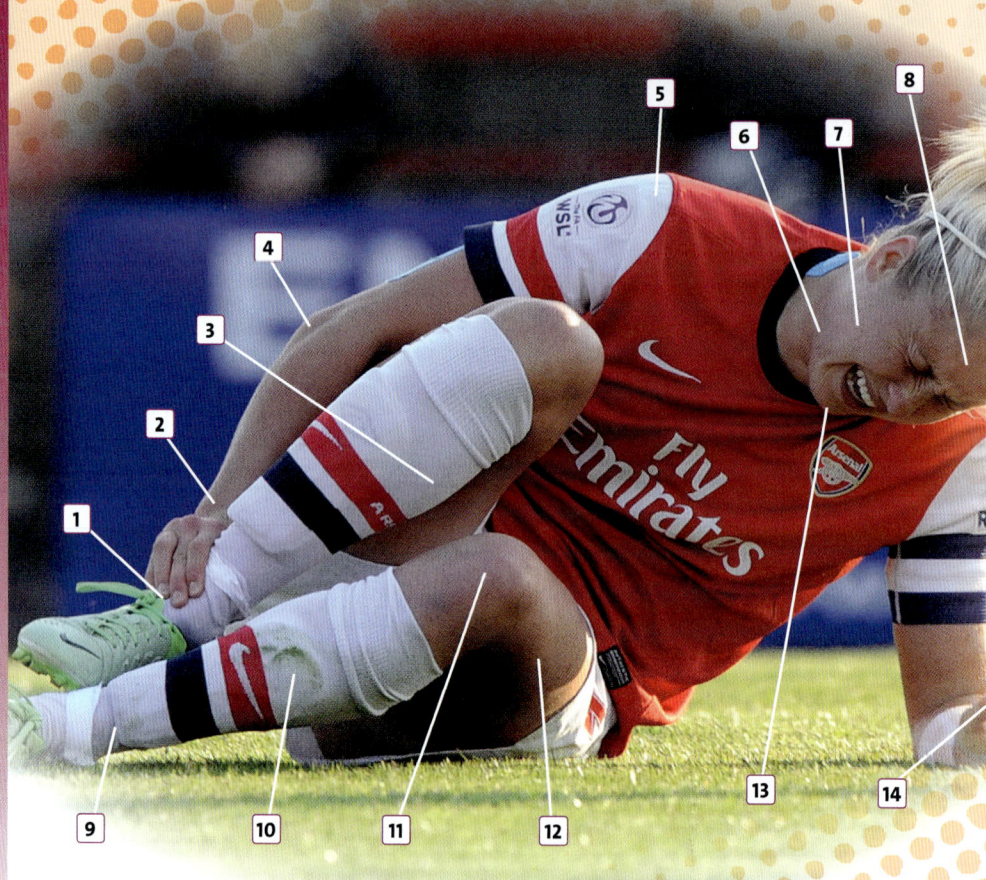

1 **SPEAKING** Describe the photo. How is the footballer feeling?
What has happened, do you think?

2 **VOCABULARY** Match 1–14 in the photo with parts of the body from the list below.
Check the meaning of all the words in the list.

Parts of the body ankle blood bottom brain calf cheek chin
elbow eyebrow eyelid forehead heart heel hip intestine jaw
kidney knee lip lung muscle nail rib scalp shin shoulder skin
skull spine stomach thigh throat thumb toe waist wrist

3 **SPEAKING** Work in pairs. Which parts of the body in the list in exercise 2 …

1 are inside your body?
2 are part of your head or neck?
3 are part of your arm or hand?
4 are part of your leg or foot?
5 are between your neck and the top of your legs?
6 do you have two of?
7 are bones?

4 **SPEAKING** Work in pairs. Describe one of the parts of the body in the list in
exercise 2. Can your partner guess what it is?

I've got two of them. They're inside my body. I use them to breathe.   Your lungs.

HOW MUCH DO YOU KNOW ABOUT
the human body?

1 What is the most common blood type?
a AB-
b B-
c O+

2 How much do fingernails grow per month?
a 0.75 mm
b 1.5 mm
c 3 mm

3 Where exactly is your heart?
a On the left of your chest.
b In the middle of your chest.
c In the middle of your chest, a bit to the left.

4 How long are the human intestines?
a 3.5 m
b 8.5 m
c 13.5 m

5 How many bones do you have when you are born?
a 206
b 300
c 426

6 How many hairs are there on the human scalp?
a 90,000–150,000
b 150,000–190,000
c 190,000–250,000

7 What is the human body's biggest organ?
a liver   b brain   c skin

8 What is the average thickness of human skin?
a 1–2 mm   b 2–3 mm   c 3–4 mm

9 Where is the largest muscle in your body?
a in your bottom
b in your thigh
c in your jaw

5 **SPEAKING** Work in pairs or small groups. Do the body quiz above.

6 🎧 **1.26** Listen and check your answers to the quiz.

7 🎧 **1.27** **VOCABULARY** Listen to four dialogues between doctors and their patients. Complete the table using the words below to complete the treatments.

Treatments antibiotics bandage cream
dressing medicine painkillers X-ray

Patient	1	2	3	4
Part of the body injured				
When				
Treatment				

> **RECYCLE!** Present perfect and past simple
>
> a We use the present perfect for:
> 1 giving news, when we do not say exactly when the event happened.
> 2 talking about experiences.
>
> b When we ask for or give specific information about the news or experience, we use the past simple.
> *'I've broken my wrist. I fell off my bike.'*
> *'Have you ever broken your leg?' 'Yes, I broke my left leg last year.'*

8 🎧 **1.27** Read the Recycle! box. Complete the extracts from the dialogues with the verbs in brackets. Use the present perfect or past simple. Listen again and check your answers.

Dialogue 1
a My ankle really hurts. I think I _____ (twist) it.
b Yes, it's a bit swollen. You _____ (sprain) it.

Dialogue 2
c I _____ (have) an accident. I _____ (bang) my head.
d I _____ (trip) over the cat and _____ (hit) my head on the corner of a table.

Dialogue 3
e I _____ (hurt) my thumb. I _____ (trap) it in the car door.
f You _____ certainly _____ (bruise) it.
g It's really painful. Do you think I _____ (break) it?

Dialogue 4
h I _____ (burn) my hand. I _____ (pick up) a very hot saucepan.
i When _____ it _____ (happen)?

9 **SPEAKING** Work in pairs. Ask and answer about experiences using the present perfect and the phrases below. If the answer is 'yes', give more information.

Accidents and injuries bang your head   break a bone
bruise yourself badly   burn yourself   cut yourself badly
have a bad nosebleed   have a black eye
sprain your wrist   twist your ankle

> Have you ever broken a bone?

> No, I haven't. / Yes, I have. I broke my arm when I was ten. I was climbing a tree and I fell to the ground.

Grammar

Speculating and predicting

I can speculate and make predictions about the future.

1 SPEAKING Look at the photo and the title of the article. What do you think the article is about?

2 Read the article and check your ideas.

BIO-PRINTING

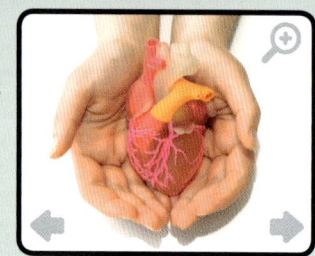

It is already possible to 'print' three-dimensional objects out of plastic and metal using a 3-D printer. Now scientists are developing printers that will be able to print human organs and body parts. If they are successful, doctors could save millions of lives. At the moment, scientists are able to print human tissue and bone, but the printing of whole organs will probably be a reality by 2025. Doctors are certain that bio-printing will revolutionise the treatment of cancer and heart disease. Moreover, if we can produce organs such as hearts and kidneys, patients won't die while they're waiting for an organ donor. The technology is very expensive and the cost might not come down for a while. But when it does, bio-printing could play an important part in all our lives.

3 Match the highlighted structures in the article in exercise 2 with rules a–d in the Learn this! box below.

> **LEARN THIS!** Speculating and predicting
>
> **a** We use *will / won't* to make predictions.
> *Scientists will find a cure for cancer.*
>
> **b** We can use phrases with *will / won't* to make the predictions stronger or weaker.
> *I'm (fairly) sure / I think / I don't think / I doubt scientists will find a cure for cancer.*
> *Scientists will definitely / probably find a cure for cancer.*
>
> **c** We use *may / might / could* + infinitive without *to* to talk about possibility in the future.
> *Scientists may / might / could find a cure for cancer.*
>
> **d** We use *may not / might not* for the negative. We do not use *could not*.

➡ **Grammar Builder 3.1** page 131

4 SPEAKING Work in pairs. Make predictions about your partner's future life using the prompts. Use *will / may / might / could* and phrases from the Learn this! box above. Your partner says if he / she agrees or not.

1 what / study at university?
2 when / leave home?
3 what job / do?
4 when / get married?
5 how many children / have?
6 what type of car / drive?

> I think you'll study maths at university.

> No, I definitely won't study maths. I might study history.

5 Study the examples in the Learn this! box below and complete the rules with the correct verbs and tenses.

> **LEARN THIS!** First conditional
>
> **a** We form the first conditional with the ¹_____ in the *if* clause and ²_____ / *won't* + infinitive without *to* in the main clause.
> *If I pass all my exams, I'll go to university.*
>
> **b** We can make predictions with the first conditional.
> *You'll cut yourself if you aren't careful with that knife.*
>
> **c** We can use *may* / ³_____ / *could* in the main clause to make the prediction less certain.
> *You might cut yourself if you aren't careful.*

➡ **Grammar Builder 3.2** page 131

6 Underline one first conditional sentence with *will / won't* and one with *could* in the article in exercise 2.

7 Complete the article below with the correct form of the verbs in brackets. Use the first conditional. In gaps 4 and 6, use a modal verb to make the prediction less certain.

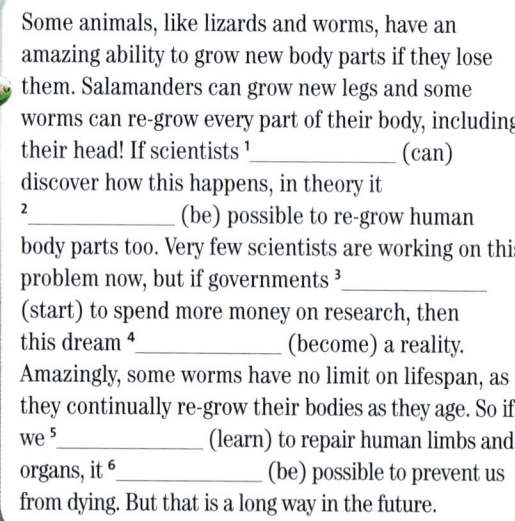

Some animals, like lizards and worms, have an amazing ability to grow new body parts if they lose them. Salamanders can grow new legs and some worms can re-grow every part of their body, including their head! If scientists ¹_____ (can) discover how this happens, in theory it ²_____ (be) possible to re-grow human body parts too. Very few scientists are working on this problem now, but if governments ³_____ (start) to spend more money on research, then this dream ⁴_____ (become) a reality. Amazingly, some worms have no limit on lifespan, as they continually re-grow their bodies as they age. So if we ⁵_____ (learn) to repair human limbs and organs, it ⁶_____ (be) possible to prevent us from dying. But that is a long way in the future.

8 SPEAKING Work in pairs. Ask and answer using the first conditional and the ideas below.

1 you feel ill tomorrow morning
2 the weather is fine at the weekend
3 there's a long power cut this evening
4 you get poor marks in your next English test
5 your best friend forgets your birthday
6 your own ideas

> What will you do if you feel ill tomorrow morning?

> I'll visit the doctor. / I won't come to school.

Listening
The body's limits
I can listen for specific information.

A

B

1 SPEAKING Describe and compare the photos. What are the similarities and differences between the activities? Which looks more challenging, in your opinion? Use the words below to help you.

become dehydrated   carry   climber   cold   desert
equipment   food and water   frostbite   heat
high altitude   oxygen   survive   temperature   tent

> **Listening Strategy**
> Some listening tasks may involve listening out for numbers, dates and measurements. Make sure you know how to pronounce these so that you can identify the information when you hear it.

2 🎧**1.28** **SPEAKING** Read the Listening Strategy. Then try to say the numbers and measurements below. Listen and check.

Large numbers: 4,500 100,000 250,000 2.5 million
Small numbers: 0 0.6 0.04 2.08
Years: 1500 1535 2000 2015 2150 the 1980s
Fractions: $\frac{1}{2}$ $\frac{1}{3}$ $\frac{1}{4}$ $\frac{1}{5}$ $\frac{1}{10}$ $\frac{3}{8}$ $1\frac{2}{3}$
Percentages: 50% 57%
Ratios and ranges: 2:1 10:1 aged 18–25
from 0–100 in 3.1 seconds
Temperature: -40°C 0°C 5°C 15°C

3 🎧**1.29** Read and listen to the article. Complete the article with numbers and measurements from exercise 2.

There are many amazing stories of human survival, but actually our bodies are very fragile and do not cope well with extremes. Polar explorers can cope with temperatures of ¹_____ , but only if they keep warm. Most people will collapse if their body temperature drops by only ²_____ , and if it drops by ³_____ , they'll die. Heat can be just as dangerous. Temperatures of 35°C are safe, provided humidity is not above ⁴_____ . High altitudes are dangerous too. We pass out when the pressure falls below ⁵_____ of normal atmospheric pressure. This happens at about ⁶_____ metres. Climbers can go higher because their bodies gradually get used to it, but no one survives for long at 8,000 metres. At high altitudes, lack of oxygen is another problem. At ground level, about ⁷_____ of the air is oxygen. If that falls below ⁸_____ , we die.

4 🎧**1.30** Read the sentences. Each one contains a mistake with a number. Listen and correct the mistakes.

1 Normal body temperature for humans is 36.5–37.5°C.
2 An increase of just 5°C above normal body temperature can make you feel unwell.
3 About a quarter of people who go to Accident and Emergency have a fever.
4 You can get frostbite if the temperature of your skin falls to 10°C or below.
5 In 2000, a Norwegian woman survived after her body temperature had fallen to 30.7°C.
6 Less than 30% of adults whose temperature drops below 28°C survive.

5 🎧**1.31** Listen to an interview with a scientist. Which of the people he talks about tested the body's limits deliberately?

6 🎧**1.31** Read the sentences aloud, paying attention to the numbers. Then listen again and decide whether the sentences are true or false. Write T or F and correct the false sentences.

1 When a Russian space capsule had a major problem in 1971, the cosmonauts died in less than 30 seconds. ___
2 In 1966, a scientist passed out after 15 seconds in a vacuum. ___
3 The scientist passed out for 27 seconds. ___
4 In the 1960s, Randy Gardner stayed awake for more than 250 hours. ___
5 After staying awake for so long, Randy Gardner then slept for almost 50 hours. ___

7 SPEAKING Discuss the questions in pairs.

1 Have you ever been awake all night or most of the night? If so, when / where / why?
2 Have you ever felt very cold? If so, when / where / why?
3 Have you ever experienced high altitude? If so, when / where / why? How did it feel?

Future continuous and future perfect
I can talk about events in the future and when they will happen.

NOW   20,000 YEARS FROM NOW   60,000 YEARS FROM NOW   100,000 YEARS FROM NOW

1 What differences can you see between the first and last pair of photos?

2 Read the article. Did you mention any differences in exercise 1 that are not mentioned in the text?

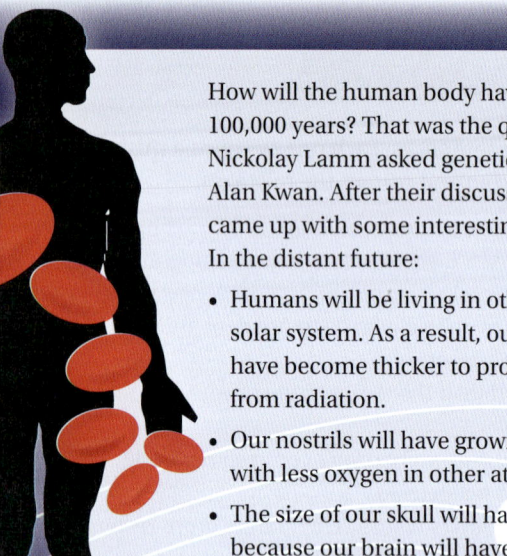

How will the human body have changed in 100,000 years? That was the question artist Nickolay Lamm asked genetics expert Dr Alan Kwan. After their discussion, Mr Lamm came up with some interesting predictions. In the distant future:

- Humans will be living in other parts of the solar system. As a result, our eyelids will have become thicker to protect our eyes from radiation.

- Our nostrils will have grown larger to cope with less oxygen in other atmospheres.

- The size of our skull will have increased because our brain will have got larger.

- We will be using a nano-chip inside our head to receive images and sound for entertainment and communication.

3 Read the Learn this! box. Complete the examples and rules. How many more examples of each tense can you find in the article in exercise 2?

> **LEARN THIS!** Future perfect and future continuous
>
> **a** We form the future perfect with *will have* + past participle.
> By the weekend, he ¹_____ left hospital.
>
> **b** We form the future continuous with *will be* + *-ing* form.
> This time next month, he ²_____ playing football again.
>
> **c** We use the future ³_____ to talk about a completed action in the future.
>
> **d** We use the future ⁴_____ to talk about an action in progress in the future.

➜ **Grammar Builder 3.3** page 132

4 Complete the sentences using the correct future continuous or future perfect form of the verbs in brackets.

1 Five hours from now, we _____ (finish) this English lesson.
2 My brother is at university, but in two years' time, he _____ (work).
3 Hopefully, I _____ (not live) with my parents when I'm thirty.
4 I'm sure the party will be a big surprise for her. Nobody _____ (tell) her about it.
5 According to the weather forecast, the sun _____ (shine) all day tomorrow.
6 I'm looking forward to the Argentina match – but I'm sad that Messi _____ (not play).

5 Read the Learn this! box. Add two more time expressions from the article in exercise 2.

> **LEARN THIS!** Future time expressions
> When we talk about the distant future, we can say:
> - about 100 years from now
> - in 1,000 / 10,000 / a million years' time
> - within 10 / 50 / 100 years
> - by the end of the decade / the century / the next century / the millennium
> - a few hundred / thousand years into the future
> - in the foreseeable future / in the long term

6 Read the prompts. Then write predictions using the future continuous or future perfect and a suitable time expression. Start with *I think ...* or *I don't think ...* .

1 scientists / find a cure for most diseases
I think / don't think scientists will have found a cure for most diseases by the end of the century.
2 most people / live to 200
3 new diseases / appear
4 a human / run 100 m in five seconds
5 computers / manage all major companies
6 the Earth / fight wars against other planets

7 **SPEAKING** Work in pairs. Discuss your predictions from exercise 6 using the phrases below to help you. Try to give reasons for your opinions.

Asking for a response   Do you agree?
What's your view / opinion?   What do you think?

Offering a response   I'm not sure I agree.
I think / don't think you're right.   That's what I think too.

Word families

I can recognise different words formed from the same base.

1 VOCABULARY In pairs, read the adjectives below and talk about situations in which you experience those feelings.

Adjectives to describe feelings afraid anxious ashamed cross depressed disgusted envious proud surprised

> I sometimes feel afraid if I see a very large spider.

> I always get anxious when …

2 Read the article and look at the pictures. Match the underlined words in the article with pictures 1–4.

A gut feeling?

Emotions do not just occur in your mind; they also have a physical effect on your body. A group of scientists from Finland decided to find out which emotions affect which parts of the body. They asked 701 volunteers to colour in silhouettes in response to emotional words, stories and videos. The results show that the people generally experience emotions like anger, envy and <u>shame</u> in similar ways.

For example, when you're angry, you probably feel that <u>anger</u> mostly in your chest and head. But if you feel ashamed, you probably notice it in your face and, in particular, your cheeks. <u>Depression</u> makes your whole body feel less active, whereas <u>happiness</u> affects your whole body in a positive way.

▼ 'Hot' colours like yellow and red show an increase in activity, while blue shows the opposite. Black is neutral.

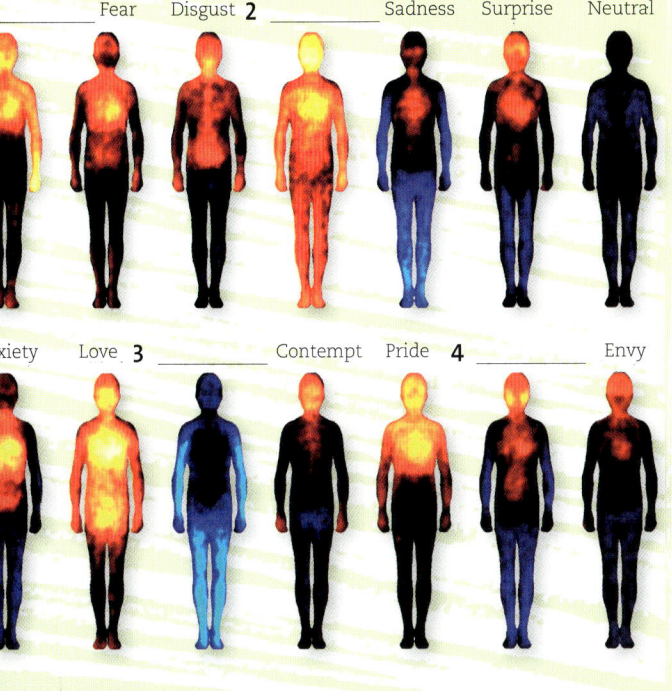

3 Complete the table with words from exercises 1 and 2.

Noun	Adjective		Noun	Adjective
1 _____	angry		5 _____	happy
anxiety	2 _____		pride	6 _____
3 _____	ashamed		7 _____	sad
4 _____	envious		8 _____	surprised

LEARN THIS! Word families

a Some nouns are formed by adding a suffix like *-ness* or *-ment* to an adjective.
sad – sadness   content – contentment

b Common adjective endings are *-ed, -ing, -ous, -ful, -less, -y* and *-al*.
surprised / surprising   suspicious   hopeful / hopeless   dirty   political

c Most adverbs are formed by adding *-ly* to an adjective.
cross – crossly   happy – happily

d We can change the meaning of many adjectives and adverbs by adding a prefix.
surprisingly – unsurprisingly

4 Read the Learn this! box. In pairs, write down two more examples for each rule (a–d). Use a dictionary to help you if necessary.

5 Complete the sentences with the adjective or adverb related to the noun in brackets.

1 He told me _____ (anger) not to be late again.
2 Liam is _____ (hope) that he'll pass all his exams.
3 I was _____ (surprise), but I tried not to show it.
4 We waited _____ (anxiety) for news of his arrival.
5 He looked for his wallet, but _____ (sadness) he couldn't find it.
6 That's a good mark for this exam – don't be _____ (shame) of it.

6 USE OF ENGLISH Complete each sentence with a word related to the word in brackets. You may need to add a prefix. Use a dictionary to help you if necessary.

1 She didn't seem *anxious* (anxiety) at all.
2 He stared _____ (envy) at his friend's new bike.
3 Her neighbour is always very bad-tempered, so she found his angry reaction _____ (surprise).
4 You ought to feel no _____ (ashamed) about asking for help.
5 They _____ (pride) carried their country's flag.
6 My sister was _____ (annoy) late.
7 He didn't try to hide his _____ (happy) – he just cried.

7 SPEAKING Discuss the questions in pairs.

1 Do you think money can make people happy? Why? / Why not?
2 When is pride good? When is it bad?
3 Is fear ever a good emotion? If so, when?

Body clock

I can understand an article about the human body clock.

1 SPEAKING Work in pairs. Ask and answer the questions.

1 What time do you usually go to bed a) on weekdays and b) at the weekend?
2 What time do you usually get up a) on weekdays and b) at the weekend?
3 Have those times changed much since you were younger?

> **Reading Strategy**
>
> When matching questions with texts, follow these steps:
>
> 1 Read the text to get a general idea of the meaning.
> 2 Read the task's lead-in line very carefully (*In which period of the day* ...). Then read all the options carefully.
> 3 Read the paragraphs of the text carefully one by one and match them to the correct option.
> 4 If you can't find the answer, leave it for now and come back to it later.

2 Read the Reading Strategy. Then read the article to get an idea of the general meaning. Which is the best summary: a, b, c or d?

The writer's main purpose is to explain:

a why children need more sleep than adults.
b why we should always get lots of sleep.
c why our bodies feel more or less tired at different times of day.
d why some people feel more alert than others.

3 Match the paragraphs (A–H) with questions 1–10 below. Two of the paragraphs match more than one question.

In which period of the day ...
1 do you completely stop digesting food? _____
2 is it best to be physically active? _____
3 do our bodies have difficulty digesting certain foods? _____
4 are older people more likely to have accidents? _____
5 does your body contain the most melatonin? _____
6 are you best at remembering things over short periods of time? _____
7 are you at your strongest physically? _____
8 does your body stop making melatonin? _____
9 is your body at its coolest? _____
10 does your body begin to become cooler? _____

4 Read the article again and answer the questions.

1 How much more sleep does a young child need than an adolescent?
2 What's the difference between 'larks' and 'owls'?
3 Why is it better not to exercise early in the morning?
4 When do sportspeople think is a good time to try to break a record?
5 If you want to lose weight, which is more important: when you eat or how much you eat?
6 Why is it not a good idea to use gadgets such as tablets and mobiles late at night?

> **LEARN THIS!** Homonyms
>
> Homonyms are words that have the same spelling or pronunciation but a different meaning or part of speech.
>
> **bank 1** a place where you keep money **2** the side of a river
>
> **walk 1** a noun **2** a verb

5 VOCABULARY Read the Learn this! box. Then look at the highlighted words in the article. What part of speech are they?

6 Find a homonym for each of the highlighted words in the article. If the meaning is different, translate the words. Use a dictionary to help you.

exercise (verb) homonym: exercise (noun)

➤➤ **Vocabulary Builder** Homonyms: page 122

7 SPEAKING Work in pairs. Ask and answer.

1 Do you get enough sleep? If not, why not?
2 How do you feel if you don't get enough sleep? What things are more difficult to do?
3 Do you use gadgets such as mobiles late at night? What for? Do you find that they keep you awake?
4 When are you most alert? Are you a 'lark', an 'owl', or in between the two? Explain your answer.

NIGHT AND DAY

🎧 1.32

HOW MUCH SLEEP DO WE NEED?

- Young children need more sleep than adults and tend to wake up earlier. A typical ten-year-old needs about ten hours' sleep.
- As you reach adolescence, your body clock changes. Most teenagers need about nine hours' sleep, but wake up later.
- As an adult, you'll need about eight to eight and a half hours' sleep a night.
- When we are much older, in our 70s and 80s, we're less able to sleep deeply and we usually need less sleep.

OUR PERSONAL BODY CLOCK

Each of us has our own personal body clock, which makes us more alert in the morning or more alert in the evening. You might be a 'lark' who likes to go to bed early and get up early, or you might be an 'owl' who prefers to go to bed late and get up late. Or somewhere in between.

A **6 A.M. – 9 A.M.** Your body is waking up. It stops producing melatonin, the hormone which makes you feel sleepy. Blood vessels are stiffer and less flexible. Your blood is thicker and stickier and your blood pressure is at its highest, so it's not the best time to exercise.

B **9 A.M. – 12 P.M.** You're at your most alert at this time in the morning. Tests show that short-term memory is at its best right now. It's a good time to get a lot of work done, because you'll experience a big dip after lunch.

C **12 P.M. – 3 P.M.** Your stomach is full and working hard after lunch. You become much less alert and probably feel a bit sleepy. More road accidents happen at this time of day than at any other, particularly involving older people.

D **3 P.M. – 6 P.M.** This is a very good time to exercise. Body temperature increases in the late afternoon. Your heart and lungs work better and muscles are six per cent stronger than at their lowest point in the day. Some sportspeople believe that if you try to break a world record at this time of day, you'll have a greater chance of success.

E **6 P.M. – 9 P.M.** By now you'll be getting hungry. But don't eat too late! In the evening, our bodies struggle to digest fats and sugars. Studies show that people will lose more weight if they have their main meal at lunchtime rather than in the evening. (But how much you eat is always more important than when you eat.)

F **9 P.M. – 12 A.M.** It's getting near to bedtime. Your body temperature is falling and your body clock is telling you that it's time for bed. Your body is producing lots of melatonin to help you go to sleep. It can be difficult to sleep with the light on because light reduces the amount of melatonin in your body. Blue light is particularly effective at keeping us awake. And mobile phones, computer screens and flat-screen TVs emit large amounts of blue light. So turn off those gadgets!

G **12 A.M. – 3 A.M.** Your body really wants to be asleep. Melatonin reaches its maximum level. Your stomach has stopped working and your brain is at rest. If you stay awake much longer, your powers of concentration will decrease sharply.

H **3 A.M. – 6 A.M.** Melatonin levels are still high, and you are in deep sleep. Your body temperature is much cooler than at any other time of the day. As dawn approaches, your melatonin levels will decrease and your body will prepare to wake up.

3G Speaking
Photo description
I can describe photos and answer questions.

1 Look at the photos. Which fitness class would you prefer to do? Why?

> **Speaking Strategy**
>
> Try to give your photo description a simple structure:
>
> **1** Say what the photo shows in general. If you are unsure, use phrases like '*It looks to me as if …*', or '*The photo appears to show …*'.
>
> **2** Talk about some of the interesting details in the photo.
>
> **3** Add a personal opinion or reaction.

2 🎧 **1.33** Read the Speaking Strategy. Then listen to two students describing the photos in exercise 1. Which student follows the strategy better? Explain your answer.

3 **KEY PHRASES** Look at the useful phrases below. Are you more likely to use them for general or detailed comments?

Identifying people in photos		
The man / woman / boy / girl	wearing / in / with	a yellow T-shirt purple leggings a red top casual / smart clothes
	with	a beard / a moustache a ponytail his / her foot in the air his / her hands on his / her hips bare feet
	who is	jumping / crouching / walking / running holding (some weights) on the ground

➥ **Vocabulary Builder** Describing appearance: page 122

4 🎧 **1.33** **KEY PHRASES** Listen again. Which of the underlined phrases from the list below does each student use?

> **Speculating about photos**
>
> It looks like some kind of dance class.
> They're in a park, or maybe in the countryside.
> I think it's a fitness class of some kind.
> There's a sort of climbing frame.
> It's most likely in the evening.
> Two men are doing pull-ups, or something like that.
> She's the instructor, I would say.
> I'd say that she's tired.

5 🎧 **1.34** Read question 1 below. Then listen to a student's answer. Which photo from exercise 1 is he referring to? How do you know?

> **1** Do you think the people are enjoying the class? Why do you think so?

6 **SPEAKING** In pairs, ask and answer the same question about the other photo in exercise 1.

7 Read questions 2 and 3 below. Then look at phrases a–h. Which phrases would be useful for each of the questions?

> **2** Do you think men care as much about their appearance as women? Why do you think that?
>
> **3** Tell me about an occasion when you wanted to look your best.

a I remember once when …
b As I see it, …
c A few months ago, …
d My view is that …
e The way I look at it, …
f Some time last year, …
g In my opinion, …
h On one occasion, …

8 🎧 **1.35** Listen to three students answering questions 2 and 3 from exercise 7. Answer the questions below.

1 What is each student's overall answer to question 2: yes, no, or maybe?

2 Which student does not really give reasons for his or her answer to question 2?

3 What three occasions do the students mention for question 3? Choose from:

a family party   a festival   a friend's party
a job interview   a school performance   a wedding

9 **SPEAKING** Work in pairs. Ask and answer the questions in exercise 7.

10 **SPEAKING** Work in pairs. Turn to page 144 and do the speaking task. Use phrases from this lesson.

3H Writing

An opinion essay

I can write an opinion essay.

1 SPEAKING Discuss the questions in pairs. Give reasons for your opinions.

1 Do you think most teenagers have a healthy lifestyle?
2 Do you have a healthy lifestyle? Why? / Why not?

2 Read the task below. What two different elements does the task contain?

Many people agree that teenagers don't get enough exercise. Write an essay in which you give your own view of the problem and propose ways of solving it.

3 Read the essay. What is the writer's opinion about the problem? How many solutions does she propose?

Most people agree that the lack of exercise in teenagers' lives is a serious problem. But what are the causes of this problem and what can we do to address them?

I strongly believe that today's teenagers spend too much time playing on electronic gadgets. They hardly ever do outdoor activities and this is why many of them do not get enough exercise. What is more, many teenagers are overweight and this makes them less willing to do exercise.

In order to tackle this problem, a number of measures are necessary. In my view, it is unrealistic to limit the amount of time teenagers spend on gadgets. What I propose instead is that we make sure school canteens only serve healthy food. Furthermore, I would strongly recommend that we give all teenagers free membership of their local sports facilities.

To conclude, lack of exercise can cause long-term health problems, so it is vital that we act now. It seems to me that the measures I propose will begin to remedy the situation.

Writing Strategy

1 Divide your essay into an introduction, main body and conclusion.
2 If the task has more than one element, deal with them in different paragraphs within the main body.
3 Use formal language.
4 Support opinions with evidence or examples.

4 Read the Writing Strategy. Does the writer follow all of the advice? Give examples.

5 KEY PHRASES Complete the useful phrases with the words below. Then translate them and find ten of them in the text in exercise 3.

agree   common   conclusion   In order to   my   only
opinion   propose   said   see   seems
solution   sum   vital   What   widely   would

1 **Introducing your opinions**
I (strongly) believe that   In my ¹_____ ,
It ²_____ to me that   As I ³_____ it,
In ⁴_____ view,

2 **Introducing other people's opinions**
It is a ⁵_____ held view that
It is often ⁶_____ that   It is a ⁷_____ belief that
Most people ⁸_____ that

3 **Making an additional point**
⁹_____ is more,   Not ¹⁰_____ that, but
Moreover,   Furthermore,

4 **Introducing proposals and solutions**
One ¹¹_____ might be to
What I ¹²_____ (instead) is that
I ¹³_____ strongly recommend that
It is ¹⁴_____ that
¹⁵_____ tackle this problem, … I suggest that

5 **Concluding**
To ¹⁶_____ up,   In ¹⁷_____ ,   To conclude,

6 SPEAKING Work in pairs. Read the task below and discuss questions 1–3. Write notes.

Some people believe that doing sport at school is a distraction from more important work. Write an essay in which you give your own opinion about this issue and propose ways for students to do more sport at school without causing problems for their studies.

1 Which sports do you do at school? How often?
2 Are there other subjects that are more important than sport? Which ones? Why?
3 How could more sport be added to the school timetable without affecting other subjects?

7 Using your notes from exercise 6, write a paragraph plan for your essay. Use the essay in exercise 3 as a model and follow the advice in the Writing Strategy.

8 Write your essay. Follow your paragraph plan from exercise 7 and the advice in the Writing Strategy. Use phrases from exercise 5.

CHECK YOUR WORK

 Have you …
• followed all the advice in the Writing Strategy?
• included phrases from exercise 5?
• checked your spelling and grammar?

Reading

1 Read the strategy above. Then read extracts 1 and 2 below, which have missing sentences. Try to predict what each missing sentence is about. Then look at A–D and choose the sentences that are closest to your prediction.

   1 Be careful when you choose a leisure activity because some activities take up a lot of time or effort. ___ Find out what an activity needs before you begin, and you won't have wasted your time.
   2 If you think you have hurt yourself while exercising, stop immediately. ___ As a result, they end up with worse injuries, so it takes them much longer to get better.

   A This is important if a doctor has told you to rest.
   B This means that you may become discouraged and give up because it is too demanding.
   C Too many people try to continue, despite the pain.
   D Then they find that it doesn't interest them as much as they thought it would.

2 Read the text. Five sentences have been removed. Choose the correct sentences (A–G) to fill the gaps (1–5). There are two extra sentences.

Hobbies and leisure activities are an ideal way to de-stress, meet people and develop your creativity. But if you don't have a lot of spare time, it can be a challenge to find one that suits your tastes and fits into your busy life. Of course, some readers ask why they should take up a hobby at all. ¹___ They don't realise that being more active and doing something really enjoyable can improve their energy levels and their mood.

One strategy for finding the right leisure activity is to think about what you enjoyed when you were a young child. ²___ Now here's your chance to try again. Perhaps you wish you could spend time exploring on your bicycle again, or wonder why you stopped drawing cartoons. Think about going back to similar activities.

Another approach is to think about the hobbies your friends have taken up. ³___ Training together will give both of you a boost in motivation. Or if you see a friend's paintings and you fancy doing some painting as well, give it a try.

Something to keep in mind is that an activity may not interest you after you've tried it. ⁴___ So don't beg your parents to pay for a lot of equipment or a whole year's lessons right away. Begin slowly, borrow what you need, and see if the activity is really right for you. If you still enjoy an activity after a few weeks of starting it, it might be the right hobby for you. ⁵___ And if you complete it, perhaps you can ask for some equipment for your next birthday present.

A Most people try activities they think they will be good at.
B Actually, lots of people give hobbies up within a couple of months of starting them.
C If you are interested when a classmate talks about her martial arts class, ask if you can join her.
D Only then is the time to pay for the full course.
E Parents may also have good ideas for activities too.
F After an exhausting day at school, all they want to do is sit in front of the TV or go online.
G Do you regret giving up those music lessons when you were ten?

Listening

3 Read the strategy above. Then read extracts 1 and 2 and match them with descriptions a–f. Match each extract with two descriptions. What do you think is the situation in each case?

🎧1 I couldn't believe it when I woke up and saw that my leg was broken, my skis were gone and I was all alone. I was terrified, but fortunately someone found me!

🎧2 OK, now bend and touch your toes. Good … that's right! Now stand up straight, relax your arms and jump up and down ten times – that's one, two, three …

This person …
a uses the first person (*I*). ___
b is enthusiastic. ___
c is patient. ___
d describes personal feelings. ___
e is impatient. ___
f uses the imperative. ___

4 🎧 1.36 You will hear four people talking about body-related subjects. You will hear the audio twice. Match sentences A–E with speakers 1–4. There is one extra sentence.

A This speaker talks about the result of a past situation. ___
B This speaker wants to advertise a solution to a problem. ___
C This speaker asks for advice about a problem. ___
D This speaker gives instructions to a group. ___
E This speaker predicts the future results of a problem. ___

Exam Skills Trainer

Use of English

5 Read the strategy above. Then read the text below and complete the missing gaps with ONE word only.

Holidays in the mountains

Many people enjoy spending their holidays hiking or climbing in the mountains. Their reasons vary. Some like being outdoors because [1]_____ is relaxing; others enjoy the positive effects of exercise and fresh air on their mental and physical well-being. Some people even choose the challenge of climbing a mountain summit for the feeling of achievement at the end. Whatever your motivation, it is important to plan and prepare carefully and [2]_____ some time before the trip doing physical training, particularly [3]_____ you are planning to go on long hikes at high altitudes.

Mountain trips can bring health challenges such [4]_____ altitude sickness. This can be mild, where you might simply develop [5]_____ headache, but in some cases people need medical attention. It is also important to take into account sudden changes in weather conditions, which can be very unpredictable. If the temperature drops below 0°C, you [6]_____ easily get frostbite. It is advisable to use cream on your hands and face before your trip, and make sure you wear warm gloves and socks. Hikers and climbers may also feel unwell because of dehydration, so drinking plenty of water before and during your trip is one of the [7]_____ important things to remember. Spending a day hiking or climbing may be more demanding on your body [8]_____ you think. You ought to rest well after each trip to help your muscles recover for the following day.

Speaking

6 Read the strategy above. You are planning to spend a weekend doing an activity with a group of friends. Compare the different activities A–D, including the different aspects given.

A going roller skating in the park
B skating in an indoor ice rink with an instructor
C going swimming in a water park with water slides
D swimming in the sea at a nearby beach

Which activity ...
- is better for people who are not into sport?
- is safer?
- seems more fun?
- is better to do in a big group?
- is more affordable for teenagers?

7 Work in pairs. You and a friend want to go cycling this weekend, but where? You have two options (A and B) to choose from. Agree on the one which you consider more appropriate, and explain why you rejected the other one.

8 Work in pairs. Answer questions 1 and 2.

1 What indoor activities are most popular with teenagers in your country? Why?
2 Why do you think being active is important for young people?

Writing

9 Read the strategy above. Then read the writing task below. Choose the correct options in the sentences. Then complete the sentences using your own ideas. Think of extra details you could add for each point.

Some people believe that teenagers do not have healthy eating habits. Write an opinion essay in which you give your own opinion about this issue and propose what could be done to make young people eat more healthily.

1 In my **conclusion** / **idea** / **view**, teenagers ...
2 I **suggest** / **see** / **summarise** that ...
3 To **tackle** / **propose** / **conclude** this problem we need to ...
4 To **sum up** / **believe** / **recommend**, I think ...

10 Read the task below and write an opinion essay.

Many people believe that teenagers spend too much time on social media. Write an essay in which you give your own opinion about this issue and propose solutions to it.

4 Home

Unit map

● **Vocabulary**
Types of home
Parts of a house and garden
Describing houses and rooms
Compound nouns
In the house

● **Word Skills**
do, *make* and *take*

● **Grammar**
Comparison
Imaginary situations
I wish ... , if only ...

● **Listening**
Young and homeless

● **Reading** Alternative living

● **Speaking**
Photo comparison and discussion

● **Writing** An email

● **Culture 4** Royal palaces

● **Vocabulary Builder** page 123

● **Grammar Builder and Reference** page 132

● **Extra Speaking Task** page 144

4A Vocabulary

Describing houses and homes
I can describe houses and homes.

A

1 **2.02** **VOCABULARY** Look at the photos. What types of homes are they? Listen and choose from the words below. What type of home do you live in?

Types of home bungalow detached house farmhouse flat houseboat mansion mobile home semi-detached house terraced house thatched cottage villa

2 **SPEAKING** Which of the homes in the photos would you most like to live in? Why? In your opinion, what are the advantages and disadvantages of living in each type of home?

3 **2.03** **VOCABULARY** Work in pairs. Listen to the words below. Put them into two groups: those that are more likely to be a) part of a house and b) in a garden.

Parts of a house and garden attic balcony basement cellar conservatory drive extension fence flower bed garage gate hall hedge landing lawn path patio pond porch shutters sliding doors stairs swimming pool

Parts of a house: attic, …

4 How many more rooms and other parts of a house or garden can you think of?

5 Which is the odd one out? Explain why. Sometimes more than one answer is possible.

1 cellar basement attic
2 detached house bungalow mansion
3 lawn path porch
4 detached house semi-detached house terraced house
5 fence gate hedge
6 houseboat mobile home villa
7 pond swimming pool patio
8 cottage houseboat farmhouse

6 **2.04** Listen to an estate agent showing someone round a house. Which seven parts of the house are mentioned in the dialogue?

7 VOCABULARY Match nine of the words below with meanings 1–8. Check the meaning of all the words.

Describing houses and rooms   beautifully restored
charming   contemporary   conveniently located
cosy   cramped   dilapidated   impressive
peaceful   popular / lively area   remote   spacious
substantial   tiny

1 uncomfortably small
2 very small
3 quiet
4 far from other places
5 modern
6 in a good location
7 in very bad condition
8 large (two words)

8 🎧**2.04** Listen again. Complete the sentences with words and phrases from the list in exercise 7.

1 It's _____ near to the shops.
2 We're in a very _____ of town.
3 On the right is the living room. _____, isn't it?
4 'It's _____.' 'It certainly isn't _____, but I wouldn't say it's _____.'
5 The back fence is very _____ .
6 There's a _____ view from the window.
7 It could be _____ .

9 🎧**2.05** Listen to four people describing their homes. Match sentences a–e with speakers 1–4. There is one extra sentence.

This home:
a is not as modern as the owners would like. ___
b did not cost very much. ___
c is very dilapidated. ___
d has got wonderful views. ___
e is in a remote location. ___

10 🎧**2.05** **SPEAKING** Listen again. What types of home were described in exercise 9? Which one appeals to you most? Which appeals least? Why?

RECYCLE! *some, any, much* and *many*
• We use *some* in affirmative sentences.
• We use *any* in negative sentences and questions.
• We use *much* with uncountable nouns and *many* with plural countable nouns.

11 🎧**2.05** Read the Recycle! box. Circle the correct words to complete the sentences. Then listen again and check.

1 a It was in a pretty poor state and needed **some** / **any** work doing on it.
  b Unfortunately, there aren't **some** / **any** spaces for boats near the centre.
2 a You reach it through **some** / **any** glass sliding doors from the living room.
  b Unfortunately, my parents don't earn **much** / **many** money, so we can't afford to move.
3 There aren't **much** / **many** people living nearby.
4 They also need to insulate the roof so we don't waste **some** / **any** energy.

12 SPEAKING Work in pairs. Describe your home to your partner. Use the phrases below to help you.

Describing where you live
It's a flat / detached house / terraced house.
It's in the town centre / on the outskirts / in the suburbs.
There's a park / There are some shops nearby.
It's got ... (bedrooms).
There is ... (other rooms).
There's / There isn't a garden / drive, etc.
It's a bit / very (adjective).

Comparison

I can make comparisons using a variety of structures.

1 **SPEAKING** Describe the photo. What are the people doing, do you think? What might they be saying?

2 Read the dialogue, ignoring the gaps, and check your ideas from exercise 1.

Jenny I think this flat is the best we've seen so far. They're all quite expensive – rents seem to be getting higher and higher. But this one's the least expensive and it's the ¹_____ (near) to the city centre.

Beth But it's the one with the fewest rooms and the least space.

Jenny So you prefer the flat in the ²_____ (bad) location and with the ³_____ (high) rent?

Beth The location isn't as bad as you think. It's ⁴_____ (far) from the centre than the other two, but you can get to the train station and the university more easily. And it's much ⁵_____ (spacious) than the other two flats.

Jenny Can we afford it, though? The more we spend on rent, the less we'll have for other things.

Beth Actually, it's less expensive than it seems because the rent includes all the bills.

3 Complete the dialogue in exercise 2 with the comparative or superlative form of the adjectives in brackets. What are the rules for forming a) comparative adjectives and b) superlative adjectives?

> **LEARN THIS!** Comparative and superlative forms
>
> **a** We often use a superlative with the present perfect.
> *That's the biggest mansion I've ever seen.*
>
> **b** We can make comparisons with simple nouns (*The kitchen is bigger than the bathroom.*) and also with clauses (*Houses are cheaper than they used to be.*).
>
> **c** We use double comparatives to emphasise that something is changing.
> *Property is getting cheaper and cheaper.*
>
> **d** We use *The ...* , *the ...* and comparatives to say that one thing changes with another.
> *The closer you are to the centre, the more you pay in rent.*
>
> **e** We usually use *more* and *most* to form comparative and superlative adverbs. However, we add *-er* and *-est* to some short adverbs.
> *The flat sold more quickly than I expected.*
> *Houses sell faster in the spring.*
>
> **f** Like *more* and *most*, we can use *less* and *least* with long adjectives, adverbs and uncountable nouns.
> *This is the least spacious house in the road.*
> *There's less space in my room than in yours.*
>
> **g** We use *fewer* and *fewest* with countable nouns.
> *Which flat has the fewest rooms?*
> *There are fewer big flats in the town centre.*

4 Read the Learn this! box. Match each highlighted phrase in the dialogue with a rule (a–g).

➡ **Grammar Builder 4.1** page 132

5 🎧 **2.06** Look at the table. Then listen and decide if the sentences are true or false. Correct the false sentences in two different ways.

1 Flat 1 has got the highest rent.
False. Flat 1 has got the lowest rent. Flat 3 has got the highest rent.

	Flat 1	Flat 2	Flat 3
Rent per month	£200	£250	£300
From centre	1.5 km	2 km	500 m
From station	3 km	2 km	1 km
Size	1,002 m	1,102 m	1,302 m
Rooms	3	5	4
Comfort	★★★★	★★★	★★★★★

6 **USE OF ENGLISH** Complete the second sentence so that it means the same as the first using the word in brackets and the correct comparative or superlative form.

1 Houses sell less fast in December. (slowly)
Houses _____ .

2 The cottage isn't as spacious as the villa. (less)
The cottage _____ .

3 Houses are becoming increasingly expensive. (more)
Houses _____ .

4 As the flat gets older, it becomes more dilapidated. (the)
The _____ .

5 I didn't expect the mansion to be so cheap. (than)
The mansion _____ .

6 I've never seen a cosier living room! (the)
This is _____ !

7 **SPEAKING** Work in pairs. Ask and answer using a superlative form (*-est / most / least*) and the present perfect with *ever*.

1 impressive building / visit
2 interesting person / know
3 stressful exam / take
4 long book / read
5 exciting film / see
6 expensive thing / buy

> What's the most impressive building you've ever visited?

4C Listening
Young and homeless
I can recognise paraphrases of simple verbs in a recording.

1 SPEAKING Work in pairs. Look at the photo, title and slogan opposite. What happens on a 'Big Sleep Out', do you think?

2 Read the text and check your ideas from exercise 1.

> **Listening Strategy 1**
>
> When you listen to a recording, remember that many ideas will be expressed differently in the task. For example, a simple verb in the task may be expressed by a phrase in the recording:
>
> *sleep well → get a good night's sleep*

3 Read Listening Strategy 1. Complete the definitions with the words below.

contact   enjoy   help   ignore   talk   try

1 to give somebody a hand = to _____ somebody
2 to turn a blind eye to something = to _____ something
3 to make a big effort = to _____ hard
4 to have the time of your life = to _____ yourself a lot
5 to have a word with somebody = to _____ to somebody
6 to get in touch with somebody = to _____ somebody

4 🎧 **2.07** Listen to three short recordings. Answer the questions. Use the verbs and phrases in exercise 3 to help you.

Speaker 1
1 Did she enjoy her Big Sleep Out?
2 Did she talk to the organisers?

Speaker 2
3 Does he think the organisers tried hard to publicise the event this year?
4 Did they contact the local newspaper last year?

Speaker 3
5 Does she think politicians ignore the problem of homelessness?
6 Did she help at the office of a charity?

> **Listening Strategy 2**
>
> Pay attention to whether the language you hear is formal or informal. This can be an important clue to the context.

5 🎧 **2.08** Read Listening Strategy 2. Then listen to five recordings. Which excerpts contain formal language? Use the table below to help you identify them.

Formal	Informal
increase sharply	go up a lot
offer / require assistance	need help
a high priority	very important
make a proposal	suggest something
currently	at the moment
gain employment	find a job

THE BIG SLEEP OUT
RAISING MONEY FOR PEOPLE WHO SLEEP ROUGH

Nobody knows exactly how many young people in the UK are homeless, but the figure may be as high as 75,000. Many of them are teenagers who don't live with their families. While the majority of homeless people are unemployed, some have jobs but are still unable to afford accommodation, especially in places where rents are very high, like London. The Big Sleep Out is a charity event which raises money to tackle homelessness among young people. Big Sleep Outs happen all over the country. People who are not homeless choose to sleep rough for one night. This raises a lot of money each year and reminds politicians to look for a solution to the problem.

6 🎧 **2.08** Listen again. Choose the correct answers (a–c).

1 Who is Speaker 1 speaking to?
   a An audience at a conference.
   b A friend who works for a charity.
   c A young homeless person.
2 Speaker 2 thinks that older people
   a care more about homelessness.
   b are more likely to take part in the Big Sleep Out.
   c often don't have time to think about homelessness.
3 Who does Speaker 3 work for?
   a a youth hostel
   b a local business
   c a city council
4 What does Speaker 4 dislike most about being homeless?
   a Receiving unkind comments.
   b Seeing people fight.
   c Spending too much time on his own.
5 Why does Speaker 5 avoid the High Street at night?
   a She thinks it is dangerous.
   b The homeless people make her anxious.
   c She does not know what to say to the homeless people.

7 SPEAKING Discuss these questions with your partner.

1 What would be the worst thing about being homeless? Think about:

   the weather   other people's attitudes   being alone
   being uncomfortable   personal safety   hygiene

2 What should governments do to tackle the problem of homelessness?
3 What can individuals do to help the homeless?

> I think the worst thing would be not having a bed / feeling cold all the time / not being able to wash …

Imaginary situations

I can talk about imaginary situations and things I would like to change.

1 SPEAKING Read the fact file about Castle Howard, a stately home in the north of England. Would you like to live in a house like this? Why? / Why not?

🌸 **Built around 1700, it has 145 rooms.**

🌸 **It is the private home of the Howard family, who have lived there for over 300 years.**

🌸 **It has been open to the public since 1952.**

2 🎧 **2.09** Read and listen to the dialogue. What two outdoor and indoor changes do the speakers mention?

Alfie This is an amazing place. I wish I lived here.
Macy Me too. If only I were a member of the Howard family!
Alfie But if it were my house, I wouldn't allow people to visit.
Macy That's mean! You'd get bored on your own.
Alfie Oh, I'd let my friends visit, of course. But not the public.
Macy If you had a party, you could invite hundreds of people!
Alfie I know. The parties would be better if I made a few changes, though.
Macy What kind of changes?
Alfie Well, if those trees weren't there, there'd be room for a swimming pool!
Macy You could make some changes inside as well. I mean, look at this corridor.
Alfie The Antique Passage, you mean?
Macy Yes. If you took away all the statues, you could build a great bowling alley there!

3 Read the Learn this! box and complete it. Underline all the examples of the second conditional in the dialogue in exercise 2.

> **LEARN THIS! Second conditional**
>
> We use the second conditional to talk about an imaginary situation or event and its result.
>
> We use the ¹_____ tense for the situation or event and ²_____ + infinitive without *to* for the result.

4 Complete these second conditional sentences using the verbs in brackets.

1 If I _____ (live) in a mansion, I _____ (have) parties every week.
2 If you _____ (visit) me, you _____ (sleep) in a huge bedroom.
3 We _____ (can) go on long bike rides if the weather _____ (be) good.
4 If the weather _____ (not be) good, we _____ (watch) movies in the Great Hall.
5 If we _____ (play) hide-and-seek, we _____ (not find) each other for hours.

➡ **Grammar Builder 4.2** page 134

5 Read the Learn this! box and complete it. Underline one example of *I wish …* and one example of *If only …* in the dialogue in exercise 2.

> **LEARN THIS!** *I wish … , If only …*
>
> **a** We use *I wish …* and *If only …* with the past simple to say that we want a situation to be different from how it really is.
> I wish I ¹_____ a brother. (But I haven't got one.)
> If only you ²_____ nearer. (But you live far away.)
>
> **b** We use *I wish …* and *If only …* with *would(n't)* + infinitive without *to* to say that we want somebody to behave differently.
> I wish you ³_____ borrow my clothes! It's annoying!
> If only she ⁴_____ spend more time on her homework!

6 Explain the difference in meaning between these two sentences.

a I wish my penfriend spoke English.
b I wish my penfriend would speak English.

> **! LOOK OUT!**
>
> In second conditional sentences and after *If only …* or *I wish …* , we often use *were* instead of *was*.
> I wish I were a little bit taller.

7 Read the Look out! box. Then complete the first line of each mini-dialogue with the verbs in brackets. Use the past simple or *would / could* + infinitive without *to*. Complete the other lines with the second conditional.

A I wish my dad ¹_____ (come) home.
B Why?
A Because he ²_____ (give) us a lift into town if he ³_____ (be) here.

A If only you ⁴_____ (live) near the town centre.
B Why?
A Because if your house ⁵_____ (be) near the centre, we ⁶_____ (get) the same bus to school.

A I wish my parents' friends ⁷_____ (leave).
B Why?
A Because if they ⁸_____ (not be) in the house, we ⁹_____ (can) turn the music up to full volume!

➡ **Grammar Builder 4.3** page 134

8 SPEAKING In pairs, talk about what you would do if you:

1 owned Castle Howard.
2 had a swimming pool in your garden.
3 gave a party for hundreds of people.
4 had to allow the public into your home.

> If I owned Castle Howard, I would …

Word Skills
do, *make* and *take*
I can use 'do', 'make' and 'take' correctly.

1 SPEAKING Work in pairs. Imagine you were trying to sell the house in the photo. How would you describe it? Use the words below to help you.

Nouns cliff glass metal ocean rock view
Adjectives modern spacious spectacular unique

2 Work in pairs. Complete the dialogue in an estate agent's using the infinitive without *to* of these verbs: *do, make, take*.

Agent	Good morning. What can I ¹_____ for you?
Woman	Can I ask you about that amazing house that's built on a cliff?
Agent	Yes, of course. You can ²_____ a look at some more pictures on my computer.
Woman	Amazing! Are there any pictures of the inside?
Agent	Yes – and they're just as impressive. ³_____ this one, for example. Look at the view from that sofa!
Woman	I love it. Can I ⁴_____ an appointment to look around?
Agent	I'm afraid you can't ⁵_____ that. The house doesn't exist yet! You need to choose a location first. But the house would only ⁶_____ twelve weeks to build, according to Modscape, the company that supplies them.
Woman	I see. I need to find somewhere soon, so I'll have to ⁷_____ up my mind quickly.
Agent	Can I ask what you ⁸_____ ?
Woman	I'm a yoga teacher.
Agent	Where do you teach?
Woman	At the local sports centre. But if I moved to a bigger house, I'd want to ⁹_____ one room into a yoga studio.
Agent	Well, this house would be a great place to ¹⁰_____ yoga! Just ¹¹_____ your yoga mat outside onto the cliff. Imagine the sunrise over the waves, the solitude …
Woman	I suppose you would be alone there … except for all the people who stop to ¹²_____ photos of your house!

3 🎧 **2.10** Listen and check your answers. Do you think the woman is keen on buying the house? Why? / Why not?

> **LEARN THIS!** *do, make* and *take*
> The verbs *do, make* and *take* are very common in English. They each have a basic meaning:
> - *do* = to perform an action or activity
> - *make* = to create or cause something
> - *take* = to move something from one place to another
>
> However, the verbs have other meanings and are used in a large number of phrases. You need to check these in a dictionary.

4 Read the Learn this! box. Which examples of *do, make* and *take* in the dialogue in exercise 2 match the basic meanings in the Learn this! box?

5 DICTIONARY WORK Read a short extract from a dictionary entry for *take*. Answer the questions.

> **take** /teɪk/ *verb* (**pt took** /tʊk/; **pp taken** /'teɪkən/)
> ▶ PHOTOGRAPH to photograph sth: *I **took** some nice **photos** of the wedding.*
> ▶ MEASUREMENT to measure sth: *The doctor **took** my temperature.*
> ▶ EAT / DRINK to swallow sth: ***Take** two **tablets** four times a day.* • *Do you **take** sugar in tea?*

1 What do 'pt' and 'pp' stand for?
2 How many different meanings are included?
3 How are the different meanings separated?
4 Why are some words in the examples in bold? Is it to show a grammatical rule, a useful collocation, or a spelling rule?

6 USE OF ENGLISH Choose the word (A, B or C) that fits the gap in both sentences (a and b). Use a dictionary to check the meanings of the verbs.

1 a I ___ French classes for a year, but I can't speak it well.
  b I ___ my Spanish exam last week and passed.
  A did   B made   C took
2 a Thanks for inviting me to your party, but I'm afraid I can't ___ it.
  b What's the time? I ___ it 7.30.
  A do   B make   C take
3 a The waves are ___ a lot of damage to the cliffs.
  b He was ___ 150 km/h when the police stopped him.
  A doing   B making   C taking
4 a That noise has been going on all night. I can't ___ it any more!
  b I wish you would ___ your schoolwork more seriously.
  A do   B make   C take

➤➤ **Vocabulary Builder** Collocations: *do* or *make*: page 123

7 SPEAKING Tell your partner about a time when you:

1 did your best.
2 took it easy.
3 had to make do.
4 didn't take something seriously.

Alternative living

I can understand an article about alternative houses.

1 SPEAKING Look at the photos and the titles of texts A–D. What do you think the texts are about?

2 Quickly read texts A–D and check your ideas.

> **Reading Strategy**
>
> When you find evidence in the text that supports an answer, underline it and note which question it refers to. If you do that, you can find it again easily when you are checking all your answers at the end.

3 Read the Reading Strategy. Match two of the texts with the photos below. Say what evidence you found to support your answers.

4 Match the texts (A–D) with the sentences (1–7) below. Three texts match with two sentences. Make a note of the evidence you found to support your answers.

1 There is information on the internet to show people how to build these homes. ___
2 The builder of these homes uses only recycled parts. ___
3 The builder of these homes was inspired by a historical figure. ___
4 The designer gives practical help to people who want to build homes like these. ___
5 These homes are powered by renewable energy. ___
6 These homes can be found in two European countries. ___
7 These homes can be put together to make a block of flats. ___

[1]

[2]

CHARDSON

5 Work in pairs. Tell each other where you found the evidence for each answer in exercise 4. Do you agree?

6 **VOCABULARY** Match a–j with 1–10 to make compound nouns. They are all in the texts. Which two are written as one word?

Compound nouns

1	rubbish	a	bed
2	sofa	b	scraper
3	front	c	containers
4	sky	d	door
5	dining	e	dump
6	solar	f	estate
7	rain	g	flat
8	shipping	h	table
9	housing	i	panels
10	studio	j	water

7 Read the text again. Answer the questions.

1 Where does Gregory Kloehn find the parts to make his houses?
2 What does Gregory sometimes use as a front door?
3 How long has Dee Williams been living in her tiny house?
4 What is the architect of the micro-house famous for?
5 In what way is the micro-house energy-efficient?
6 Apart from the UK, in which country have containers been made into flats?

8 **SPEAKING** Work in pairs. Discuss these questions.

1 Which home is the most original and clever, do you think? Why?
2 Which is the most useful from a social point of view? Why?
3 Which of the homes would you like to live in? Why?
4 Which of the homes would you not like to live in? Why not?

🎧 2.11

A *Living sculptures*

Gregory Kloehn is a sculptor with a difference. Not only are his sculptures created from bits of rubbish, but each of his unique creations offers a homeless person somewhere to live.

5 Gregory works in California, where there are a lot of people living on the streets. Each of his sculptures is no bigger than the average sofa, but the tiny, one-roomed shelters are as wonderful as mansions for a person who is sleeping rough.

10 Gregory searches on rubbish dumps to find pieces to use. A washing machine door is as good as a normal window. A fridge door can make a fine front door, and has useful shelves on the inside. And each home is on wheels so that it can be pushed around easily.

15 Gregory used to make sculptures for rich people. Now he knows that his creations really make a difference to people's lives. And he has also inspired other people to start building.

B *Build your own tiny home*

If you wanted your own house, would you build it yourself?
20 Some Americans are now building miniature homes for themselves in order to live more cheaply and in a more ecological way than usual. And with wheels on their home, they can go anywhere! Part of the fun is making it yourself – even if you don't know how.

25 'Most people who are interested in tiny houses don't have any building experience,' says Ryan Mitchell, founder of TheTinyLife.com website, who organises conferences for interested people, and one of the conference speakers is Dee Williams, who has been living in her cosy wooden
30 home since 2004. She wishes that more help had been available then. 'I didn't know anyone else who was building a little house at the time, anywhere,' she says. Now you can find thousands of instructional videos on YouTube, if you want to make your own!

C *The designer micro-house*

35 Italian architect Renzo Piano is famous for designing Europe's tallest skyscraper, the Shard in London. Now he has gone to the other extreme: he's designed the smallest house possible. It's just two and a half by three metres and can be carried on a lorry.

The interior is divided into two halves. There's a living room in
40 the front with a sofa and folding table. At the back of the house, there's a small kitchen with a cooker and fridge, a shower and a toilet. It's really energy-efficient, with solar panels on the roof and a container to collect rainwater, so the house is incredibly cheap to run. The house is called 'Diogene', named after the Greek
45 philosopher Diogenes who rejected luxury by living in a large ceramic jar! The Diogene is currently on display in Germany. And at just £17,000, this designer house isn't as expensive as many family cars, so a lot of people are interested in it.

D *Well-contained housing*

If you heard that they were putting homeless people into
50 shipping containers, you might be shocked. But that's exactly what is happening in Brighton, England.

The Brighton Housing Trust has been inspired by a similar housing estate in the Netherlands. It is developing 36 studio flats in the town centre, using old shipping
55 containers. The flats will have a window at each end and a toilet and shower room in the middle. On one side there'll be a kitchen and small dining table, and on the other side a living room with a sofa bed.

At 24 square metres, they are smaller than a shared room
60 in a homeless hostel. But they are much more desirable and certainly spacious enough for one person. They are also stackable. The containers will sit on top of one another with stairs connecting them. And in future, if somebody wants to move them, they can simply pick
65 them up and take them to another site.

Photo comparison and discussion

I can describe, compare and contrast photos.

A   B

1 SPEAKING Which items from below can you see in the photos?

In the house bedside table bookcase bunk bed curtains cushion double bed duvet fridge hook kitchen cupboard lamp microwave pillow shelf sofa

> In photo B there's a lamp on the bedside table.

➡ **Vocabulary Builder** In the house: page 123

> **Speaking Strategy 1**
> When comparing and contrasting photos, use a variety of comparative and superlative forms, including negative structures like *less comfortable than* and *not as big as*.

2 Read Speaking Strategy 1. Then complete the sentences that contrast photos A and B. Use comparative structures.

1 The room in photo A is _____ tidy _____ the room in photo B.
2 The bed in photo B looks _____ comfortable.
3 The room in photo A isn't _____ bright _____ the room in photo B.
4 The room in photo B is one of _____ nicest rooms I've _____ seen.

> Compare and contrast the photos of student accommodation and say which you would prefer to live in.

3 🎧 **2.12** Read the task above. Then listen to a student doing the task. Which room does she prefer? Do you agree? Why? / Why not?

4 🎧 **2.12** Choose the best words to complete the sentences. Then listen again and check your answers.

1 Photo A is of a room in a hostel, I think, **unless / whereas** the second shows a small flat.
2 There are bunk beds in the room in the hostel, **but / when** the other room has got a double bed.
3 **While / When** photo A shows a rather untidy room, the room in photo B is very tidy.
4 The room in the hostel looks quite cosy. **However, / Whereas** the furniture looks a bit old and worn out.
5 I like the idea of sharing with other students, **although / despite** the lack of privacy.

> In his / her gap year, a friend is going to spend three months studying English at a British university. He / She can stay with a host family or in university accommodation with other foreign students. Your friend asks you for advice on the best option. Discuss these points:
> • convenience and cost
> • social life
> • opportunities to practise your English
> • getting to know Britain and British culture

5 Read the task above. For each of the four points, think of one advantage of staying with a host family and one advantage of staying in university accommodation.

> From the point of view of location and convenience, the university accommodation would be better because …

> From the point of view of cost, a host family would be better because …

6 🎧 **2.13** Listen to two students doing the task. Did they mention any of your ideas from exercise 5? Do you agree with their opinions? Why? / Why not?

> **Speaking Strategy 2**
> When giving your opinion, you will have to think as you speak. Learn phrases that create time for you to formulate opinions. They will also make you sound more fluent.

7 KEY PHRASES Read Speaking Strategy 2. Then complete the phrases with the words below.

considered else point see suppose think thinking

Phrases for gaining time
Let me [1]_____ .
Actually, now I come to [2]_____ about it, …
[3]_____ about it, …
All things [4]_____ , …
I [5]_____ the thing is, …
What [6]_____ ? Well, …
That's a good [7]_____ .

8 🎧 **2.13** Listen again to both answers. Which phrases from exercise 7 did the students use?

> In your gap year, you are going to spend three months in the UK studying English. You are looking for a flat to rent. Ask your friend for advice. Discuss these points:
> • location   • cost
> • meals   • sharing with other students

9 Work in pairs. Read the task above and make notes for each of the four points that you have to cover.

10 SPEAKING Work in pairs. Do the task in exercise 9.

11 SPEAKING Work in pairs. Turn to page 144 and do the photo comparison task.

An email

I can write an email to a friend about a new home.

1 SPEAKING Work in pairs. If you could move to any city in the world, where would you choose? Why?

2 Read the email. Do you think Ellie is happy or unhappy with her new home? Find evidence in her email.

✉ **To:** anna@email.com

Hi Anna,

Hope everything is OK with you. We've just moved to a new flat nearer the centre of town. It's brilliant being so close to the shops, and the flat is bigger than our old one. It's quite noisy, though, as there is a lot of traffic. I'd rather it was further from the main road. I met one of our neighbours yesterday. She is about my age and she is very friendly. She has invited me to a party next weekend. Can you go with me? I hope so. To be honest, I'd rather not go alone. Also, would it be OK if I used your bike for a few days? Mine is at the bike shop and I'd rather cycle to school than get the bus.

Got to go now. I'd better finish my homework before bed. I look forward to receiving your reply.

Love,

Ellie

---

3 Read the task below. Does the email in exercise 2 cover all four points in the task? Match sentences in the text with each point.

You have recently moved to a new flat in a city centre. Write an email to a friend. Include the following:
- Say why you like your new flat.
- Mention something you would like to be different.
- Mention meeting a new neighbour and describe him / her.
- Ask permission to use something belonging to your friend.

1 *It's brilliant being . . .*
2 *. . .*

Writing Strategy

When you write an informal email or letter:
- You should avoid formal language.
- You can use contractions (*you're, it's*, etc.).
- You sometimes omit words like *I, I'm* or *I've* at the start of a sentence (*Hope you're well, Got to go now*, etc.).

---

4 Read the Writing Strategy. Then read Ellie's email again and underline:

1 a piece of formal language. How could you make it informal?
2 three different contractions. Can you find any more places where Ellie could have used contractions?
3 an example of a sentence with words omitted at the start. What exactly has been omitted?

LEARN THIS! *would rather, had better*

a We use *would rather (not)* + infinitive without *to* to express a preference.
I'd rather (not) stay out late tonight.

b We use *would rather* + subject + past simple to say we would prefer a situation to be different.
She'd rather her bedroom had bigger windows.

c We use *had better* + infinitive without *to* to say what we or somebody else should do.
I'd / You'd better go straight home – it's 8 p.m.

---

5 Read the Learn this! box. Circle three examples of *would rather* and an example of *had better* in Ellie's email.

➼ **Grammar Builder 4.4** page 135

6 Read the task below. Make notes for each of the four points in the task.

You have recently moved to a house in the country. Write an email to a friend. Include the following:
- Describe the advantages of being in the country.
- Mention something you would change.
- Mention something that went wrong during the move.
- Ask if you can stay a night at your friend's house.

1 *fresh air, beautiful scenery, etc.*

7 KEY PHRASES Complete the useful phrases for starting and ending a letter or email. Find two more in Ellie's email.

all are from going hi hope love touch write

Starting an email	
I ¹_____ you're well.	How's everything ³_____?
I hope ²_____ is well.	How ⁴_____ you?
Ending an email	
That's all ⁵_____ me.	Say ⁸_____ to (Ben)
Keep in ⁶_____.	for me.
Please ⁷_____ soon.	Give (Zoe) my ⁹_____.

8 Write your email using your notes from exercise 6 and phrases from exercise 7.

CHECK YOUR WORK

Have you ...
- included all four points from the task?
- used appropriate language (see the Writing Strategy)?
- included appropriate phrases for starting and ending the email?

5 Technology

Unit map

● Vocabulary
Digital activities
Computing verbs
Computing: useful collocations
Gadgets
Expressing opinions
Verb–noun collocations
School subjects

● Word Skills
Adjective + preposition

● Grammar
Quantifiers
Modals in the past

● Listening
Navigation nightmare

● Reading Clever machines

● Speaking Photo comparison

● Writing An internet forum post

● Culture 5 Benjamin Franklin

● Vocabulary Builder page 123

● Grammar Builder and Reference page 135

● Extra Speaking Task page 144

5A Vocabulary
Computing
I can talk about computers and communication technology.

1 VOCABULARY How many of these things do you use a computer or tablet for? What else do you use them for?

Digital activities do your homework   download music   follow people on Twitter
play games   read / write a blog   shop   use social networking sites (e.g. Facebook)

2 SPEAKING Work in pairs. Ask and answer about the activities in exercise 1. Use *How often … ?* Give extra information in your answer.

> How often do you download music?

> Not very often. I usually listen to music online. What about you?

3 VOCABULARY Complete the quiz questions with the verbs below.

Computing verbs comment   forward   install   log on   print
~~program~~   rate   search   set up   subscribe   update   upload

How tech-savvy are you?

**Answer 1, 2, 3 or 4 for each question.
Make a note of your scores.**

1 = I don't know what you're talking about.
2 = No, I don't think I can do that.
3 = I've never done that, but I think I know how.
4 = Yes, I can do that.

Do you know how to …

a ¹*program* a simple game?

b ² _____ a video clip to YouTube?

c use Google to ³_____ within a specific website?

d ⁴_____ your profile on a social networking site?

e post, ⁵_____ on and ⁶_____ contributions on a social networking site?

f ⁷_____ a new email account?

g ⁸_____ to a Wi-Fi hotspot with your tablet or phone when you're away from home?

h ⁹_____ to a YouTube channel?

i ¹⁰_____ a text message you've received from one friend to another friend?

j ¹¹_____ a document directly from your phone?

k ¹²_____ an app on your phone?

4 SPEAKING Work in pairs. Ask and answer the quiz questions. Calculate your partner's score. Then tell your partner how tech-savvy he or she is. Compare your results with your partner's.

11–16 You are not at all tech-savvy. That's fine, but be careful not to get left behind! There are lots of ways in which computers and smartphones can make life easier.

17–22 You have a basic knowledge of computer technology, but you'd probably rather make a phone call than send a text, meet face-to-face than chat online, and read a paper book than use an e-reader.

23–33 You understand technology and are pretty good at using it. You probably aren't the first to hear about new gadgets, apps and websites, but you are willing and quick to learn.

34–44 You are plugged in – a real computer geek! You can handle any gadget or software. That's fantastic, but make sure there's lots of personal contact with friends and family in your life too.

5 **2.14** **VOCABULARY** Match a–e with 1–5 and f–j with 6–10. Then listen and check.

Computing: useful collocations

1	open / close	a the trash, the recycle bin
2	save	b a page, a menu, a document
3	enter	c your password, your username, your name, your address
4	scroll up / down	
5	empty	d a document, a file, a photo, your work
		e an app, a new window, a folder, a file, a document
6	check / uncheck	f a link
7	follow	g a box
8	copy and paste	h a button, an icon, a link
9	create	i text, a photo, a file, a document, a link, a folder
10	click / double click on	j an account, a document, a file, a link, a folder

6 **2.15** Listen to three helpline dialogues. Circle the correct answers (a–c).

1 The customer doesn't know how to
  a enter his payment details.
  b add items to the basket.
  c get money off something he wants to buy.
2 The technical support assistant advises the woman to
  a send the email to the bank, then remove it from her computer.
  b click on the link in the email.
  c choose a new password.
3 The man can
  a send emails, but can't receive them.
  b receive emails, but can't send them.
  c send and receive emails from one email account, but not from another.

RECYCLE! Imperatives

We form imperatives with the infinitive of the verb without *to*. We form the negative with *don't*.

Please reply to my email. Don't click on that link.

We put *always* and *never* before the verb in affirmative imperatives.

Never click on links in spam email.

7 **2.15** Read the Recycle! box. Then listen again and complete the sentences with the affirmative or negative imperative of the verbs below.

click on   delete   enter   follow   log on

Dialogue 1
¹_____ that button just yet. ²_____ the discount code first.
Dialogue 2
And then you should ³_____ the email. And whatever you do, ⁴_____ any links contained in the email.
Dialogue 3
⁵_____ to your email account. Once you've got it, you can reset your password.

8 SPEAKING Work in pairs. Give each other instructions on how to do four of these things. Use words from exercises 3, 5 and 7 to help you, and use the imperative.

1 buy and download a song
2 watch a YouTube clip
3 create a new document
4 buy something online
5 comment on a Facebook post
6 add an emoji to a text message
7 set up an event on a social networking site
8 your ideas

To download a song, first open iTunes. Then click on the iTunes Store icon. Then type the name …

5B Grammar
Quantifiers
I can use quantifiers correctly.

1 SPEAKING Look at the photo and the title of the text. What do you think all the man's wearable gadgets are for?

2 Read the text and check your ideas.

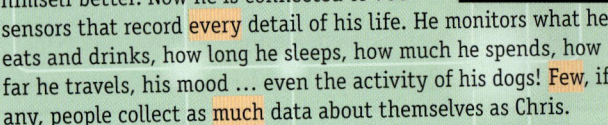

MR CONNECTED

Chris Dancy loves technology. A few years ago, he noticed that he had very little information about his habits, health and lifestyle, and he wanted to lose some weight. So he bought some gadgets that could collect this information and help him understand himself better. Now he is connected to 700 sensors that record every detail of his life. He monitors what he eats and drinks, how long he sleeps, how much he spends, how far he travels, his mood ... even the activity of his dogs! Few, if any, people collect as much data about themselves as Chris.

Most of his gadgets are attached to him. He wears gadgets on both arms, a heart rate monitor and a device that counts calories. He has a smartwatch too, which he can wear on either wrist. His house and car are also full of gadgets. Every one of them sends data to his computer, and at the end of each day Chris spends a little time analysing it. The smartwatch is the only gadget he wears all the time. He doesn't wear all of his gadgets 24/7, but he has so many systems that automatically track his activity that there aren't any days when there is no monitoring at all. Is there any information about himself that he doesn't have? If there is, it must be impossible to collect!

3 Study the highlighted quantifiers and the type of noun they go with in the text in exercise 2. Then read the **Learn this!** box. Complete the table with the quantifiers below.

a few   a little   all   any   any   both
each   every   many   no   some

LEARN THIS! Quantifiers

¹_____ , ²_____ , *either*	+ singular countable noun
most, little, some, much, ³_____ , ⁴_____ , ⁵_____ , ⁶_____	+ uncountable noun
no, few, all, most, ⁷_____ , ⁸_____ , ⁹_____ , ¹⁰_____ , ¹¹_____	+ plural noun

! LOOK OUT!
We can use most quantifiers with *of* before a determiner (e.g. *the, his, these*) and a noun.
All of my friends have got phones.

However, we cannot use *of* with *every* or *no*. Instead, we use *every one of* and *none of* with a plural verb or with a singular verb (in formal style).
None of my friends have / has got a tablet.

4 Read the **Look out!** box and underline three examples of *of* with quantifiers in the text in exercise 2.

5 Study the sentences below. What is the difference between *few* and *a few*, *little* and *a little*?

1 a I've got few high-tech gadgets. I want more!
  b I've got a few high-tech gadgets. I love them!
2 a Unfortunately, I have little time for computer games.
  b I have a little time. Let's play a computer game.

➜ **Grammar Builder 5.1** page 135

6 Complete the sentences with the quantifiers below.

any both few little most none some

1 Unfortunately, there are _____ tablets at school, so we don't often use them.
2 _____ of the students use social media. That's how they stay in touch with one another.
3 I downloaded _____ music from Amazon last night.
4 There aren't _____ interactive whiteboards in our school.
5 You need to hold the games console controller with _____ hands.
6 _____ of my friends know the answer. I'll have to ask a teacher.
7 Jason's always on his computer. He spends _____ time on other hobbies.

7 USE OF ENGLISH Rewrite the sentences so they have a similar meaning. Use the word(s) in brackets.

1 I don't have much IT homework this weekend. (little)
2 Almost all of the students own a computer. (most)
3 Not many of my friends use Twitter. (few)
4 Sam loves Facebook and Ben loves Facebook. (both)
5 I will text you on Saturday or on Sunday. (either)
6 There aren't any documents in the folder. (no)
7 Marlon has a gadget on his left wrist and his right wrist. (each)
8 I downloaded all the apps to my new phone. (every one)
9 I don't spend a lot of time using social media. (much)
10 I haven't got any gadgets that are expensive. (none)

8 Write sentences about the students in your class. Make predictions using *all of them, most of them, some of them, a few of them, very few of them* and *none of them*.

1 use Facebook
2 own a computer
3 download music
4 have a smartphone
5 shop online
6 have a YouTube channel
7 have broadband
8 visit chatrooms

> Most of them use Facebook.

9 SPEAKING Read your sentences from exercise 8 to the class. Compare your predictions with other students' ideas. Then find out which are correct by a show of hands.

> I think most of them use Facebook.

> No, I think some of them use Facebook.

Navigation nightmare

I can distinguish fact from opinion.

1 SPEAKING Work in pairs. Look at the photo and explain the meaning of the headlines below. Why do you think people make this kind of mistake?

A **Driver followed satnav to edge of 100-ft drop**

B **GPS failure leaves woman in Zagreb two days later**

C **SATNAV ERROR LEAVES SHOPPERS IN WRONG COUNTRY**

D **Satnav leads woman into river**

2 🎧2.16 Listen to two people discussing a news item. Which of the headlines in exercise 1 are they talking about?

> **Listening Strategy**
>
> You may have to distinguish fact from opinion in a listening task. Listen for clues to help you decide. An opinion might begin with a verb connected with thinking (e.g. *think, believe, expect, reckon*) or a phrase for introducing opinions (*in my view, as I see it*, etc.).

3 🎧2.16 Read the Listening Strategy. Then listen again and decide whether each sentence below is a fact or an opinion. Which words introduce the opinions?

1 Sabine Moreau began her journey in Belgium.
2 She travelled through six different countries before arriving in Croatia.
3 She wanted to spend a couple of days on her own.
4 Her son contacted the police.
5 Ms Moreau invented the story about following her satnav by mistake.
6 Hundreds of people follow their satnavs without thinking and end up at the wrong destination.

4 VOCABULARY Work in pairs. Match three of the gadgets in the list with photos A–C below. Check that you understand the meaning of all the other words.

Gadgets Bluetooth headset   Bluetooth speaker
camcorder   digital radio   games console   memory stick
MP3 player   satnav   smartphone   smartwatch   tablet

5 🎧2.17 Listen to five dialogues. Which gadgets from exercise 4 are mentioned in each one?

6 🎧2.17 Listen again. Choose the correct answers (a–c).

1 It is a fact, not an opinion, that the problem
  a was caused by a child.
  b cannot be solved in the shop.
  c will take several days to solve.
2 Where does the dialogue take place?
  a Outside the man's house.
  b Outside the Victoria Hotel.
  c Outside the Empire Hotel.
3 Why is the girl angry with the boy?
  a He won't let her use his MP3 player.
  b He accused her of stealing something from a friend.
  c He accidentally deleted something that she wanted.
4 The dialogue takes place a short while before
  a a dance performance.
  b a football match.
  c a social event.
5 It is an opinion, not a fact, that the girl playing the game
  a needs to cross the river.
  b does not have a high score.
  c does not have a lot of time left.

7 SPEAKING Discuss the questions with your partner. Use the phrases below to help you.

Expressing opinions   I believe that …   I think that …
In my opinion, …   In my view, …   As I see it, …
It seems to me that …   I'd say that …

1 Do you think people depend too much on technology? Give examples.
2 Do you think any of the gadgets in exercise 4 will have disappeared fifty years from now? Explain your opinion.
3 Do you think it's wrong to copy songs and films from friends rather than buying them? Why? / Why not?

A

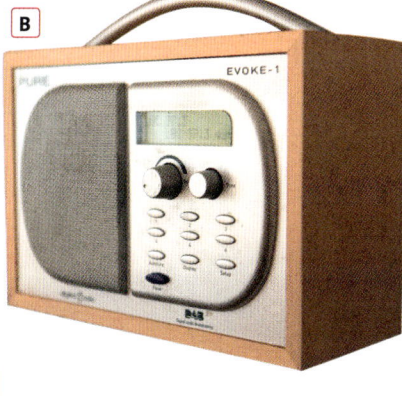

B

C

Modals in the past
I can use past modals correctly.

1 Read the dialogue. Who has a problem with their phone: Freya, Archie or both? Explain your answer.

Freya Hi, Archie. I didn't understand that email you sent me yesterday.

Archie I didn't send any emails yesterday.

Freya Well, you might have sent it earlier. But I got it yesterday.

Archie I can't have sent you an email. My phone hasn't been working for a week.

Freya Somebody must have used your account. The email had a link to a competition, but when I clicked on it, nothing happened.

Archie Oh no! You shouldn't have clicked on the link. You've possibly downloaded some malware onto your phone.

Freya That's terrible! You should have warned me earlier.

Archie I didn't know! Anyway, you might not have downloaded anything. It's possible that you were lucky. You just need to wait and see.

Freya Anyway, you need to warn your other friends. That email could have gone to everybody in your address book!

2 🎧 **2.18** Listen to the dialogue in exercise 1. How is *have* pronounced?

LEARN THIS! Modal verbs

a We use *may / might / could have* + past participle for speculating about past events.
She may / might / could have gone home hours ago.
(= It's possible she went home hours ago.)

b We use *may / might not have* + past participle (but not *could not have*) as the negative.
She didn't phone. She might / may not have known my number. (= It's possible she didn't know it.)

c We use *must have* and *can't / couldn't have* + past participle to make logical deductions about the past.
You can't / couldn't have seen Louis in town. He lives abroad now. (= It's not possible that you saw him.)
You must have seen somebody who looks like him. (= That is the only possible explanation.)

d We use *should / shouldn't have* + past participle to criticise past actions.
You should have phoned her before you went out.
You shouldn't have used all the credit on your phone.

---

3 Read the Learn this! box. Underline the past modal verbs in the dialogue in exercise 1.

4 Find two more sentences in the dialogue in exercise 1 which could be expressed using *may / might / could have*. Rewrite them with the correct past modal verb.

➡ **Grammar Builder 5.2** page 136

---

5 **USE OF ENGLISH** For each mini-dialogue, write the option (a–c) that makes the most sense in the gap.

1 **Bill** I can't find my camera.
Ben ___
Bill Yes, maybe. I'll look there tomorrow.
a You should have kept it in a safe place.
b You might have left it at school.
c You couldn't have lost it.

2 **Alex** She didn't get my email.
Kat ___
Alex I'm sure I did. I checked before I sent it.
a You might have sent it to the wrong address.
b You should have sent it to a different address.
c You can't have sent it to the right address.

3 **Clare** My dad wasn't answering his phone.
Liz ___
Clare But he always has it.
a He should have been at work.
b He might not have gone to work.
c He can't have taken his phone to work.

6 **USE OF ENGLISH** Complete the second sentence so that it means the same as the first. Include the word in brackets.

1 It was a bad idea for you to lend Jake your phone. (shouldn't)
You _____ Jake your phone.

2 It's possible that Fraser deleted your messages by accident. (could)
Fraser _____ by accident.

3 The only possible explanation is that you sent that email to the wrong person. (must)
You _____ to the wrong person.

4 It's possible that I didn't dial the correct number. (may)
I _____ the correct number.

5 Leaving your phone on was a bad idea. (should)
You _____ your phone off.

6 It's not possible that Tom phoned Kim. (can't)
Tom _____ Kim.

7 **SPEAKING** In pairs, describe the photo. Say what might / must / can't have happened.

5E Word Skills

Adjective + preposition

I can use the correct prepositions after adjectives.

1 SPEAKING Work in pairs. Which of these activities do you spend a lot of time doing? Do you think you might do any of them too much? Give reasons for your answers.

- checking your phone for messages
- taking photos of yourself
- browsing social networking sites
- watching video clips online
- playing video games

2 Read the article. Do you think the son was addicted to playing video games? Find evidence for your opinion.

According to a Chinese blog, a man has hired gamers to find his son in an online game and kill his character.

The man was unhappy with his son for not finding a job and was also worried about the amount of time the 23-year-old spent playing games online. So he found some other gamers who were particularly good at online combat games and paid them to kill his son's character. His son became aware of the situation when people kept attacking him. He was so curious about it that he asked one of his attackers to explain. Apparently, the son was shocked at the answer, but he was not particularly angry with his father. After all, people who play online combat games are used to being killed!

We are probably all familiar with stories of video game addiction. However, many experts are not sure that it is a real condition. They point out that spending a lot of time doing something is not the same as being addicted to it. It only becomes an addiction when it is harmful to family life, friendships or work.

LEARN THIS! Adjective + preposition

Many adjectives are followed by certain prepositions: *in, at, of, with*, etc.

to be obsessed with / successful in / sensitive to something

You need to learn these adjective + preposition combinations as they do not follow any rules. A good dictionary will tell you which preposition to use with which adjective.

3 Read the Learn this! box. Then underline these adjectives in the text in exercise 2. Which prepositions follow them?

addicted   angry   aware   curious   familiar
good   harmful   shocked   unhappy   worried

LOOK OUT!

Some adjectives can be followed by more than one preposition with no difference in use or meaning.

to be annoyed at / with somebody or something

But with some adjectives, the preposition changes depending on the type or meaning of the word which follows.

to be unhappy with somebody / about something

4 DICTIONARY WORK Read the Look out! box. Then read the dictionary entry. Which two prepositions can be used after the adjective *similar*? Does the choice of preposition depend on the meaning or on the type of word which follows?

> **similar** /ˈsɪmələ(r)/ *adj* **similar (to sth/sb); similar (in sth)** like sth/sb but not exactly the same: *My phone is similar to my brother's.* • *Our houses are very similar in size.*

5 Circle the correct prepositions to go with these adjectives. Use a dictionary to help you.

1 dissatisfied **in / with**
2 responsible **for / in**
3 obsessed **of / with**
4 sensitive **for / to**
5 pleased **to / with**
6 successful **in / to**

6 USE OF ENGLISH Complete the text with the correct prepositions. All of the adjectives are in exercises 2–5.

selfie (n):
a picture taken of a person by that person

A teenager in the UK, Danny Bowman, became addicted ¹_____ 'selfies' and spent up to ten hours a day taking around 200 photos of himself with his phone. This was a true case of addiction: it was harmful ²_____ his education and his friendships and responsible ³_____ several health problems. Experts are aware ⁴_____ the condition and say it is becoming more and more common. Danny first posted selfies on Facebook when he was fifteen and soon became obsessed ⁵_____ reading his friends' comments. Although he was pleased ⁶_____ many of the things his friends wrote, he was also very sensitive ⁷_____ criticism. Before long, he was feeling very dissatisfied ⁸_____ his appearance. He took more and more photos of himself. His parents became very worried ⁹_____ his behaviour. Because they were both mental health nurses, they were familiar ¹⁰_____ addictions. They knew that Danny needed help. Now, after months of hospital treatment, Danny has been successful ¹¹_____ beating his addiction. But it's a growing problem, with many other cases similar ¹²_____ Danny's.

7 SPEAKING Work in pairs. Tell your partner about something that you are (or have been):

1 successful in.
2 excited about.
3 satisfied with.
4 curious about.
5 pleased with.
6 good at.
7 angry about.
8 keen on.

> I was really successful in my recent music exam.

Clever machines
I can understand a text about artificial intelligence.

1 **SPEAKING** Read the conversation between a human and a computer at the beginning of the article. Is it obvious which is the computer and which the human?

2 Now scan the text and find out which is the computer. Check your ideas from exercise 1.

> **Reading Strategy**
> In a multiple-choice question, the correct option will match the meaning of the text but use different words. It is therefore important not to *automatically* assume that a multiple-choice option which contains words from the text is correct.

3 Read the Reading Strategy. Then complete these tasks.

1 Look at question 1 in exercise 4. Read the second paragraph of the text (lines 8–23).
2 Circle the correct answer and identify the part of the text which gives the answer.
3 How many words from that part of the text does the correct answer contain?
4 Which words are used in the text instead of the words in the question?

Testing intelligence

🎧 2.19

A Hello there.
B How are you?
A I am doing very well. How are you?
B Fine.
A Glad to hear it. What's new?
B Nothin'.
A Fair enough. What do you want to talk about?
B I dunno.
A You don't know what you want to talk about?! Humans are not too intelligent at times.
B Says the one who doesn't know my name.
A You have not yet told me your name.
B MY NAME IS A.A.R.D.V.A.R.K.
A No, it isn't. What is your real name?

This conversation is between a real human and a computer program called Mitsuku. Programs like Mitsuku are called 'chatbots'. Mitsuku was the winner of the Loebner Prize in 2013, an annual competition
5 to find a program that can pass the Turing test. The test, designed to measure artificial intelligence, was invented by British mathematician Alan Turing.

Fifty or sixty years ago, computers were very simple machines, but even then scientists believed that one
10 day machines would be able to 'think' and that they would probably be as intelligent as humans. The question was, 'How can we measure the intelligence of a machine?' Alan Turing, who had helped to break the German Enigma code during the Second World War,
15 came up with an answer. He said we need to ask, 'Can this computer talk? Can it have a conversation like a human?' If it can, he argued, then it is intelligent and it can think. In a Turing test, judges sit at a screen and have a chatroom conversation with the chatbot program.
20 They don't know if they are chatting with another person or with a chatbot. After exchanging messages for five minutes, the judge decides if he or she is chatting with a human or a machine.

4 Read the rest of the text. Choose the correct answers (a–d).

1 Around the middle of the last century, scientists
   a tried to build computers that were as intelligent as humans.
   b built a machine that could have a conversation with a human.
   c thought that computers could never be as intelligent as humans.
   d thought that in the future computers and people might be equally clever.

2 According to the Turing test, a computer that could think would be able to
   a break the Enigma code.
   b talk to people like an ordinary person does.
   c chat with another computer.
   d have a chatroom conversation for a minimum of five minutes.

3 Chatbots that enter the Loebner competition
   a have a 30% chance of winning.
   b share prize money of $100,000.
   c need to appear human to about a third of the judges.
   d will never win the big money prize.

4 The main criticism of the Turing test is that
   a Turing focused on the wrong type of intelligence.
   b the winner simply has to copy human behaviour.
   c Google and NASA computers can also achieve amazing things with the help of chatbots.
   d chatbots are designed to do things that we can't do.

5 The writer of the text
   a agrees with the critics of the Turing test.
   b is more impressed with search engines than chatbots.
   c does not express a personal opinion on the validity of the Turing test.
   d believes that people are just very complex robots.

5 SPEAKING Do you agree that a search engine like Google is more impressive than a chatbot that can seem human? Why? / Why not?

6 VOCABULARY Complete the verb–noun collocations with the nouns below. They are all in the text.

Verb–noun collocations an answer a code a competition a conversation a prize a test a website messages

1 pass _____
2 break _____
3 come up with _____
4 have _____
5 exchange _____
6 enter _____
7 win _____
8 search _____

➡ **Vocabulary Builder** Verb–noun collocations: page 123

7 SPEAKING Work in pairs. Imagine that you were going to chat with a chatbot. Think of six questions that you would ask or requests you would make. Try to think of questions that would reveal that it was not human.

8 SPEAKING Share your ideas with another pair or with the class. Vote on the best ideas.

We would ask, 'Tell me how to boil an egg.'

9 INTERNET RESEARCH Complete the following tasks.

1 Search online for the websites of chatbots such as Mitsuku, A.L.I.C.E., Jabberwacky chatbot and Elbot.
2 Have an online conversation with one of them. Use your ideas from exercises 7 and 8.
3 Write down the questions you ask and the chatbot's replies.
4 Bring them into school and discuss them with your class. How convincingly human are the chatbots?

Turing predicted that by the year 2000, the average person 'will not have more than a 70% chance of making the right identification'. In other words, computers would trick the judges 30% of the time. An American called Hugh Loebner was fascinated by Turing's idea, and in the early 1990s he offered a prize of $100,000 to the creator of the first chatbot to pass the Turing test. In order to win the $100,000, a chatbot must convince at least 30% of the judges that it is human. Many chatbots have entered the competition, but so far no chatbot has won the big money prize. Mitsuku, however, came very close. In the conversation at the beginning of this article, Mitsuku is A and the real human is B. You can tell that A is not human because at one point in the conversation, A says 'Humans are not too intelligent at times.' Although Mitsuku failed to win the $100,000, it certainly won't be long before a chatbot is able to fool the Loebner judges into thinking that it is a real person.

But is the Turing test a good way to decide if a machine is intelligent? Critics argue that the chatbots in the competition are merely imitating humans. Humans are the only animals on Earth that can speak, and that's why Turing chose to focus on it. But what is really impressive, critics say, is machines that do things that we can't do. For example, it is amazing that Google can search hundreds of millions of websites for a single word in a matter of seconds, or that a NASA computer can control a rocket on a journey from Earth to Jupiter. Even some of the things that smartphone apps can do are extremely impressive. Those achievements are far more interesting and useful than a chatbot's. A chatbot is really nothing more than a successful liar, so the argument goes.

Fans of the Turing test, on the other hand, feel that humans are themselves machines. It's just that our brains are far more complex than computers. As philosopher and scientist Daniel Dennett said in a recent interview, 'It's not impossible to have a conscious robot. You're looking at one.'

Photo comparison
I can compare photos and answer questions.

1 SPEAKING Look at photo A of students using their tablets in a lesson. Speculate about the questions below.

1 What subject is it? (Choose from the list below.)
2 What has the teacher asked them to do?
3 What are they doing with their tablets?

> It may / might / could be …

> They may / might / could be (+ -ing) …

> Their teacher may / might / could have asked them to …

School subjects art   design and technology   drama
English   geography   history   I.C.T. (computing)
maths   music   P.E. (physical education)
R.E. (religious education)   science

2 🎧 2.20 Listen to a student describing photo A. Does she agree with your ideas from exercise 1?

3 🎧 2.20 KEY PHRASES Listen again. Which of the phrases below does the candidate use for speculating?

Speculating
It looks to me / doesn't look to me as if they …
They look / don't look (to me) as if / as though they're …
They look / don't look like they're (+ -ing) …
They seem quite (+ adj) …
They don't look / don't seem very (+ adj) …

4 SPEAKING Work in pairs. Take turns to describe photo B. Include some speculation in your description.

These photos (A and B) show students in lessons. Compare and contrast the photos. Include the following points:
• Typical school subjects at primary level.
• A typical classroom in a primary school.
• Why it is important for students to enjoy lessons.

5 🎧 2.21 Read the task above. Listen to a student doing the task. Which of the three points does he forget to mention?

A

B

Speaking Strategy
When you have to compare and contrast photos, try to find at least two things the photos have in common and at least two differences. Learn some key phrases for expressing these similarities and differences.

6 🎧 2.21 KEY PHRASES Read the Speaking Strategy. Then listen again. What is the missing word in each of the phrases below?

Comparing photos
The common theme in the photos is ¹_____ .
Both photos show a ²_____ of some kind.
In the first photo, the students are outside, whereas in the second photo they're in a ³_____ .
Unlike the second photo, the first photo does not show the ⁴_____ .
In the second photo, they're listening to the teacher rather than looking at ⁵_____ .

7 SPEAKING In pairs, discuss questions 1 and 2 below. Use evidence from the photos in your discussion if possible.

1 Do you think using smartphones and tablets is a good way for students to learn?
2 Do you think it is possible to learn without a teacher?

8 🎧 2.22 Now listen to the student answering the questions from exercise 7. Does he agree or disagree with your opinions? Does he mention any of the same evidence?

9 🎧 2.22 KEY PHRASES Listen again. Which of the phrases below does the student use to introduce his opinions?

Introducing opinions
It seems to me that …
In my opinion / view, …
Personally, I think / don't think that …
I believe that …
The way I see it, …
For me, the important thing is (that) …

10 SPEAKING Turn to page 144 and do the speaking task. Use phrases from this lesson.

5H Writing
An internet forum post
I can write an internet forum post about a new gadget.

1 SPEAKING Ask and answer the questions about internet forums.

1 What is an internet forum?
2 Have you ever contributed to one? If so, what type of forum was it? Why did you contribute?

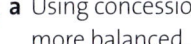
Writing Strategy
Each point in the task will ask you to do a different thing, such as describe, recommend, relate, express an opinion, suggest, etc. Read the task carefully and make sure that you understand exactly what you are being asked to do.

2 Read the Writing Strategy and the task below. Identify the verbs in each point that tell you what you should do.

You recently bought a new computer. Write a forum post in which you:
- Describe your experience of using the computer.
- Compare it with another computer you have used.
- Present the opinions of people who think teenagers rely too much on computers.
- Ask other contributors to react to your post.

3 Read the forum posts. Did both writers cover all four points in the way described in the task? Explain your answers.

LEARN THIS! Concession clauses
a Using concession clauses can make your arguments more balanced.
b We can use *although* or *even though* to introduce a concession clause. The clause can come before or after the main clause.
The computer is quite powerful even though it's quite small.
Although it's quite small, the computer is quite powerful.
c *In spite of* and *despite* also express concession, but are followed by a noun or *-ing* form, not a clause.
In spite of / Despite its size, it's still quite powerful.

4 Read the Learn this! box. Underline four examples of concession clauses in the forum posts.

➤➤ **Grammar Builder 5.3** page 136

5 Read the task below. Identify the key words in the four points that tell you what you should do.

You recently bought a new tablet. Write a forum post in which you:
- Describe the tablet and some of its features.
- Give other forum contributors brief instructions on how to use it or one of its features (e.g. taking a photo).
- Give your overall opinion of the tablet.
- Explain how it helps you with your schoolwork.

Techspot forum

Sam245

Last month I bought a new laptop. I use it every day for schoolwork and for accessing social media. I research topics for homework, and I also access the school website and submit my homework online. It's also great for messaging my friends.

I used to have a desktop computer. Although it was powerful, it was very slow and it didn't have much storage. Despite its small size, the laptop is lightning-quick and has a massive 1TB hard drive.

Unfortunately my parents are always telling me to get off the computer. They think that teenagers should spend less time interacting with people via a screen and more time talking face-to-face.

I'd be interested to hear what you think about this. Should we spend less time at our computers?

HollyXX

I love my new PC! It's an all-in-one desktop with a widescreen display. It's a really up-to-date model, despite the fact that I got it second-hand on eBay. It's bright green with a black keyboard and a wireless mouse.

Until now, I've always used my mum's old laptop. The screen was much smaller and the operating system was old so it was often impossible to download new software. And it had a lot less memory than my new computer.

I agree that teenagers rely a lot on computers, although I don't really think it's a serious problem. And anyway, it's difficult to say what we could do about it.

What do you think? Do you agree with me? Have you bought a new PC recently? What's it like?

➤➤ **Vocabulary Builder** Describing computer equipment: page 123

6 Brainstorm ideas for each of the four points in the task in exercise 5.

7 Write your forum post.

CHECK YOUR WORK

Have you ...
- covered all four points?
- used one or two concession clauses?
- checked the grammar and spelling?

Reading

1 Read the strategy above. Then read questions 1–5 below. Decide what kind of information the questions ask for. Write S for specific information or G for general ideas.

1 What does the writer want to convince readers of? ___
2 What happened in 2009 which 'changed everything'? ___
3 Why did the writer write to the editor of a newspaper? ___
4 How does the writer summarise her experience of house-hunting? ___
5 Where would you expect to find this text? ___

2 Read the three texts and choose the best answer (A–D).

Back in time

As she stepped into the hall after nearly thirty years of absence, she realised at once that she shouldn't have come back. The smell of wood smoke, damp stone and ancient paper brought the past back so powerfully that it nearly knocked her backwards. In an instant she felt like a young girl again, alone and frightened in the house. She remembered feeling very, very cold – not from the damp and the near-freezing temperature, but because a terrible new life was beginning. And she could do nothing to stop it.

1 What is true about the woman's feelings when she entered the house?
  A She realised that she had missed her old home.
  B She was happy to return to the house.
  C She understood that coming back was a mistake.
  D She was sad about the condition of the house.

Future home?

Every few years, trend-watchers tell us that the house of the future has arrived, and gadgets from science fiction films will soon be in every home in the country. So far they've been wrong – and after viewing the 'Home of the Future' exhibition, I suspect that they are still wrong. Why do I need a super-intelligent fridge or an internet-surfing mirror? I would much rather see my face clearly in an ordinary bathroom mirror than try to surf the internet while I'm combing my hair! If only they could design a device to stop me killing all my houseplants. If they did that, then I might be interested!

2 What was the writer's reaction to the exhibition?
  A He found it very interesting.
  B It reminded him of a science fiction film.
  C He wanted to buy the gadgets online.
  D He didn't see the use of many of the inventions.

Ackerman dream homes

Since 1893, Ackerman Homes have created some of the most charming neighbourhoods in the south of England. Our homes combine a sense of history with the most modern advances in home design and technology. Now you can have the opportunity to own a beautiful contemporary Ackerman home in our new development in Acreage Woods. Experience the quality, beauty and comfort of Ackerman Homes, the most trusted name in home building. With spacious semi-detached and detached homes from £275,000 to £425,000, we are sure that you will find what you're looking for. So why not visit us today?

3 The purpose of the text is to …
  A describe a particular home.
  B attract the interest of people who are looking for a new home.
  C outline the history of a home builder.
  D explain what makes a quality home.

Listening

3 Read the strategy above. Then look at the statement below. Choose the extract, A or B, which matches the statement.

The woman missed several previous yoga classes.

🎧 A I've only just come back to yoga after taking some time off – I found I really missed it.

🎧 B There was an emergency at home, so I couldn't come to the last class, but I don't like missing lessons.

4 🎧 **2.23** You will hear a conversation between two friends about smartphones. Are the sentences true or false? Write T or F. You will hear the recording twice.

1 Sal paid too much for her phone. ___
2 Sal's parents encouraged her to get a new phone. ___
3 Tim is not happy with his sister's use of her phone. ___
4 Sal's family avoid using their phones at dinner. ___
5 Sal does not like talking when she's eating. ___
6 Tim could cause a problem by using his phone. ___
7 Sal advises Tim not to listen to music on his phone. ___
8 Tim disagrees with Sal's suggestion. ___

Exam Skills Trainer

Use of English

5 Read the strategy above. Then complete the second sentence so that it has a similar meaning to the first sentence. You must use between two and five words, including the word given. Do not change the word given.

1 It's possible we'll sell our flat next year. (may)
   We may sell our flat next year.
2 Not many of the links on this website are useful. (few)
   There are _____ on this website.
3 It's not possible that you deleted the file. (can't)
   You _____ the file.
4 My computer has been really slow lately. (fast)
   My computer _____ it was.
5 Staying up so late was a bad idea. (shouldn't)
   You _____ stayed up so late.
6 She hasn't got any clothes that are expensive. (none)
   _____ expensive.

Speaking

6 Read the strategy above. Then look at photo A and the answer below. Choose the best words to complete the answer.

A

It seems to me that the man is homeless because he's
¹**sleeping** / **relaxing** outside on ²**the ground** / **the floor**. It looks as ³**like** / **if** it might be cold because he's under a ⁴**blanket** / **cardboard box**.
I think the man is ⁵**aware** / **unaware** that someone is taking a photo because his eyes are ⁶**half-open** / **closed** and he looks ⁷**calm** / **nervous**. I also think the man is ⁸**asleep** / **awake**, so he's probably too ⁹**excited** / **tired** to notice anything going on around him.

7 Compare and contrast the photos (A and B) which show homeless people in Britain. Include the following points:

- Where homeless people usually live.
- Why people may become homeless.
- How you think we can help homeless people.

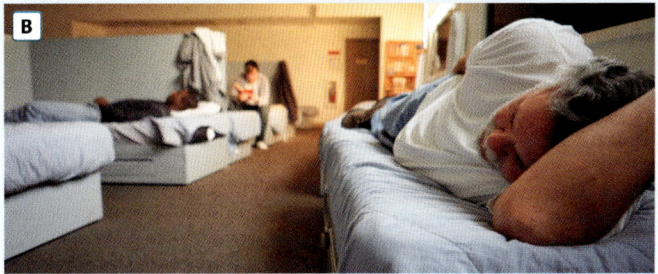

B

8 In pairs, discuss questions 1 and 2 below. Use evidence from the photos in your discussion if possible.

1 Do you think it is a problem that some people live on the street?
2 Do you think we should give money to homeless people?

Writing

9 Read the strategy above and the task below. Think of ideas for each of the four points. Write notes.

You recently bought a new MP3 player. Write a forum post in which you:
- Describe the MP3 player and its features.
- Compare it with another gadget which you can use to listen to music.
- Give other forum contributors brief instructions on how to use one of its features.
- Ask other contributors to react to your post.

10 Read the task below and write an internet forum post. You can choose to do the task below or the task in exercise 9.

You recently bought a new smartphone. Write a forum post in which you:
- Describe the smartphone and some of its features.
- Compare it with another smartphone you have used.
- Give your overall opinion of the smartphone.
- Present the opinions of people who think teenagers use smartphones too much.

6

High flyers

Unit map

● **Vocabulary**
Describing character: nouns
Describing character: adjectives
Personal qualities: phrases
Separable and inseparable phrasal verbs
Verb and preposition

● **Word Skills**
Phrasal verbs (2)

● **Grammar**
Defining relative clauses
Non-defining relative clauses

● **Listening** Nellie Bly

● **Reading** #GIRLBOSS

● **Speaking** Guided conversation

● **Writing** A for and against essay

● **Culture 6**
British public schools

● **Vocabulary Builder** page 124

● **Grammar Builder and**
 Reference page 137

6A Vocabulary

Describing character
I can describe people's character.

1 SPEAKING Describe the photos. In your opinion, which is a) the most interesting job and b) the most difficult job? Give reasons.

2 VOCABULARY Look at the list of nouns for describing character. What are the corresponding adjectives? Use a dictionary and the list of adjective endings below to help you. Sometimes, you just need to remove a noun ending to form the adjective.

Describing character: nouns ambition cheerfulness creativity enthusiasm flexibility generosity honesty idealism intelligence loyalty maturity modesty optimism patience pessimism punctuality realism self-confidence seriousness shyness sociability stubbornness sympathy thoughtfulness

Adjective endings -able / -ible -al -ant / -ent -astic / -istic -ed -est -ful -ive -ous -ual

ambitious, cheerful, . . .

3 🎧 **2.24** Listen to ten noun–adjective pairs. In which noun–adjective pairs is the stress different between the noun and the adjective?

creative creativity

A

disability support worker

B

PUNCH & JUDY

children's entertainer

LOOK OUT!

Some personal qualities are best expressed using phrases.

have a good sense of humour   show lots of initiative
have physical courage   have lots of / no common sense
be good at communicating   have lots of energy
have good organisational skills   lack self-confidence

4 **VOCABULARY** Read the Look out! box. What personal qualities do you need for the jobs in the photos in exercise 1, in your opinion? Use words from exercise 2 and the phrases in the Look out! box.

> A disability support worker needs lots of patience / needs to be very patient.

> It's important for a children's entertainer to have a good sense of humour.

C

instrument maker

D

helicopter paramedic

5 🎧 **2.25** Listen to three people discussing the qualities needed for particular jobs. Which jobs are they talking about? Choose from the ones below. There are three extra jobs. Explain your choices.

hotel receptionist   nurse   police officer   sales assistant
sports coach   teacher

RECYCLE! Comparison

a Key forms:
kinder – the kindest
more practical – the most practical
less sociable – the least sociable
(not) as intelligent as

b We use double comparatives to say that something is changing.
You're getting more and more impatient!

c We use *the … the* and comparatives to say that one thing changes with another.
The more arrogant you are, the less popular you'll be.

6 🎧 **2.25** Read the Recycle! box. Complete the sentences with the correct form of the adjectives in brackets. Then listen again and check.

Dialogue 1
1 The _____ (sympathetic) you are, the _____ (good) you'll be at the job.
2 I don't think idealism is _____ (useful) as patience.
3 These days they have to work _____ and _____ (long) hours.

Dialogue 2
4 I think that _____ (important) quality is punctuality.
5 You'll certainly be _____ (popular) if you can laugh at things.

Dialogue 3
6 I think patience is less _____ (important) physical courage.
7 Which do you think is _____ (useful) quality of the three?

7 **SPEAKING** Work in pairs. Agree on which are the three most important or useful qualities when you are in the following situations. Use the adjectives and nouns from exercise 2 and the phrases from the Look out! box and exercise 6 to help you.

1 at a party
2 in a job interview
3 in your first job
4 in lessons
5 with close friends
6 at home with your family

> We think that sociability and … are useful qualities to have when you're at a party.

> It's best not to be … when you are …

Defining relative clauses
I can use defining relative clauses.

1 Read the article. What job is Harris applying for?

Harris Aslam is an ambitious young man who left school at the age of thirteen to work in his family's grocery business. Now, at the age of eighteen, he owns three shops in Kirkcaldy, Scotland, the town where he was born and brought up. But Harris has bigger ambitions and wants a new challenge. The job he is now applying for is CEO of Nisa Retail, a grocery business whose annual sales are about £1.6 billion! This is a job which usually attracts middle-aged businesspeople, not eighteen-year-olds. And indeed, Nisa Retail is looking for someone who is very experienced, so Harris might not get the job. But you have to admire his ambition!

2 Underline these relative pronouns in the article in exercise 1: *which, who, whose, where.* Which do we use a) for people, b) for things and animals, c) for places and d) to indicate possession?

> **LEARN THIS!** Defining relative clauses
>
> **a** A defining relative clause tells us which person, thing, or place we are talking about. It follows the noun and can come in the middle of a sentence. We do not put commas before or after the clause.
> *He's the police officer who arrested the man.*
> *The police officer who arrested the man is over there.*
>
> **b** In informal style, we often use *that* instead of *who* and *which*. *The boy that you saw is my brother.*
>
> **c** In very formal English, we can use *whom* instead of *who* when the pronoun is the object of the clause or follows a preposition.
> *The nurse whom the police questioned has moved abroad.*
> *Is this the man to whom you are referring?*
>
> **d** Prepositions can go at the end of a relative clause, or, in very formal style, at the start.
> *The music which I'm listening to is great.*
> *He remembered the music to which he had listened in his youth.*

3 Read the Learn this! box. Can you find examples of all four rules in the article in exercise 1?

4 Complete the text with *who, which, where* and *whose.*

This is Katie Stagliano, a girl ¹_____ idea to grow vegetables for the homeless has improved the lives of thousands of people. In 2008, she planted a seed ²_____ grew into a 20-kg cabbage. She donated it to a soup kitchen ³_____ it fed more than 275 people ⁴_____ were living on the streets. She decided to create gardens ⁵_____ she could grow vegetables ⁶_____ she would then donate to organisations ⁷_____ help homeless people. Katie's a girl ⁸_____ mission in life is simple: to help others.

5 Read rules c and d in the Learn this! box again. Then rewrite these sentences in a less formal style.

1 The car in which we drove to London belongs to my mum.
2 This is the address to which you should write.
3 The exam about which I'm worried is on Monday.
4 Chris is the friend with whom I went to Italy.
5 The man about whom I told you is over there.
6 Who is the girl to whom you were talking?

> **! LOOK OUT!**
> We can omit object pronouns, but not subject pronouns.
> *Who's the man that I saw you with?*
> → *Who's the man I saw you with?* ✓
> *Who's the man who was with you?*
> → ~~Who's the man was with you?~~ ✗

6 Read the Look out! box. Underline a relative clause in the article in exercise 1 where the object pronoun has been omitted and rewrite it with the pronoun. In which of the sentences from exercise 5 can you omit the pronoun?

➡ **Grammar Builder 6.1** page 137

7 In which sentences can we omit the relative pronouns?

1 Patience and tolerance are qualities which I admire.
2 I like people who are modest and thoughtful.
3 Punctuality is a quality which is quite rare in young people.
4 Sam's a boy who people see as good-humoured and generous.
5 I'm grateful for the sympathy which you showed.
6 Joanna is a girl who is always willing to help.

8 **USE OF ENGLISH** Choose the correct option(s) to complete the sentences. Sometimes more than one option is correct.

1 Who's the girl ___ is sitting over there?
   a which   b (no pronoun)   c who
   d whom   e that
2 Did you get the job ___ you applied for?
   a who   b that   c which
   d (no pronoun)   e for which
3 A nurse is someone ___ job is to care for people in hospital.
   a who   b whose   c of which
   d (no pronoun)   e that's
4 That's the office ___ my dad works.
   a whose   b that   c in which
   d which   e where

9 **SPEAKING** Work in pairs. Take turns to define these jobs and places of work. Use defining relative clauses.

1 a doctor   5 an engineer
2 a fire station   6 a town hall
3 an actor   7 a babysitter
4 a school   8 your ideas

> A doctor is a person who … / whose job …

6C Listening

Nellie Bly

I can listen for linking words and phrases.

1 **SPEAKING** Work in pairs. What qualities do you think you need to be a good journalist? Why? Discuss the qualities below and your own ideas.

ambitious   creative   determined   intelligent
patient   self-confident   stubborn

2 **USE OF ENGLISH** Complete the article with suitable words.

At the age of sixteen, Nellie Bly read an article in her local newspaper which argued that women were not able to do the same jobs ¹_____ men. Furious, she wrote an anonymous article in reply and sent it to the paper. The paper's editor was so impressed ²_____ he offered her a job: Nellie was now a journalist!

At that time, female journalists mostly wrote about fashion and gardening, but Nellie had other ideas. She was determined to be an investigative journalist ³_____ wrote about serious issues, like women's rights and the problems of factory workers. But when Nellie accused companies ⁴_____ treating workers badly, they refused to buy advertisements in the paper, so the editor stopped Nellie's investigations.

⁵_____ 1887, Nellie moved to the *New York World* newspaper, where the owner, Joseph Pulitzer, helped her to do undercover work. For example, Nellie pretended to be insane so that she could become a patient at a psychiatric hospital in New York and find out ⁶_____ the conditions there. As a result of Nellie's shocking discoveries, the authorities changed the way they cared ⁷_____ mentally ill patients. This was probably her greatest success ⁸_____ an investigative journalist.

3 **2.26** Listen and check your answers to exercise 2. Which of the qualities from exercise 1 do you think Nellie Bly showed? Justify your answer with evidence from the text.

> **Listening Strategy**
> When you listen to a more formal text, pay attention to linking words and phrases. These tell you how the pieces of information are connected: a contrast, a result, an example, emphasis, etc.

4 Read the Listening Strategy. Add one more phrase from the list below to each group (a–d).

for instance   for that reason   however   indeed

a **contrast:** *mind you, though,* _____
b **result:** *as a result, consequently,* _____
c **emphasis:** *in fact,* _____
d **example:** *for example,* _____

5 **2.27** Listen to six sentences and the linking words which follow. Circle the endings (a or b) that make sense.

1   a   … Nellie was not interested in that.
   b   … Nellie was happy just to have a job.
2   a   … this did not affect Nellie's ambitions.
   b   … Nellie was one of the first.
3   a   … her reports were truthful and well written.
   b   … she wrote about children who worked in factories.
4   a   … she was not popular with those people.
   b   … she was shocked by what she saw.
5   a   … the pay was not good.
   b   … they started before sunrise.
6   a   … nobody seemed to know or care.
   b   … the staff did not treat the patients well.

6 **2.28** Listen and check your answers to exercise 5.

7 **2.29** Listen to a radio interview about Nellie Bly's most famous adventure: a trip around the world. What are the missing places on the map (A–C)?

8 **2.29** Listen again. Are these sentences true or false? Write T or F.

1   Nellie's adventure was Joseph Pulitzer's idea. ___
2   Elizabeth Bisland worked for a different newspaper. ___
3   Nellie began her journey in 1888. ___
4   Nellie and Elizabeth travelled together some of the way. ___
5   Bad weather nearly caused Nellie to fail. ___
6   Joseph Pulitzer's money helped Nellie get home on time. ___

9 **SPEAKING** In what ways do you think Nellie Bly is a good role model? Give examples from her life to support your opinions. Use the phrases below and your own ideas.

discover the truth   follow her dream   help the poor
make a difference   win the race

Non-defining relative clauses

I can use non-defining relative clauses.

1 **SPEAKING** Discuss the questions below, which were asked in job interviews at Google. Do you think they are fair questions for a job interview? Why? / Why not?

1 How many golf balls can fit in a school bus?
2 How many times a day do a clock's hands cross?

2 Read the article. Do you think this interview was fair? Why? / Why not?

> A graduate was shocked at being asked to dance at a job interview. Alan Bacon, who left university in July, had been looking for a job for several months. He prepared thoroughly for the interview, which was for a job with a major retailer. But Alan, whose degree is in film and TV studies, was not expecting it to include dancing. 'I felt so embarrassed,' he said. The retailer has apologised and said that they are investigating managers at the store in Cardiff, where the interview took place. They also offered Mr Bacon another interview, which he has declined.

3 Look at the highlighted examples of non-defining relative clauses in the text. Circle the correct words to complete the Learn this! box.

> **LEARN THIS!** Non-defining relative clauses
>
> **a** In non-defining relative clauses, we use *who*, *which*, *where* and *whose*, but we do not use *that*.
>
> **b** A non-defining relative clause:
> - comes immediately **¹before / after** a noun and gives us information about that noun.
> - adds extra information to the sentence; the sentence **²makes sense / does not make sense** without it.
>   *Alan Bacon, who had to dance at an interview, now has a great job.*
> - **³has / doesn't have** a comma at the start. It has a comma or a full stop at the end.

4 Complete sentences 1–5 with phrases a–e. You need to add the correct relative pronoun (*who*, *which*, *where* or *whose*) at the start of each phrase.

1 Our neighbours, ___ , want to give up their jobs.
2 We spent a week in New York, ___ .
3 My cousin Grace, ___ , wants to be a doctor.
4 Wal-Mart, ___ , is an American company.
5 We bought this furniture at IKEA, ___ .

a _____ my mother used to live
b _____ is a Swedish company
c _____ mother is a nurse
d _____ both work in London
e _____ is the largest retailer in the world

➡ **Grammar Builder 6.2** page 137

5 **USE OF ENGLISH** Complete the second sentence in each pair so that it means the same as the first.

1 Ben lives in San Francisco and his dad works for Apple.
  Ben, _____ Apple, lives in San Francisco.
2 Lucy is a talented chef and has a lot of experience.
  Lucy, _____ chef, has a lot of experience.
3 My sister used to study in Madrid and now works there.
  My sister works in Madrid, _____ study.
4 My job used to be relaxing, but it's now very stressful.
  My job, _____ relaxing, is now very stressful.
5 I sat next to Laura at school and now she's a TV star.
  Laura, _____ at school, is now a TV star.

6 Rewrite each pair of sentences as a single sentence with a non-defining relative clause.

1 She was exhausted after the interview. It lasted two hours.
  She was exhausted after the interview, which lasted two hours.
2 My local department store has offered me a job. Two of my friends work there.
3 My neighbour is going for an interview at Google. Her degree was in computing.
4 Completing the training course means she can teach English abroad. It lasted six months.
5 I'll never forget my first job. It was in a toy factory.
6 My violin teacher helped me get a place at music college. He wanted me to be a professional musician.
7 I studied at the London School of Economics. My father had been a student there.
8 Jemma wants to study languages at university. Her dad is French.

7 **SPEAKING** Work in pairs. Agree on one piece of extra information to add to each sentence as a non-defining relative clause.

1 Einstein developed the general theory of relativity.
  Einstein, who was born in Germany, developed the general theory of relativity.
2 Silicon Valley is in California.
3 The Statue of Liberty was designed by a Frenchman.
4 Lionel Messi was born in Argentina.
5 *The Hunger Games* was made into a film in 2012.

8 **SPEAKING** Compare your sentences with another pair. Did they add the same information?

> Einstein, who was born in Germany, was a famous scientist.

Phrasal verbs (2)

I can use separable and inseparable phrasal verbs correctly.

1 Read the article. What is the problem Boyan Slat is trying to solve? What is his solution?

There are very few people who come up with a world-changing idea during their lifetime – but to come up with it while you are still a student is even more unusual. But that is exactly what Dutch teenager Boyan Slat has done. *Environmental Impact* magazine interviewed him.

EIM What is the problem that you identified?

BS Every year, millions of tonnes of plastic end up in the oceans, where the waves break it up into tiny pieces. This pollution kills millions of sea creatures every year.

EIM Hasn't there been any action to stop it?

BS Very little, even though campaigners have been calling for it for years.

EIM And you've worked out a way to tackle the problem.

BS Yes. My invention would float on the surface of the ocean and gradually clean it up by collecting around 20 billion tonnes of plastic from the water.

EIM What would you do with all that plastic?

BS Rather than throwing this away, it could be recycled and sold for about $500 million a year.

EIM And how would your floating invention be powered?

BS It would take energy from the waves and sun, so it would never run out of it!

2 Circle the correct words to complete the Learn this! box. Use the examples in the box and the article in exercise 1 to help you.

> **LEARN THIS!** Separable and inseparable phrasal verbs
>
> **a** Two-part phrasal verbs can be separable or inseparable. With separable phrasal verbs, the object can come before or after the particle (*for, up, with*, etc.).
> *We must work out the answer.*
> OR *We must work the answer out.*
>
> **b** When the object is a pronoun (*her, it, them*, etc.) it can only come ¹**after / before** the particle.
> *We must work it out.*
>
> **c** With inseparable phrasal verbs, the object always comes ²**after / before** the particle, even when it is a pronoun.
> *She looks after her dad. She looks after him.*
>
> **d** Three-part phrasal verbs are always ³**separable / inseparable**.
> *We won't run out of energy. We won't run out of it.*

3 Find the phrasal verbs in the article in exercise 1. Are they separable or inseparable? How do you know?

4 DICTIONARY WORK Read the dictionary entries. Then answer the questions below.

> **PHR V** **look after sb/sth/yourself** to be responsible for or take care of sb/sth/yourself: *I'll go back to work if I can find somebody to look after the children.* • *The old lady's son looked after all her financial affairs.*
> **look down on sb/sth** to think that you are better than sb/sth
> **look sth up** to search for information in a book: *to look up a word in a dictionary*
> **look up to sb** to respect and admire sb

1 Which phrasal verbs are two-part and which are three-part?
2 Which two-part phrasal verb is separable and which is inseparable? How do you know?

5 VOCABULARY Match the phrasal verbs below with definitions 1–9. Is each phrasal verb separable or inseparable?

Separable and inseparable phrasal verbs ask sb out bring sth up call sth off come across sth count on sb ~~give sth up~~ hold sb up take after sb turn into sth

1 stop doing something *give sth up (separable)*
2 mention something
3 be similar to somebody (a parent or older relative)
4 rely on somebody
5 delay somebody
6 invite somebody to go on a date (e.g. to the cinema)
7 find something accidentally
8 become something else
9 cancel something

6 Complete each question using a phrasal verb from exercise 4 or 5. Complete the follow-up question with the same phrasal verb and the correct pronoun.

1 Which person from history do you _____ to?
   Why do you _____ ?
   Which person from history do you look up to? Why do …
2 Which food or habit would you like to _____ ?
   Why do you want to _____ ?
3 If you could _____ a famous person, who would you choose? Why would you want to _____ ?
4 Have you ever _____ some money in the street? If so, what did you do when you _____ ?
5 Which member of your family do you _____ ?
   In what way do you _____ ?

7 SPEAKING Work in pairs. Ask and answer the questions and follow-up questions from exercise 6.

> Which person from history do you look up to?
>
> I look up to …
>
> Why do you look up to him / her?
>
> Because …

Reading

#GIRLBOSS

I can understand a text about a fashion entrepreneur.

1 Look at the title of the article and the images. What kind of business do you think the woman runs? Give reasons.

2 Read the article and answer the questions.

1 How did she get into trouble with a) the police and b) eBay?
2 Describe a typical a) Nasty Gal customer and b) Nasty Gal employee.

Rags to RICHES

🎧 2.30 Sophia Amoruso is the highly successful CEO of Nasty Gal, an online fashion retailer with over 550,000 customers in 150 countries. But Sophia is not your average entrepreneur and certainly nothing like the
5 majority of CEOs that you come across in today's business world.

Amoruso hated school and left home at the age of seventeen. She did a variety of boring jobs, spent a couple of years hitch-hiking around, and then got
10 arrested for shoplifting. ¹__ There, she got a job in a shoe shop, from which she was soon sacked. Her next job was on the reception desk at an art school, checking student IDs. While sitting at her computer, she spent hours visiting shopping sites such as eBay and
15 the social networking site MySpace. She was interested in fashion and photography and thought that selling clothes on eBay might be an amusing way to make money. So she resigned from her job and bought a book called *Starting an eBay Business for Dummies*.
20 She decided to start buying and selling vintage designer clothes – clothes that would appeal to fashion-conscious women like herself in their late teens and early twenties. Having named her eBay store 'Nasty Gal Vintage', she

began visiting second-hand clothes shops and charity shops, and spent hours searching for designer clothes 25 that other people had rejected. ²__ For example, she bought a Chanel jacket at a Salvation Army store for $8 and sold it on eBay for $1,000. She also searched for second-hand clothes online. For example, she found Yves Saint Laurent clothes by googling misspellings of 30 the designer's name. She reasoned that anyone who couldn't spell the name probably had no idea how much the clothes were worth!

Amoruso realised that people were more likely to visit her eBay shop if her clothes were worn by real 35 people rather than photographed hanging on a door or thrown across a bed. As she explained, 'Put it on the right girl, with the right hair and the right attitude, showing people how they could wear it – that was everything.' ³__ She had hardly any money to spend 40 on wages, so she paid them in hamburgers!

In 2007, eBay suspended her account because other eBay sellers had complained about the links on her eBay page to her MySpace page, where she had also begun to sell her clothes. ⁴__ Customers were flocking 45 to her MySpace page, and she had already learned all

Reading Strategy

When you are doing a gapped-sentence task:

1 Fill in the easiest gaps first.

2 When you have filled all the gaps, try the extra sentences in each gap again to make sure they don't fit.

3 Read the whole text again, checking your answers.

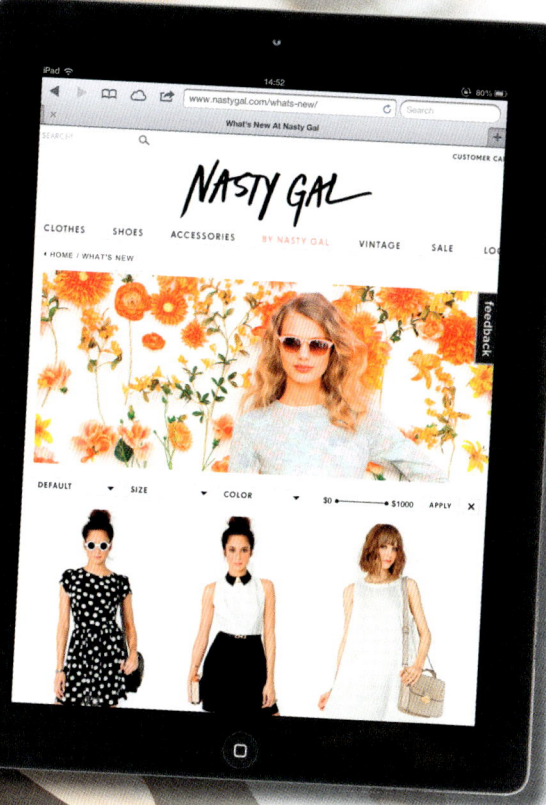

she could from her time on eBay – to respond to every customer comment and to really understand the people who were buying her clothes and
50 what they liked about them. This has allowed her to build up a large group of incredibly loyal customers. Most are women in their twenties who come back again and again to her online store. Half of Nasty Gal's business comes from customers
55 who are returning for a second, third or fourth visit.
^{5}___ From a small office in Amoruso's aunt's house in 2006, Nasty Gal has moved to enormous offices and warehouses in Los Angeles with over 350 employees, 75% of whom are women. Even
60 Amoruso's mother works for Nasty Gal, but only part-time!

Amoruso isn't going to stop there, however. ^{6}___ She knows how much time and effort has gone into building the business and has no time for
65 people who think success like hers comes easily. 'A lot of people in my generation don't seem to understand that you have to work your way up,' she writes in her book *#GIRLBOSS*.

3 Read the **Reading Strategy**. Match sentences A–H with gaps 1–6 in the text. There are two extra sentences.

A So she employed her MySpace friends as models.

B All the clothes she bought were very expensive and certainly would not appeal to teenagers or young women.

C That is quite rare in retail stores, whether online or on the high street.

D Luckily, the police didn't charge her and she moved to San Francisco.

E She has big plans for Nasty Gal and is prepared to work hard for it.

F She knows that her success is due in large part to luck and not to her own efforts and talents.

G Occasionally, she came across something really valuable that other customers had evidently missed.

H But she didn't worry about that. She had no regrets about leaving the auction site.

4 Read the text again. Are the sentences true or false? Write T or F.

1 Amoruso resigned from the job in the shoe shop because she found it boring. ___

2 She hoped to attract women of her own age to her eBay store. ___

3 She found all the clothes for her eBay store by searching online. ___

4 She found one valuable item of clothing by accidentally misspelling the designer's name. ___

5 She couldn't afford to employ professional models. ___

6 Amoruso thinks that many young people's expectations are too high when they first start work. ___

5 **VOCABULARY** Complete the verb + preposition combinations with the words below. Check your answers in the text and in the sentences in exercise 3.

Verb and preposition about   about   as   at   for   for   for   on   to   to

1 arrest somebody _____ (a crime) (line 10)

2 sit _____ (a desk, a computer, etc.) (line 13)

3 appeal _____ somebody (line 21)

4 search _____ something (line 25)

5 employ somebody _____ a (name of a job) (sentence A)

6 spend money _____ something (line 40)

7 complain _____ something (line 43)

8 worry _____ something (sentence H)

9 respond _____ something / someone (line 47)

10 work _____ (a business, etc.) (line 60)

➡ **Vocabulary Builder** Verb plus preposition: page 124

6 **SPEAKING** Work in pairs or small groups. Discuss these questions and report your ideas to the class.

1 Is Sophia Amoruso a good role model for young people? Why? / Why not?

2 Do you agree with the opinion Amoruso expresses in the last paragraph of the text? Why? / Why not?

3 Would you like to be an entrepreneur? Why? / Why not? If so, what kind of business would you like to start?

4 Do you think it's as easy for a woman to succeed in business as it is for a man? Give reasons.

6G Speaking
Guided conversation
I can exchange information about jobs.

1 SPEAKING Why do people go abroad to work? Think of at least three reasons.

2 SPEAKING Compare and contrast the photos of people working abroad. What are the people doing?

Speaking Strategy

Make sure that you refer to all of the points in the task. You may need to move the conversation on in order to cover all of the topics. Use phrases like:

Moving on to the question of ...
Another thing I wanted to ask / know is ...
Something else I'd like to talk about is ...
Could I ask you about ... ?
Speaking of X, ... (if X has been mentioned)
That reminds me, ... (if there is a link with something you want to say or ask)

3 🎧 **2.31** Read the Speaking Strategy above and the task below. Then listen to a student doing the task. Which phrases from the strategy does she use?

You have moved to the UK and are looking for work. You have seen a job advert for hotel staff. Discuss the job with the hotel manager. Cover these four points:
- responsibilities
- personal qualities required
- hours of work and salary
- if accommodation is included

4 🎧 **2.31** **KEY PHRASES** Listen again. Complete the questions that the student asked with the phrases below.

Indirect questions   Could you tell me ... ?
I was wondering ...   I'd like to know ...   May I ask ... ?
I'd be interested to know ...   I'd like to know ...

1 ... if I could discuss it with you.
2 ... what the job involves.
3 ... what I would be doing in the restaurant?
4 ... when I would start and finish work exactly.
5 ... what the salary is?
6 ... if accommodation is included.

LEARN THIS! Indirect questions

a We often use indirect questions to sound more polite in formal situations. They begin with phrases like the ones in exercise 4.
Could you tell me what the time is?

b We use *if* or *whether* to turn a *yes / no* question into an indirect question.
Is accommodation included?
I'd like to know if accommodation is included.

c In an indirect question, the word order and verb form are the same as in a direct statement.
Is the job well paid? → *Could you tell me if the job is well paid?*

5 Read the Learn this! box. Why does the student choose to use indirect questions in exercise 4?

➡ **Grammar Builder 6.3** page 138

6 Write the direct questions that correspond to the indirect questions in exercise 4.

1 *Could I discuss it with you?*

7 Read the task below and think of at least six direct questions that you could ask the café manager. Make sure you cover all four points in the task.

What does the job involve?

You have moved to the UK and are looking for work. You have seen a job advert for waiters and kitchen staff in a café. Discuss the jobs with the manager of the café. Cover these four points:
- responsibilities
- experience required
- your personal qualities
- hours of work and salary

➡ **Vocabulary Builder** Working and employment conditions: page 124

8 Rewrite the questions from exercise 7 as indirect questions. Use a variety of structures from exercise 4.

Could you tell me what the job involves?

9 Work in pairs. Swap the questions you wrote in exercise 8 and write answers to them. Use the phrases below to help you.

Could you tell me what the job involves?
– It involves greeting customers and taking orders.
– Sometimes you will have to work in the kitchen.

10 SPEAKING Take turns to do the task in exercise 7. Use the questions and answers you prepared in exercises 8 and 9.

I saw a job advert for ... and I was wondering if I could discuss it with you.

6H Writing
A for and against essay
I can write a for and against essay about education and work.

1 SPEAKING In pairs, read the definition of *vocational*. Then think of three jobs for which you would need to do a vocational degree.

> **vocational** /vəʊˈkeɪʃənl/ *adj* (of education or training) preparing students for a particular job: *Vocational courses such as costume design and catering are becoming very popular.*

2 Read the task and the essay. Do you agree with the writer's general opinion? Why? / Why not?

> Students should be encouraged to choose vocational courses at university instead of more traditional courses. Discuss.

Some people maintain that the benefits of vocational courses are greater than those of more traditional ones. That is the question we need to consider. It is certainly true that the workplace is becoming more competitive. A vocational course may be a more direct route into employment compared to traditional courses. It is also undeniable that certain jobs (for example nurse, hairdresser) are only available to people with a vocational qualification. On the other hand, choosing a vocational course means deciding what job you want to do when you are still at school. Many people believe this is too early. How can a teenager know what job is right for him or her? Another problem is that vocational courses only focus on what you need to learn for a particular job. Is it not better for students to explore other interests while at university? On balance, I do not believe that students should choose vocational courses unless they are sure what career they want to follow. It is wiser to opt for a course that really interests you.

3 Look at the paragraph plan for a for and against essay. Then decide where the paragraph breaks should come in the essay in exercise 2.

Paragraph 1: Introduction
Paragraph 2: Arguments for
Paragraph 3: Arguments against
Paragraph 4: Conclusion (the writer's opinion)

4 Look at the essay in exercise 2 again. What phrase does the writer use to:

1 introduce the first argument for?
2 introduce the second argument for?
3 introduce the first argument against?
4 introduce the second argument against?
5 begin the conclusion?

> **Writing Strategy**
> Rhetorical questions can make an essay more persuasive, provided you only include one or two. You do not have to answer the questions, but always make sure that the expected answer is clear, e.g.
>
> *Some people work long hours for very low pay. How can this be right?* (Expected answer: *It can't be right.*)

5 Read the Writing Strategy. Underline two rhetorical questions in the essay in exercise 2. What are the expected answers?

> **LEARN THIS! Preparatory *it***
> We often use *it* to avoid beginning a sentence with an infinitive, an *-ing* form or a clause, which can all sound unnatural or too formal. We use:
>
> *it* + *be* + adjective + an infinitive or a clause.
>
> It's important <u>to book</u> in advance.
> It's surprising <u>that she hasn't phoned</u>.

6 Read the Learn this! box. In the model essay, circle three examples of preparatory *it*.

> ➡ Grammar Builder 6.4 page 138

7 Read the task. Then plan your essay following the paragraph plan below.

> More students should choose to do voluntary work during the long holidays rather than work for money. Discuss.

Paragraph 1: Introduction (*rephrase the statement in the task*)
Paragraph 2: Arguments for (*include two*)
Paragraph 3: Arguments against (*include two*)
Paragraph 4: Conclusion (*state your opinion*)

8 Write your essay using your plan from exercise 7. Include one or two rhetorical questions.

> **CHECK YOUR WORK**
> Have you ...
> • followed your paragraph plan carefully?
> • presented both sides of the argument?
> • included at least one rhetorical question?
> • checked the spelling and grammar?

7 Artists

Talking about the arts
I can talk about the arts.

Unit map

Vocabulary
Art forms
Artists
Artistic activities
Cultural activities
Musical genres
Aspects of music
Cultural events and shows

Word Skills
Indefinite pronouns

Grammar
The passive
have something done

Listening
Poetry in motion

The Lost Generation
by Jonathan Reed
I am part of a lost generation.

Reading Graffiti's softer side

Speaking
Photo comparison and role-play

Writing Article: a book review

Culture 7 Charles Dickens

Vocabulary Builder page 124

Grammar Builder and Reference page 138

Extra Speaking Task page 144

1 **VOCABULARY** Match the photos (A–H) with art forms from the list below. In your opinion, which art form needs the most skill and which the least? Give reasons, using the phrases below to help you.

Art forms ballet cartoon classical music dance drawing mime musical
novel opera painting play poem pop music sculpture sitcom

You have to (be able to) … in order to …
It's very difficult to … / It isn't that difficult to … / It's relatively easy to …
It doesn't take much practice to … / It takes a lot of practice to …

2 Put the art forms in exercise 1 into four groups. Some can go in more than one group.

A literature   B music   C performing arts   D visual arts

3 **VOCABULARY** Work in pairs. Match the famous people (1–12) with the types of artist below.

Artists actor composer conductor dancer / choreographer director
novelist opera singer painter playwright poet pop singer sculptor

1 Tennessee Williams
2 William Wordsworth
3 John Steinbeck
4 Pablo Picasso
5 Auguste Rodin
6 Adele
7 George Lucas
8 Antonio Vivaldi
9 Jennifer Aniston
10 Fred Astaire
11 Luciano Pavarotti
12 Claudio Abbado

Arts quiz

4 VOCABULARY Choose six of the artists in exercise 3. Can you name a work with which each artist is associated? Use the verbs below to help you.

Artistic activities act appear in carve compose conduct create dance direct draw paint perform play sing write

Pablo Picasso painted Guernica.

5 Complete the arts quiz with the correct form of words from exercises 1, 3 and 4.

6 SPEAKING Work in pairs. Do the arts quiz. Write your answers. Then check your answers at the bottom of the page.

7 🎧 **3.02** Listen to four people talking about cultural events. Match sentences A–E with the speakers (1–4). There is one extra sentence.

This person:

A thought that they might change their mind about something. ___
B was persuaded to go to the event by someone else. ___
C was disappointed with the experience, but is planning to try it again. ___
D was surprised by how good the event was. ___
E organised the outing to the event. ___

> **RECYCLE! Articles**
>
> **a** We use *a / an* when we mention something for the first time, but *the* when we mention it again.
> **b** We use *a / an* to mean 'per' or 'in each', e.g. *once a day*.
> **c** We use *the* i) when it is clear what we are talking about, ii) with superlatives and iii) in certain phrases, e.g. *go to the cinema*.
> **d** We do not use an article i) when we make generalisations, or ii) in certain phrases after prepositions, e.g. *at home*, *by bus*, *at university*.

8 🎧 **3.02** Read the Recycle! box. Complete the sentences with *a / an*, *the* or *–* (no article). Then listen again and check.

Speaker 1
1 I'm not a big fan of _____ modern art.
2 I didn't really understand what _____ artist was trying to say.
Speaker 2
3 It was _____ first time I'd been to a festival.
4 _____ field we were camping in turned into _____ sea of mud.
Speaker 3
5 Last month I went to _____ theatre with my family.
6 I'd already seen it _____ couple of times on _____ DVD.
Speaker 4
7 I hardly ever watch or listen to _____ musicals – maybe about once _____ year, if that.
8 I booked really good seats right at _____ front. It was _____ amazing experience!

9 SPEAKING Work in pairs. Take turns to tell each other about the last time you did one of the things below. Include points 1–4 and add extra information and detail.

Cultural activities went to a rock concert visited an art gallery read a novel read a poem went to the theatre saw a musical listened to a song watched a sitcom went to a classical concert / opera / ballet

1 When was it?
2 Where was it?
3 Who did you go with?
4 Did you enjoy it? Why? / Why not?

1 Which Italian Renaissance artist [1]_____ the *Mona Lisa*?
  a Michelangelo
  b Leonardo da Vinci
  c Caravaggio

2 Which Russian [2]_____ wrote the music for the [3]_____ *Swan Lake*?
  a Shostakovich
  b Rachmaninov
  c Tchaikovsky

3 Which of these films was not [4]_____ by Steven Spielberg?
  a *Jaws*
  b *2001: A Space Odyssey*
  c *Schindler's List*

4 Which Shakespeare [5]_____ inspired the [6]_____ *West Side Story*?
  a *Romeo and Juliet*
  b *Julius Caesar*
  c *A Midsummer Night's Dream*

5 Which famous [7]_____ cut off part of his ear?
  a Monet
  b Cézanne
  c Van Gogh

6 Which British [8]_____ sang on the 2011 hit *Someone Like You*?
  a Adele
  b Ellie Goulding
  c Calvin Harris

7 Which [9]_____ played Katniss in the *Hunger Games* films?
  a Emma Watson
  b Jennifer Lawrence
  c Keira Knightley

8 Which English [10]_____ wrote *Oliver Twist*?
  a Charles Dickens
  b Jane Austen
  c George Orwell

9 Which of these film series did actor Robert Pattinson not [11]_____ ?
  a *Harry Potter*
  b *Twilight*
  c *The Hobbit*

10 What is the name of the famous [12]_____ in the photo?
  a *Mark*
  b *David*
  c *Anthony*

6a 7b 8a 9c 10b
1b 2c 3b 4a 5c

The passive

I can identify and use different forms of the passive.

REAL OR FAKE?

News reader Artist Wolfgang Beltracchi has made millions of pounds from his paintings. However, many of the paintings are not signed with his own name, but with the names of other famous painters. He is the world's most successful forger, and has fooled the art world for over thirty years. Our reporter Jade Quinn has been investigating. How was he finally caught, Jade?

JQ He used the wrong kind of paint in a forgery of a Campendonk painting. The painting had been bought by a company who sent it to a forensic art scientist in London. He identified a type of paint which wasn't being used when Campendonk was alive.

NR That was careless! What happened to Beltracchi?

JQ He was prosecuted and sent to prison for six years.

NR Fifty-eight of his paintings have been identified by police as forgeries and several more are being examined by experts. Are there any more?

JQ Beltracchi himself claims that he has forged hundreds of paintings, but he won't say which ones, so they might never be discovered.

NR What has he done with the money he earned from the forgeries?

JQ He's spent a lot of it, but some of it will be returned to the people who bought his forgeries.

NR Does he still paint in the style of famous artists?

JQ Yes, but now he signs the paintings with his own name.

1 **SPEAKING** Discuss this question.

Why is a perfect forgery worth less than an original work of art?

2 Read the article above. Was it right to send Beltracchi to prison? Why? / Why not?

3 Match the highlighted passive forms in the article with 1–9 below. Then find two examples of 9.

1 present simple passive	5 present perfect passive
2 present continuous passive	6 past perfect passive
3 past simple passive	7 *will* + passive
4 past continuous passive	8 modal verb + passive
	9 *by* + agent

4 Study the passive forms in the article. Complete the rules in the Learn this! box. Use *action, by, infinitive, subject* and the verb *be*.

> **LEARN THIS!** The passive
>
> **a** We form the passive with ¹_____ and the past participle of the verb.
>
> **b** We use a passive ²_____ after modal verbs.
>
> **c** The object of an active verb can become the ³_____ of a passive verb.
> *They make films in Hollywood.* (films = object)
> *Films are made in Hollywood.* (films = subject)
>
> **d** We use the passive when we want to focus on the ⁴_____ itself, or when we do not know who or what performed the action.
>
> **e** When we want to say who or what performed the action in a passive sentence, we use ⁵_____ .

➡ Grammar Builder 7.1 page 138

5 Make the active sentences passive. Use *by* where necessary.

1 William Shakespeare wrote *Macbeth*.
Macbeth was written by William Shakespeare.
2 They are performing a ballet at the concert hall this evening.
3 Does Lady Gaga design the costumes?
4 How many *Hobbit* films have they made?
5 The artist ought to sign the painting.
6 Thousands of people will visit the gallery this year.

6 Complete the text with the verbs in brackets. Use active or passive verbs, as appropriate.

John Myatt is a British artist. He makes copies of famous works of art, but they ¹_____ (not sell) as originals. They ²_____ (paint) with ordinary decorator's paint, and the word 'fake' ³_____ (write) on the back. But it wasn't always like that. In the 1990s, Myatt ⁴_____ (forge) about 200 paintings. In 1998, he ⁵_____ (catch) and ⁶_____ (send) to prison for a year. Since his release from jail, Myatt ⁷_____ (be) very successful, and his paintings ⁸_____ (buy) by wealthy people all over the world. He ⁹_____ (be) now a rich man!

7 Write down five questions about famous works of art including songs, films, books, etc. Use the passive form of the verbs below to help you.

compose   direct   paint   perform   sing   write

Who was Avatar directed by?
Who were the Harry Potter novels written by?

8 **SPEAKING** Work in pairs. Take turns to ask the questions you wrote in exercise 7. Answer in full sentences, using the passive.

> Who was *E.T.* directed by?

> *E.T.* was directed by Steven Spielberg.

9 **INTERNET RESEARCH** Find out about a work of art that you like, and describe it using at least three passive structures. Do not include the name of the work or of the artist. Present your description to the class. Can the class guess what the work is and who it is by?

> It was painted by a Spanish artist ...

Listening
Poetry in motion
I can listen for implications and subtext.

1 SPEAKING Work in pairs. Do you know any poems, lines of poetry or song lyrics by heart in your own language? Were they written recently or a long time ago? Why do you remember them?

2 🎧 3.03 Read and listen to the poem. Do you think its message is optimistic or pessimistic? What do you think the last line is telling us to do?

3 Match the underlined words in the poem with definitions a–h.

a a period of time in history
b not interested in anything
c in the right order
d people who are the same age
e an easy solution, but not a good one
f not clever or intelligent
g something that is typical or usual
h lazy – not wanting to do anything

4 🎧 3.04 Listen to the poem again. How does starting with the last line change the meaning? Which version of the poem do you agree with more?

> **Listening Strategy**
> Sometimes the information you need for a listening task is implied rather than stated directly. For example, if somebody says 'I wish I was back home', it implies they are not happy with their current situation.

5 🎧 3.05 Read the **Listening Strategy**. Then listen to five short extracts and circle the correct implication: a or b.

1 a He wishes he hadn't gone to the gym.
  b He was much stronger in the past.
2 a She is a big fan of Robbie Williams.
  b She is not a big fan of Robbie Williams.
3 a He often tries food from other countries.
  b He rarely tries food from other countries.
4 a She thought the hotel was good.
  b She didn't think the hotel was very good.
5 a He does not like the jumper very much.
  b His sister does not usually buy him a birthday present.

6 🎧 3.06 Listen to five speakers. Match sentences A–F below with the speakers (1–5). There is one extra sentence.

This speaker believes that:
A sad topics make better poetry. ___
B poetry was better in previous eras. ___
C men are not as good as women at writing poems. ___
D poetry is still popular with young people. ___
E young people like poetry more than adults do. ___
F good poems tell us about the poet's feelings. ___

7 🎧 3.06 Listen again. Circle the words which best sum up the speakers' opinions.

1 These days, rap artists **are / aren't** the best poets.
2 Writing poems for greetings cards **would / wouldn't** be a good job.
3 A good poem **has / doesn't have** to rhyme and make sense.
4 Learning poems by heart **is / isn't** a waste of time.
5 Poems **are / aren't** always a true reflection of the poet's feelings.

8 SPEAKING Work in pairs. Discuss the opinions in exercise 7. Do you agree with the affirmative or negative version? Give reasons.

> I think / don't think rap artists are the best poets these days because …

The Lost Generation

by Jonathan Reed

I am part of a lost generation.
And I refuse to believe that
I can change the world.
I realize this may be a shock, but
'Happiness comes from within'
Is a lie, and
'Money will make me happy'
So in 30 years, I will tell my children
They are not the most important thing in my life.
My employer will know that
I have my priorities <u>straight</u> because
Work
Is more important than
Family
I tell you this:
Once upon a time
Families stayed together
But this will not be true in my <u>era</u>.
This is a <u>quick fix</u> society
Experts tell me
Thirty years from now, I will be celebrating the tenth anniversary of my divorce.
I do not concede that
I will live in a country of my own making.
In the future,
Environmental destruction will be <u>the norm</u>.
No longer can it be said that
My <u>peers</u> and I care about this Earth.
It will be evident that
My generation is <u>apathetic</u> and <u>lethargic</u>.
It is <u>foolish</u> to presume that
There is hope.
And all of this will come true unless we reverse it.

7D Grammar

have something done

I can use the structure 'have something done'.

1 SPEAKING Work in pairs. Look at the photo. Do you like the tattoo? Is it a form of art? Does it tell you anything about the woman's personality or not?

2 Read the article. Why do some people think it is necessary to hide their tattoos when they have an interview?

Amanda recently had a colourful butterfly tattooed on her wrist. Brad had the names of his two daughters tattooed on his neck under his hair. His friend Doug had his back decorated with a large tattoo of a shield. For the people themselves, these examples of body art are meaningful and important. Nevertheless, they deliberately had them done in places that can easily be hidden. Why? Because they want to give themselves the best possible chance of getting a job, and many employers have a negative attitude towards tattoos and other forms of body art (piercings, body painting, etc.). That is because many employers do not think that decorating yourself with tattoos is acceptable. But when these employers were young themselves, back in the 1980s, they probably had their hair dyed a bright colour to shock their parents! Fashions change, but younger generations always have the desire to be different.

LEARN THIS! *have something done*

a You can use the structure *have* + object + past participle to say that you arranged for somebody to do something for you. (You did not do it yourself.)
She had her hair dyed.
I haven't had my eyes tested for years.

b You can also use the structure for unpleasant things that somebody or something has done to you.
He had his nose broken in a rugby game.

3 Read the Learn this! box. What examples of *have something done* can you find in the article in exercise 2?

4 Use the prompts to write sentences with the correct form of *have something done*. Then match each sentence with rule a or b in the Learn this! box.

1 Olivia / her hair / dye / red / for charity ___
2 Josh / his bike / steal / at the weekend ___
3 the house / its roof / blow off / in the storm ___
4 we / the carpets / clean / after the party last weekend ___
5 my sister / always / her nails / do / on Fridays ___
6 she / her visa application / refuse / last month ___

➡ **Grammar Builder 7.2** page 139

5 SPEAKING Discuss this question with your partner.

Imagine you are going to get a new haircut. Where would you have it done? How would you have it cut?

6 Read the second Learn this! box. Underline two example of use a and two examples of use b in the text in exercise 2.

LEARN THIS! Reflexive pronouns (*myself, himself, themselves*, etc.)

a We use a reflexive pronoun when the object of a verb is the same as the subject.
I gave myself a birthday present.
NOT *I gave me a birthday present.* ✗

b We sometimes use a reflexive pronoun for emphasis. The sentence makes sense without a reflexive pronoun, but is clearer with it.
I built that wall myself. (The builders didn't do it.)

7 Complete the sentences with the correct reflexive pronouns. Which are there to add clarity and emphasis?

1 If you eat any more popcorn, you'll make _____ ill.
2 On the farm, we only eat what we produce _____ .
3 When the screen broke on my smartphone, I replaced it _____ .
4 I got the information from the internet, but I wrote the essay _____ .
5 The medicine was horrible, but I forced _____ to drink it.
6 If you think waterskiing looks easy, you should try it _____ .
7 My grandmother taught _____ Chinese when she was seventy.

➡ **Grammar Builder 7.3** page 139

8 SPEAKING Work in pairs. Which of these things has your partner done or experienced? Use *Have you ever had your ... ?* Ask follow-up questions if appropriate.

1 ears / pierce
2 phone / steal
3 hair / dye
4 portrait / paint
5 email account / hack
6 nails / do
7 bedroom / decorate
8 fortune / tell

7E | Word Skills

Indefinite pronouns
I can use indefinite pronouns.

1 🎧 **3.07** **VOCABULARY** Work in pairs. Listen to the musical excerpts. Match the excerpts (1–9) with the musical genres below.

Musical genres blues classical country and western folk heavy metal hip hop / rap jazz pop / rock techno

1 *heavy metal*

2 Read the article. What is unusual about John Cage's most famous composition?

Experimental music by John Cage

Most composers want their music to contain something different – a distinctive melody or rhythm, or an unusual harmony which no one has thought of before. But has anyone gone further than composer John Cage in the search for originality?

In 1951, John Cage wanted to find somewhere he could experience complete silence. He went inside a special soundproof room and expected to hear nothing, but instead heard two sounds, one high-pitched and one low-pitched. Later, the sound engineer explained that the first was the sound of his nervous system and the second was the sound of his blood circulating. Cage realised that nowhere is completely silent – you can always hear something. A year later, he composed his most famous piece: 4'33" ('four minutes and thirty-three seconds'). In this piece, the performer walks on stage and then … nothing happens. He or she does not play anything at all. Everybody in the audience listens to nothing for exactly four minutes and 33 seconds. Then the performer bows and everyone applauds!

3 Complete the table with indefinite pronouns from the article in exercise 2.

Indefinite pronouns			
1 _____	2 _____	someone	3 _____
nobody	anybody	somebody	4 _____
5 _____	anywhere	6 _____	everywhere
7 _____	8 _____	9 _____	everything

4 Read the Learn this! box. Complete it with the words below. Use the article in exercise 2 to help you.

affirmative (×2)   -body   negative   plural   questions   singular

> **LEARN THIS!** Indefinite pronouns
>
> **a** We use indefinite pronouns beginning with *some-* in ¹_____ sentences. We use pronouns beginning with *any-* in ²_____ sentences and ³_____ .
>
> **b** Indefinite pronouns ending in *-one* and in ⁴_____ mean the same.
>
> **c** Pronouns beginning with *no-* have a negative meaning, but take an ⁵_____ verb form (singular).
> *Nobody lives in that house.*
>
> **d** Pronouns beginning with *every-* have a plural meaning, but take a ⁶_____ verb form.
> *Everybody knows what happened.*
> But if we refer back to *everyone* or *everybody*, we treat them as ⁷_____ .
> *Everybody is doing their best.*
> *Everyone is here, aren't they?*

> **LOOK OUT!**
> We use indefinite pronouns with *some-* when we make offers and requests, even though they are questions.
> *Would you like something to eat?*
> *Can I talk to somebody about this job?*

5 Read the Look out! box. Complete the dialogue with the correct indefinite pronouns.

Amelia Are you doing ¹_____ this weekend?
Jake No, I'm not.
Amelia Would you like to do ²_____ together, then? How about the cinema?
Jake Not the cinema. There's ³_____ I want to see. Let's go ⁴_____ different for a change. We could see some live music.
Amelia Is there ⁵_____ in town that has live music?
Jake Yes – the Oxygen Arena. I can find the programme online. Wait a moment …
Amelia Is ⁶_____ good playing?
Jake There's ⁷_____ well known, I'm afraid. But this band might be OK – Purple Dawn. They play hip hop.
Amelia I'll ask James. He knows ⁸_____ about hip hop.

6 **SPEAKING** Work in pairs. Discuss what kind of music you enjoy listening to and in what situations. Try to explain your choices using the words below.

Aspects of music beat chorus harmony lyrics melody / tune rhythm speed / tempo verse

> When I want something to dance to, I listen to techno or anything with a good beat.

Reading

Graffiti's softer side

I can understand a text about street art.

1 SPEAKING Work in pairs. Choose one of the photos and describe it to your partner. Use the words below to help you.

Nouns boxer   branch   bus   cover   message   parking meter   statue   street   tree trunk   wool   writing

Verbs attach   cover   knit

Adjectives brightly coloured   patterned   striped

> In the first photo there's a tree in the street …

2 Read the article and match the photos (A–D) with two of the artists.

Jessie Hemmons A __

Magda Sayeg __ __

Agata Oleksiak __ __

Reading Strategy

1 Multiple-choice questions are always in the same order as the information in the text.

2 If there is a question testing the main idea of the text, or the writer's overall opinion, it will come last.

3 The correct option will match the meaning of the text but use different words. Make sure the other options are not right or are not mentioned in the text.

4 If you can't decide between the options, an intelligent guess is better than no answer.

3 Read the Reading Strategy. Is there a question about the main idea or the writer's overall opinion in the questions in exercise 4?

4 For questions 1–6, circle the correct answers (a–d).

1 Jessie Hemmons 'yarn bombed' the statue of Rocky because
   a she wants people to take photos of it.
   b she thinks too many tourists come and see it.
   c she wants more people to go and see the paintings in the museum.
   d tourists find it annoying.

2 Why did Magda Sayeg knit a cover for the door handle of her shop?
   a For her own amusement.
   b To attract customers.
   c Because someone passing the shop suggested it.
   d To set an example to other yarn bombers.

3 Jessie thinks that yarn bombing is different from other forms of street art because
   a its popularity has spread via the internet.
   b it's temporary and soon disappears.
   c it looks much nicer.
   d it's less masculine.

4 What is the police's usual attitude to yarn bombing?
   a They make it clear that it is against the law.
   b They think that yarn bombers are strange people.
   c They hardly ever try to arrest yarn bombers.
   d They tolerate professional artists, but not amateurs.

5 Agata Oleksiak isn't very pleased
   a because she was prevented from knitting covers for objects in a museum.
   b because people don't realise that she started yarn bombing before anyone else.
   c if galleries don't accept her work.
   d if people don't see the difference between her work and yarn bombing.

6 What is the writer's overall opinion of yarn bombing?
   a It is wrong because it's against the law.
   b The writer doesn't express a personal view.
   c It's a more feminine version of graffiti.
   d It deserves to be called 'art'.

5 VOCABULARY In paragraphs 1 and 2, underline ten things (excluding vehicles) that you might find in the street. How many more items can you add to the list?

6 SPEAKING Work in pairs. Discuss the questions. Use the phrases below to help you.

Arguing your point

In my opinion, …   As I see it, …
It could be argued that …   I agree with you.
I see your point, but …   That may be true, but …

1 Do you think that yarn bombing is art, or vandalism and littering? Why?

2 What about other forms of street art, such as graffiti and chalk drawings on the pavement? Are they art or vandalism? Give reasons for your opinion.

3 Tell your partner about some street art you've seen that you either liked or didn't like, and say why.

Granny graffiti

🎧 3.08

The statue of Rocky outside the Philadelphia Museum of Art is very popular with tourists, who often stop to take their photo in front of it without bothering to visit the museum itself. This irritated Jessie Hemmons, so last month the 24-year-old artist knitted a
5 bright pink jacket and put it on the statue of the boxer. She chose the colour because it attracts attention. On the front of the jacket, Jessie has knitted the words 'Go see the art'. Jessie hopes that her message will result in more people visiting the gallery.

This form of street art has become known as 'yarn bombing'.
10 The craze is believed to have started in 2005, when Magda Sayeg was working at Raye, her shop in Houston, Texas. One day she decided, just for fun, to knit a blue-and-pink cover for the shop's door handle. She loved it, and – unexpectedly – so did her customers. Pedestrians stopped on the pavement outside the
15 shop to photograph it, and even motorists slowed down to take a closer look. Their reaction inspired Magda to make covers for other objects in the street, such as a stop sign, a lamp post, a parking meter – and even an entire bus, which took a whole week to complete! She decided to set up a group of knitters, which she
20 called 'Knitta Please'. Photos of their creations kept appearing on blogs and social networking sites and the craze soon spread. There are now yarn bombing groups in dozens of countries and they have covered bus stops, bicycle racks, benches, phone boxes and even fountains! Like most types of street art, the works are
25 temporary and begin to fall apart within a few weeks, so yarn bombers photograph and film their works and upload them to the internet, where everybody can see them.

Some of the men who want to have their photos taken with Rocky are disappointed when they see the jacket, but Jessie is pleased that they react that way. She believes that most street art is done by men 30 and that yarn bombing is a more feminine activity. But not everyone approves of the new form of street art. Some people argue that if it is done without permission, then covering public objects in wool is vandalism and littering. That may be true in the eyes of the law, but the police appear to take a relatively relaxed attitude to yarn 35 bombers. They might interrupt them if they see them at work in the street, but yarn bombers say the police are more likely to find their activities amusing than view them as criminal.

However, yarn bombing has landed Polish artist Agata Oleksiak in serious trouble. Agata – or Olek, as she calls herself – has been 40 an active artist since 2003, and has covered cars and diggers in wool, as well as a whole train in her native city of Łódź. Her work has been shown in museums and galleries around the world. But when Olek knitted covers and attached them to sculptures in an underwater museum near Cancún, the Mexican authorities were 45 not very happy. Like Jessie Hemmons's jacket, Olek's covers had a political message: she wanted to draw attention to endangered species such as the whale shark. But the director of the museum claims that Olek may herself have harmed the marine life that grows on the sculptures. Olek is puzzled by the reaction. She 50 claims that her message is a positive one and sees herself as a professional artist. She believes that her creations are as good as the paintings you see in the world's best art galleries, and if anyone calls her work 'yarn bombing', she gets quite upset.

Whether you see yarn bombing as a bit of fun that brightens up 55 drab cities, or as a form of high culture with a serious message, it is a craze that is likely to continue.

Photo comparison and role-play

I can compare photos and role-play a discussion.

1 SPEAKING Work in pairs. Match photos A–C with three of the types of show below. Then choose one photo each and describe it to your partner.

Cultural events and shows an art exhibition   a circus
a classical concert   a comedy club   a magic show
a musical   an open-air theatre   a piano recital

➡ **Vocabulary Builder** Cultural events and venues: page 124

2 SPEAKING Work in pairs. Compare and contrast photos A–C from exercise 1.

> All three photos show …

> Unlike the other two photos, in photo C you can see …

> Whereas photo B shows … , the other two photos …

> You are staying with your English penfriend and want to take the family out one evening to say thank you. You and your penfriend should decide which show is most suitable and talk about the details of the outing.

3 🎧3.09 Read the task above. Then listen to a student doing the task. Which show does the student choose? Which of the details below does she also mention?

- When to go on the outing.
- How to book tickets.
- Who will pay for the tickets.
- Travelling to the show.
- What to eat and drink.

Speaking Strategy 1
Try to use a variety of expressions instead of repeating the same common verbs too often. For example, make sure you know several different ways of saying 'I like' / 'I don't like'.

4 KEY PHRASES Read Speaking Strategy 1. Then look at the phrases for expressing preferences. Tick the expression you think is strongest in each group.

Like
☐ I'm a big fan of …
☐ I'm quite into …
☐ I'm really keen on …
☐ I absolutely love …
☐ I enjoy … very much.

Dislike
☐ … is not really my thing.
☐ I'm not really into …
☐ … doesn't do anything for me.
☐ I've never been that keen on …
☐ I really can't stand …
☐ I'm not a big fan of …

Photointerest

Speaking Strategy 2
We often use one of the phrases below to introduce a preference, particularly when it is negative.
*I'm afraid …   I must say …   To be honest, …   To be frank, …
If I'm honest, …   To be blunt, …   Personally, …*

5 🎧3.09 KEY PHRASES Read Speaking Strategy 2. Then listen again. Which phrases from exercise 4 do you hear? Which ones are introduced by a phrase from the strategy?

6 SPEAKING Work in pairs. Find out your partner's preferences for the shows in exercise 1 and other types of shows you can think of. Use phrases from exercise 4 and Speaking Strategy 2 in your answers.

> What do you think of art exhibitions?

> I absolutely love them. / To be blunt, I'm not really into them.

7 SPEAKING Work in pairs. Turn to page 144 and do the speaking task. Use the strategies and the key phrases in this lesson to help you.

Writing

Article: a book review

I can write a book review.

1 SPEAKING Work in pairs. What was the last book you read? What was it about? Did you enjoy it? Why? / Why not?

Your teacher has asked you to write a book review for the school magazine. Write your review describing the book and say what you liked and didn't like about it.

2 Read the task above and the review. Did the writer enjoy the book? Did he / she have any reservations?

> **Writing Strategy 1**
>
> **1** In the first paragraph, attract the reader's attention. You can do this by addressing him / her directly, especially with questions.
>
> **2** Use an appropriate style and register for the target audience.
>
> **3** Choose a good title for your article.

3 Read the first point in Writing Strategy 1 and the first paragraph of the review again. Has the writer followed the advice? If so, say how.

4 Read the second point in the strategy and the rest of the review again. Did the writer use an appropriate style for his / her audience? How would you describe the style: a) informal and lively or b) formal and serious?

5 Read the third point in the strategy. Which title (1–5) do you think would be the best for the review? Why? Use the words and phrases below to help you.

appeal to   boring   catch your attention   main idea
pun   question   relate to the topic   snappy
target audience   too long

1 Book review: *The Hunger Games*
2 This is probably one of the best books that I have ever read
3 If I were you, I'd read this book
4 A book I really enjoyed
5 If you are hungry for a good book, read on!

> **Writing Strategy 2**
>
> **1** Give your review a logical structure. Divide it into paragraphs, each with its own topic or focus.
>
> **2** The conclusion should restate the main idea given in the introduction, but using different words. It should also include the writer's opinion and, if appropriate, a recommendation.

6 Read Writing Strategy 2. In which paragraph (A–D) does the writer …

1 restate his / her opinion of the book?
2 describe the plot and characters?
3 mention something he / she didn't like?
4 give some background information about the book?
5 give his / her opinion of the book for the first time?
6 say why he / she liked it?

A Have you ever read a book that you just couldn't put down? *The Hunger Games* was like that for me. I read it in two days! It's that good! Written by Suzanne Collins in 2006, it's sold millions of copies around the world and has been made into a film.

B It's set in the future in a place called Panem and it tells the story of Katniss, a sixteen-year-old girl who has to leave her family and compete in the Hunger Games with eleven other children. Only one child can survive the games, and Katniss is not optimistic about her chances. There are lots of twists and turns along the way. I won't give away the ending, but I guarantee you'll love it.

C What I loved about the book was the character of Katniss. She's a really strong person, but she's also very sensitive. I really identified with her. The story is very gripping too. There's quite a lot of violence, which may put some people off, but it's an important part of the story. The one criticism I have is that the games themselves don't start until chapter 10, but this didn't spoil my overall enjoyment.

D All in all, this book is a real page-turner. I absolutely loved it and I'd definitely recommend it. So if you haven't read it yet, buy it, borrow it, or steal it (just kidding!) as soon as you can. You won't be disappointed.

7 Which tense does the writer use to describe the plot and characters?

8 KEY PHRASES Complete the useful phrases with the words below. Underline them in the review.

page   recommend   set   tells   twists

> **Describing stories**
> It's ¹_____ in (place and / or time).
> It ²_____ the story of (character).
> There are lots of ³_____ and turns.
> It's a real ⁴_____ -turner.
> I would definitely ⁵_____ it.

▶▶ Vocabulary Builder Describing stories: page 124

9 Do the task in exercise 1. Follow the advice in the strategies, use the structure of the model review (see exercise 6) and use phrases from exercise 8.

> **CHECK YOUR WORK**
>
> Have you …
> • given your review a title and an interesting introduction?
> • used an appropriate style?
> • given your article a logical structure?
> • used the present tense to describe the plot and characters?
> • checked your grammar and spelling?

Exam Skills Trainer

Reading

1 Read the strategy above. Then read the article in exercise 2. Match the underlined words with the definitions (1–6).

1 to stop existing, to become impossible to see _____
2 notice taken of someone or something; seeing someone or something as interesting or important _____
3 occur or be found _____
4 lasting for a short time, not permanent _____
5 a picture, painting or photo of a person _____
6 to plan something _____

2 Read the article about a type of art. Are the sentences true or false? Write T or F.

When we think of art, we normally picture something which can <u>exist</u> for centuries. But there has always been a type of art which doesn't last. This is often referred to as 'temporary' art. Sculptures which are made of snow or ice, paintings in coloured sand, chalk drawings done on public pavements: it's not that these don't have artistic value, but they are designed to <u>disappear</u>.

Jorge Rodríguez-Gerada is a modern 'temporary' artist, and one who gets a lot of <u>attention</u> for his work. He uses groups of volunteers to help him, and his pieces take a long time to plan and create. But they are mostly talked about because the final results are so impressive. For the past few years, Rodríguez-Gerada has been creating gigantic faces in empty spaces in cities. To people on the ground, it looks like a garden is being created, and it is hard to see any kind of design in it. In fact, GPS mapping is used to <u>set out</u> the design. Then an army of workers use this master plan to create the image which the artist has planned.

In 2014, the artist created an astonishing face on the National Mall in Washington, D.C. It covered an area of 25,000 square metres, and it was created because the mall was getting new gardens, and the land wasn't going to be used for a while. The <u>portrait</u> was of a young man of mixed race, and was called *Of the Many, One*. The artist says that it showed one of the millions of faces that represent the American people. After a while, the sand and soil of the portrait were mixed together, and new lawns were planted in its place. The portrait has disappeared, but it will not easily be forgotten.

1 Temporary art is a new kind of art. ___
2 Artists use sand or chalk in their artwork so that it will exist for a long time. ___
3 Jorge Rodríguez-Gerada is an important artist in the field of temporary art. ___
4 His work is very quick to create. ___
5 He uses maps to plan his artwork. ___
6 A lot of people help him to create his art. ___
7 Jorge's artwork called *Of the Many, One* was part of a new garden design for the National Mall. ___
8 The artwork does not exist any more. ___

Listening

3 Read the strategy above and underline the key words in the question below. Then underline the information in the listening extract that helps you choose the correct answer (A–C).

What quality does the speaker value least in an employee?
A creativity
B loyalty
C self-confidence

🎧 A lot of employers think it's important to have very loyal workers. But personally, I don't find loyalty to be a very valuable quality in an employee. I like to work with people who show intelligence, thoughtfulness and creativity. People who are extremely loyal often just go along with what their boss says. They avoid asking too many questions, and I think that in the end they lose their self-confidence.

4 🎧 **3.10** You will hear a talk. Look at the questions below and choose the best answer (A–C).

1 The Gold Performance Academy
  A is a school of contemporary dance.
  B teaches people dance, drama and music.
  C specialises in classical ballet and musical theatre.
2 The Academy helps students to
  A build confidence as a performer.
  B choose the right performing art for them.
  C decide on a future career.
3 Many of the teachers at the Academy
  A have experience in the industry.
  B perform in the lessons.
  C like pop music.
4 Every year, students
  A work in a theatre during the summer.
  B design a certificate for a ceremony.
  C take part in stage performances.
5 The speaker
  A wants everyone in the audience to attend the Academy.
  B invites her audience to come to see a lesson at the Academy.
  C asks the audience to write an email to apply to the Academy.

4 Exam Skills Trainer

Use of English

Exam Strategy
Read the text without looking at the options (A–D). Try to predict what the missing answers might be. Decide what type of information is missing, e.g. which tense, modal verb or preposition. Then look at options A–D and choose the one that grammatically fits in the text. If you are not sure about an answer, cross out the ones you are sure are wrong, then choose one of the remaining answers.

5 Read the strategy above. Choose the correct option (A–D) to complete the text.

If you ask people what they think of graffiti, many say that they consider [1]___ vandalism, but some actually appreciate the images or words sprayed on walls and think of it as an art form. Interestingly, wall painting [2]___ in various forms for about the last 40,000 years. [3]___ prehistoric times, humans used to paint images of wild animals or people on the walls and ceilings of caves. There are many theories about the reasons for creating these images, but [4]___ knows for sure. Evidence shows that they were not just used to decorate the living areas, as most of the caves [5]___ inhabited at the time when the paintings were created. Many experts believe that cave paintings [6]___ a way of communicating with others.

Although today street art rarely features in art exhibitions, works of art in public places remain popular with artists all over the world. Whether they use chalk drawings, street sculptures, or graffiti, street artists use the streets as their gallery to communicate with the public more directly. There are even [7]___ walls around the world where graffiti is encouraged. For example, the famous John Lennon Wall in Prague in the Czech Republic, [8]___ was filled with graffiti featuring lyrics from the Beatles' songs. It was popular for over two decades until the wall was painted over with a single colour in 2000.

1 A as if	B it to be	C like as	D it like
2 A has existed	B had existed	C existed	D exist
3 A While	B Since	C From	D During
4 A somebody	B everybody	C nobody	D anybody
5 A aren't	B haven't been	C hadn't been	D weren't
6 A must be	B might had been	C may have been	D could have
7 A few	B a few	C little	D a little
8 A which	B where	C when	D whom

Speaking

Exam Strategy
In a role-play conversation you will need to make suggestions, express your preferences and ask for a response to something you have said. Learn a variety of phrases to help you with this.

6 Read the strategy. Match the functions (1–5) with the phrases (A–E). Can you think of one more phrase for each function?

1 suggesting ___
2 expressing doubt ___
3 expressing preferences ___
4 asking for a response ___
5 reaching a decision ___

A I think I'd rather ...
B Well, I'm not sure she's keen on ...
C What do you think about ... ?
D We seem to agree, so ...
E How about ... ?

7 You and a classmate are planning a surprise for a friend to celebrate his / her birthday. You would like to take him / her to a concert. You and your classmate should decide which show is most suitable and discuss the arrangements for the outing. Use the ideas below to help you.

- when to go to the concert
- the type of concert
- getting tickets
- transport to and from
- food and drink
- keeping the surprise a secret

Writing

Exam Strategy
When writing a book review, organise the information in a logical order. First you need to introduce the book, and then describe the setting (place and time). Next, outline the plot and describe characters. Finally, the conclusion should include your opinion and a recommendation if appropriate.

8 Read the strategy. Match the phrases (A–G) with paragraphs 1–4. Then complete the sentences about a book you have read recently.

Paragraph 1: ____________ Paragraph 3: ____________
Paragraph 2: ____________ Paragraph 4: ____________

A I'd definitely recommend it ...
B It's set in ...
C What I loved about the book is ...
D It's called ... and is written by ...
E It tells the story of ...
F The story is very ...
G I really identified with the main character, ...

9 Read the task below and write a book review.

You have decided to write a book review for the local newspaper. Describe the book and say what you liked and didn't like about it.

Unit map

● **Vocabulary**
Collocations: using a mobile phone
Phrasal verbs: phoning
Film genres
Reporting verbs
Reading matter & digital formats

● **Word Skills**
Verb patterns: reporting verbs

● **Grammar**
Reported speech
Reported questions

● **Listening**
Global network

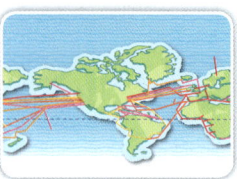

● **Reading** A novel idea

● **Speaking** Photo description

● **Writing** A narrative

● **Culture 8** Helen Keller

● **Vocabulary Builder** page 125

● **Grammar Builder and Reference** page 140

8A Vocabulary
On the phone
I can talk about using my phone.

A

1 SPEAKING Work in pairs. Choose a photo each and describe it to your partner. Then discuss the questions.

1 Do you mind if people talk on their phones in public places? Why? / Why not?
2 Do you think people rely too much on their phones? Why? / Why not?
3 Have you ever had problems getting a mobile signal? If so, where? What did you do about it?

2 KEY PHRASES Match a–f with 1–6 and g–l with 7–12.

Collocations: using a mobile phone

1 enter	**a** a number	7 leave	**g** data roaming
2 make	**b** the signal	8 top up	**h** a message
3 lose	**c** your phone	9 disable / enable	**i** a call / somebody on loudspeaker
4 put	**d** a call	10 save / add	
5 recharge	**e** your voicemail	11 put	**j** a number to the contacts list
6 listen to	**f** the phone on silent	12 run out of	**k** your mobile
			l credit

3 🎧 3.11 Listen to four phone conversations. Answer the questions.

1 **a** Who does Ryan mistake Jodie for?
  b What message does Ryan leave?
2 **c** Whose money does the boy use to top up his mobile?
  d How much does the boy top up?
3 **e** Why didn't Jake receive his messages?
  f Why didn't Jake answer his calls yesterday?
4 **g** What problem does the girl have?
  h What solution does the boy suggest?

4 🎧 **3.11** Listen again. How many of the phrases in exercise 2 can you hear?

5 **KEY PHRASES** Match the phrasal verbs (1–10) with the definitions (a–j).

Phrasal verbs: phoning

1 get through (to someone)
2 pick up the phone
3 switch something off
4 speak up
5 run out of something
6 call somebody back
7 break up
8 cut somebody off
9 hang up
10 get back to somebody

a turn something off
b phone somebody again later
c phone somebody again later
d establish contact
e stop or interrupt somebody's phone conversation
f have no more of something; finish something
g answer a call
h become unclear and difficult to understand
i end a phone call
j talk more loudly

RECYCLE! Phrasal verbs

• With separable phrasal verbs, the object can come **before** or **after** the particle, but when the object is a pronoun (*her*, *it*, *them*, etc.) it must come **before** the particle.
switch the phone off / *switch off the phone*
switch it off / *switch off it* ✗

• With inseparable verbs, the object always comes **after** the particle, even when it is a pronoun.

• Three-part phrasal verbs are always **transitive** and **inseparable**. The object always comes after the two particles.
get back to somebody

6 Read the Recycle! box and answer the questions.

1 Which phrasal verbs in exercise 5 are transitive? How do you know?
2 Which have three parts?
3 Which are separable? How do you know?

7 🎧 **3.12** Listen to a phone conversation. Answer the questions.

1 Why couldn't the two people talk earlier?
2 What two reasons do they have for ending the call?

8 🎧 **3.12** Complete the extracts from the conversation with a verb and one or two particles. Then listen again and check.

1 I've been trying to call, but I couldn't _____ .
2 The phone rang, but I couldn't _____ .
3 The teacher told me to _____ the phone _____ .
4 Can you _____ ? I can't hear you very well.
5 Look, I'm _____ credit. Can I _____ you _____ ?
6 You're _____ .
7 OK, I'll _____ and _____ you.

9 **SPEAKING** Work in pairs. Ask and answer the questions.

1 Do you have a mobile phone? If so, how long have you had it? Who pays for the calling plan and / or the calls?
2 How often do you use your phone? How long do you spend on your phone each day?
3 How many texts do you send per day, on average? Who do you send them to?
4 If you're phoning someone from your home, are you more likely to use a mobile phone or the landline? Why?
5 Would you find life difficult without mobile phones? Why? / Why not?

Grammar

Reported speech

I can use reported speech.

1 Read the text opposite. Do you think the twin sisters have a special connection or are there other explanations? Give reasons for your opinions.

2 Read the text and study the highlighted and underlined examples of reported speech. What are the speakers' original words? Complete the table with the correct tenses for the direct speech.

Direct speech	Reported speech
1	past simple
2	past continuous
3	past perfect
4	past perfect
5	could / couldn't
6	would / wouldn't

LEARN THIS! Reported speech

a These verbs do not usually change in reported speech: *might, must, should, could, would, would like.*

b The past perfect does not change in reported speech.
'I'd never been there.' She said she'd never been there.

c Verbs in subordinate clauses in the reported sentence usually change in the same way.
'I think I'm ill.' He said he thought he was ill.

d We always use a personal object with *tell*. With *say*, we do not need a personal object.
I told Jo that I'd phone. / I said (to Jo) that I'd phone.

e We often omit *that* in reported speech.
He said he'd call you.

3 Read the **Learn this!** box. Match the underlined verbs in the text with rules a–c. What are the speaker's original words?

4 Circle examples in the text of rules d and e.

LOOK OUT!

Pronouns, possessive adjectives and references to time and place usually change in reported speech.

'I'll phone you tomorrow,' he said to me.

He told me he'd phone me the following day.

now → then / at that moment
today → that day
an hour ago → an hour earlier
yesterday → the day before
last Tuesday, month, year, etc. → the Tuesday, the month, the year before, etc.
tomorrow → the following day
next week, month, etc. → the following week, month, etc.
here → there

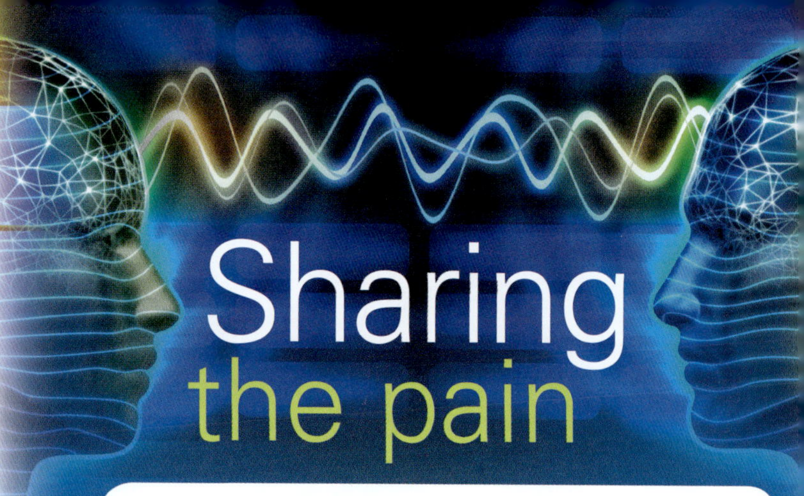

Sharing the pain

Beth and her twin sister Harriet are convinced that they are able to share experiences and feelings without seeing or speaking to each other. Here's what Beth says:

'One day I was walking in town with Harriet. She told me that her right ankle was hurting, but didn't know why. She said she hadn't twisted it or anything, but told me she couldn't put any weight on it. About a minute later, I suddenly felt a sharp pain in my right ankle! On another occasion, I told Harriet that I had watched a really good video clip on the internet the day before. I said that I would send her a link to the website where I'd found it. I told her she must watch it. Imagine my surprise when she said she had come across the same clip at the same time! She said that after she'd finished watching it, she had thought about sending me the link.'

5 Read the **Look out!** box. Underline examples of changes to pronouns, possessive adjectives and references to time in the text in exercise 1.

6 Rewrite the sentences in reported speech. (Imagine that the speakers were talking to you.)

1 'I'll call you when I get back this evening,' said Maisy.
Maisy said she would call me when she got back that evening.

2 'I might disable data roaming when I go abroad next week,' said Joel.

3 'Kelly had never had a mobile,' said Max.

4 'I haven't topped up my mobile since last month,' said Freddy.

5 'You mustn't let your battery run out,' said my mum.

6 'Liam saved your number to his phone book,' said Sally.

7 'This time next week, I'll be flying to Prague,' said Tom.

➡ **Grammar Builder 8.1** page 140

7 Write answers to these questions.

1 Where did you go last summer?
I went to …

2 What are you doing this evening?

3 Can you write with both hands?

4 Could you walk before you could talk?

5 What are you going to do at the weekend?

6 Have you been to Italy?

7 What time do you usually get to school?

8 **SPEAKING** Work in pairs. Ask the questions in exercise 7, note your partner's answers and report the answers to the class.

Martin said that he'd been to Dubrovnik the summer before.

Listening
Global network
I can identify the main idea of a listening text.

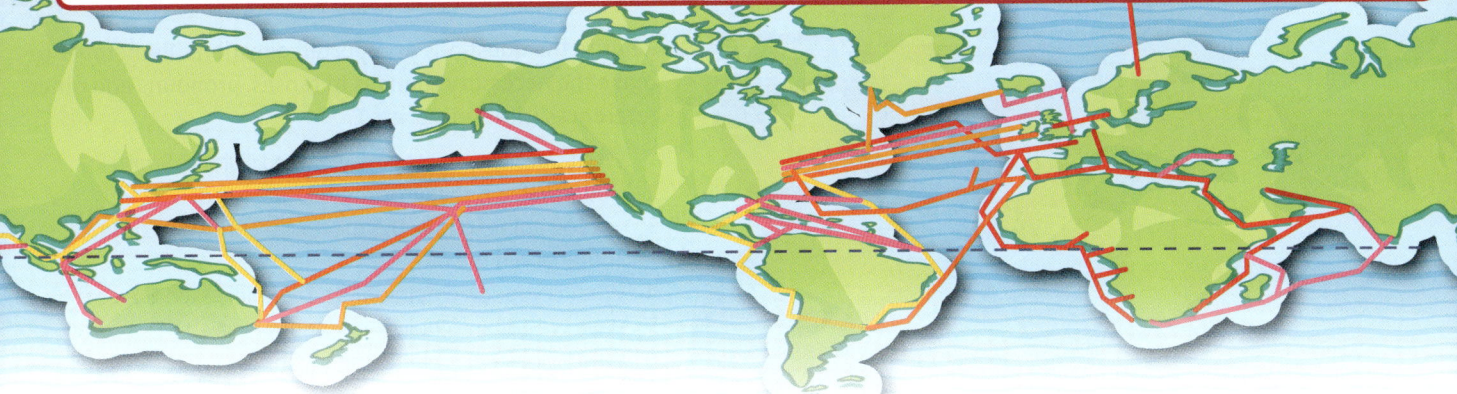

1 SPEAKING Work in pairs. What do you think the map shows? Choose from the ideas below.

undersea cables   shipping routes   ocean currents
popular cruises   weather patterns

2 🎧 **3.13** Listen to part 1 of a radio programme. Check your ideas from exercise 1.

3 🎧 **3.13** Listen again. What is the significance of these numbers?

95%   8 cm   21,000 km   60%

> **Listening Strategy 1**
> Sometimes you need to listen for the main idea (gist) rather than a specific piece of information. If this is the case, do not worry about a few unknown words. You can often understand the gist without understanding every word.

4 🎧 **3.14** Read Listening Strategy 1. Then listen to four voicemail messages. Ignore the parts you cannot hear well. Circle the correct words to sum up the main ideas.

1 Speaker 1 **will** / **won't** be able to meet Sam outside the theatre.
2 Speaker 2 **can** / **can't** come to Ava's birthday meal.
3 Speaker 3 **is** / **isn't** going to recommend a hotel in Paris.
4 Speaker 4 **has** / **hasn't** sent Emma's top back to her.

> **Listening Strategy 2**
> When you do a multiple-choice task, do not choose the correct answer based only on one or two words. Remember that the incorrect options also have some connection with what you hear.

5 🎧 **3.15** Read Listening Strategy 2. Then listen to part 2 of the radio programme from exercise 2. What is it mainly about: a, b or c?

a Improvements in communications cables from 1840 to the present day.
b Different ways of laying communications cables under the sea.
c One man's efforts to have a communications cable laid under the Atlantic Ocean.

6 🎧 **3.15** Listen again. For questions 1–5, circle the correct answers (a–d).

1 What advance in technology was made between 1840 and 1850?
 a A cable was laid under the Atlantic Ocean.
 b The electric telegraph was invented.
 c A cable was laid under the English Channel.
 d A telegraph message was sent from France to the USA.

2 For Field's first attempt to lay a cable under the Atlantic Ocean, where did the two ships begin?
 a in the middle of the Atlantic
 b on the east coast of America
 c one in America and one in Ireland
 d both on the west coast of Ireland

3 On the second attempt, how many times did the cable break?
 a once b twice c three times d six times

4 For the third attempt, the ships' starting position
 a was the same as the first attempt.
 b was the same as the second attempt.
 c was different from both previous attempts.
 d is not mentioned in the programme.

5 What period of history does the programme mainly talk about?
 a from 1840 to the present day
 b the decade 1840 to 1850
 c from 1858 to the present day
 d the two years 1857 and 1858

7 VOCABULARY Complete the phrasal verbs with the correct particles.

1 Somebody had to work _____ how to lay a cable under the Atlantic.
2 Two ships set _____ from the west coast of Ireland.
3 They repaired the cable and carried _____ their work.
4 They decided to call _____ the attempt.
5 They abandoned the attempt and the ships went _____ to port.
6 But Cyrus Field was not prepared to give _____ .

8 🎧 **3.15** Listen again and check your answers to exercise 7.

9 SPEAKING Work in pairs. Tell your partner about <u>one</u> of the following.

1 something you spent a long time trying to work out
2 an occasion when you wanted to give up, but carried on instead
3 an occasion when you set off on a journey, but had to go back for some reason

Reported questions

I can report questions correctly.

1 SPEAKING Work in pairs. How can people send messages over long distances without using electronic technology? Think of as many different ways as you can.

2 🎧**3.16** **VOCABULARY** Listen to an extract from a film. What kind of film is it? Choose from the list below. Which words were clues?

Film genres action film   comedy   horror film   musical science fiction film   war film   western

3 🎧**3.16** Work in pairs. Read the reported questions that Captain Hunter asked the woman. Then listen again and write the exact words the captain used.

1 Captain Hunter asked her when she had received the message.
   When did you receive the message?
2 He asked her who was sending the messages.
3 Then he asked her why she wanted to help them.
4 He asked her if he could trust her.
5 He also asked how she had learned to speak English.
6 Finally, he asked her whether there would be another message the following day.

4 Compare the reported questions in exercise 3 with the questions you wrote down. Circle the correct words to complete the Learn this! box.

LEARN THIS! Reported questions

a We use the verb ¹*ask* / *tell* to report a question.

b The tenses ²**change** / **don't change** as they do in reported statements.

c Pronouns and time phrases ³**change** / **don't change** in reported questions.

d The word order in a reported question is the same as a ⁴**statement** / **question** – subject before verb.

e We ⁵**use** / **don't use** *do* and *did* in reported questions.

f We use ⁶*if* / *that* or *whether* to report *yes* / *no* questions.

➡ **Grammar Builder 8.2** page 141

5 Rewrite the questions as reported questions. Remember to make the necessary changes to tenses, pronouns and other references (time, place, etc.).

1 'What does the message say?' asked Colonel Smith.
2 'How reliable is the information?' he asked.
3 'Are you going to take the message seriously?' Captain Hunter asked the colonel.
4 'What is your own opinion?' the colonel asked the captain.
5 'Have we got any choice?' the captain asked.
6 'Who will take the blame for any mistakes?' the colonel asked.
7 'Can we discuss this again tomorrow morning?' Captain Hunter asked the colonel.
8 'How many other people have you told about the messages?' the colonel asked.

6 🎧**3.17** Read and listen to another part of the film. Then complete the text below with reported speech (questions and statements).

Woman	Were the messages helpful?
Capt Hunter	They saved a lot of lives. Who sent the messages to you?
Woman	My cousin sent them from his office. He works at enemy High Command.
Capt Hunter	How did he send the messages in secret?
Woman	He used the sun and a mirror.
Capt Hunter	Why did his messages stop?
Woman	The weather turned cloudy!

The woman asked ¹*if her messages had been helpful*. Captain Hunter said ²_____ lives. He asked her ³_____ . She replied that her cousin ⁴_____ office. She said ⁵_____ High Command. The captain asked her ⁶_____ in secret. She said ⁷_____ and a mirror. The captain asked her ⁸_____ . The woman replied ⁹_____ cloudy.

7 Work in pairs. Write four questions and answers using the prompts below.

1 What sports / instruments / video games can you play?
   What sports can you play? I can play football and tennis.
2 Where do you usually go after school / at weekends / during the holidays?
3 What did you eat this morning / last night / last New Year?
4 Have you ever tried kayaking / rock climbing / Japanese food?

8 SPEAKING Work with another pair. Ask and answer your questions from exercise 7. Can the other pair remember and report them?

What sports can you play? | I can play football and tennis.

Phil asked Anna what sports she could play. Anna said that she could play football and tennis.

Word Skills

Verb patterns: reporting verbs

I can use a variety of reporting verbs correctly.

a great big fat ...
... SORRY!
from 'The Reformed Bike Theif'
(I never mistreated it)

1 **SPEAKING** Work in pairs. Find one spelling mistake in the handwritten note. Then decide what has happened. Who wrote the note and why?

2 Read the text opposite and find the answers to the questions in exercise 1.

3 **VOCABULARY** Read the Learn this! box. Underline the verbs below in the text in exercise 2. Complete the rules (a–e) with the correct verbs.

Reporting verbs accuse admit apologise beg persuade promise thank

LEARN THIS! Verb patterns

a verb + infinitive
agree / ¹_____ / offer / refuse to do something

b verb + object + infinitive
advise / ask / ²_____ / ³_____ / encourage / tell / remind somebody to do something

c verb + -ing form
⁴_____ / deny / propose / mention / suggest doing something

d verb + preposition + -ing form
insist on / ⁵_____ for / wonder about doing something

e verb + object + preposition + -ing form
⁶_____ somebody of / blame somebody for doing something / ⁷_____ somebody for / warn somebody against doing something

4 Circle the correct reporting verb to complete the sentences.

1 My parents **encouraged** / **proposed** me to play an instrument.
2 Kate **agreed** / **suggested** going out for dinner.
3 He **denied** / **refused** to tell them his real name.
4 She **agreed** / **warned** him against going to the party.
5 He **insisted on** / **offered** paying for the meal.

LOOK OUT!

We add *not* to infinitives and *-ing* forms to make them negative.

He persuaded us not to go on foot.
She apologised for not being ready.

Sometimes, sending a message to a stranger can be very powerful. When Eileen Remedios had her bike stolen, she decided to leave a note where it had been. She begged the thief to return her bike, saying it was 'old but loved'. The next day, her bike was returned with a message from the thief. He apologised for stealing the bike and signed himself 'The Reformed Bike Thief'. Eileen was amazed and delighted. She left one final message in which she thanked the thief for returning her bike.

A similar thing happened to Julie Colwell after she was nearly hit by a car while she was jogging. She shouted at the driver and accused him of driving dangerously. The driver didn't stop or reply, but the next day Julie found a note at the same place. It was from the driver. In it, he admitted driving badly and apologised for frightening her. He even said that her angry words had persuaded him to change his ways and he promised to drive more carefully in the future.

5 Read the Look out! box. Then rewrite the sentences using the verb in brackets as a reporting verb.

1 'I don't spend enough time on my homework,' Sarah said. (admit)
   Sarah admitted not spending enough time on her homework.
2 'Please, please don't lose your phone again,' John's mother said to him. (beg)
3 'My neighbours are stealing my plants,' said Mrs Brown. (accuse)
4 'I'm sorry I'm not better at cooking,' said Grace. (apologise)
5 'Maybe we shouldn't spend so much money on snacks,' Harry said. (suggest)
6 'You should take up a hobby,' Anna's parents told her. (encourage)
7 'Swimming in the river is dangerous,' said the tour guide to the tourists. (warn)
8 'I'm definitely going to pay for my own ticket,' said Ella. (insist)

6 Make notes about something:

1 you advised somebody not to do.
2 you refused to do.
3 somebody reminded you to do.
4 a friend suggested doing.
5 someone apologised to you for doing.
6 you thanked somebody for doing.
7 somebody blamed you for doing / not doing.

7 **SPEAKING** Work in pairs. Tell your partner about the things in exercise 6.

I advised my friend not to buy an expensive smartphone.

A novel idea

I can understand a text about cell phone novels.

1 VOCABULARY What types of things do you read and how do you read them? Do you prefer paper or digital formats? Use the words below to help you.

Reading matter biographies blog posts comics magazines newspapers novels poems textbooks

Digital formats blogs e-books social networking sites tweets websites zines

➡ **Vocabulary Builder** Publications: page 125

2 Read the text quickly, ignoring the gaps. What are cell phone novels and how do they work? Circle the correct answer: a, b or c.

a They are paperback novels divided into instalments and sent to mobile phones.

b They are stories in episodes written on mobile phones and uploaded onto a special website.

c They are long texts sent by friends to other friends.

> **Reading Strategy**
>
> Read the missing sentences carefully. Then read the sentences in the text that come before and after each gap. Use these two strategies when selecting which sentence fits each gap:
>
> **1** Look for vocabulary links between the sentence and the surrounding text.
>
> **2** Look for pronouns, e.g. *he*, *she*, *it* and other references and check that they match your answer choice.

3 Read the Reading Strategy. Match sentences A–H with gaps 1–6 in the text. There are two extra sentences.

A Common themes are love, tragedy and betrayal, and the stories often deal with difficult or controversial issues.

B Books are sometimes regarded as old-fashioned and difficult to read.

C In response to this trend, some smart young authors have changed the way they write.

D However, as the story progressed, the style gradually evolved into something different.

E She typed out instalments on her phone and uploaded them onto a popular website for cell phone authors.

F No money is made from cell phone novels unless they are published as books.

G It was called *Deep Love* and told the story of a teenager who contracted AIDS.

H Sentences are short and there are no descriptions of anything or anybody because there isn't space.

4 Read the text again. Are the sentences true or false? Write T or F.

1 The first cell phone novel appeared in Japan. ___

2 The success of Yoshi's first book was due mainly to advertisements on the TV and in comic books. ___

3 Most cell phone novels deal with difficult issues. ___

4 Rin did not tell her parents that she was writing a cell phone novel. ___

5 There is a lot of conversation between the characters in cell phone novels. ___

6 Cell phone novels in English have recently appeared in the USA. ___

5 Answer the questions.

1 What was the first cell phone novel about?

2 How did Rin write her cell phone novel?

3 How did the first English language cell phone novel come about?

4 What does Takatsu particularly like about this form of writing?

6 VOCABULARY Match a–k with 1–11 to make compound nouns. They are all in the text.

Compound nouns		
1 leisure	**a** series
2 cell	**b** book
3 television	**c** school
4 comic	**d** story
5 high	**e** time
6 love	**f** name
7 book	**g** phone
8 bestseller	**h** culture
9 pen	**i** contract
10 pop	**j** media
11 social	**k** list

7 SPEAKING Work in pairs or small groups. Discuss the questions.

1 Do you think cell phone novels are a good idea? Why? / Why not?

2 Would you be interested in reading one? Why? / Why not?

3 Do you think you could write one yourself? Why? / Why not?

🎧 3.18

A different type of phone book

Although books are still popular with teenagers, most of them spend more of their leisure time staring at their phone than reading a paperback. And the more versatile phones become, the more reasons young people have for looking at them. ¹__ Instead of publishing a whole book at once, they produce
5 very short chapters, which they send once a week to their readers by text message. Some even claim that this style of writing represents a new literary genre: the 'cell phone novel'.

The very first cell phone novel was written in 2003 by a man in Tokyo who called himself Yoshi. ²__ It became so popular, mainly through word of mouth,
10 that it was later published as a paperback. The book version sold 2.6 million copies and a television series, a comic book and a film were made of the story. Online companies became interested and set up websites where authors could upload their stories and readers could discuss them in forums as the stories evolved.

15 Although the idea originated in Japan, cell phone novels have also sprung up in the rest of East Asia, Europe and Africa. Many are written by high school or university students who are very familiar with the topics that teenagers are interested in. ³__ Twenty-one-year-old Rin said that she started her novel *If You* during her final year at high school and explained that it was the tragic
20 love story of two childhood friends.

Rin wrote her novel over a six-month period in spare moments, often while commuting on the train. ⁴__ Readers then voted her novel the best that year and she was offered a book contract. Her book sold 400,000 copies and was number five in the Japanese bestseller list. Rin said that her mother had had
25 no idea that she had been writing a novel and was therefore very surprised when she saw a book with her daughter's name on it.

The style of cell phone novels has evolved to suit the medium. Chapters have no more than 200 words, and often just 50–100 words. ⁵__ The text mostly consists of dialogue and the language is direct, conveying a lot in a few words.
30 Many cell phone novelists had never written fiction before and many of their readers have never read a normal novel. Other rules have evolved; for example, authors only have one name and that is a pseudonym or pen name.

In 2009, a young Japanese writer called Takatsu, who
35 lives in Canada, began writing the first English language cell phone novel, *Secondhand Memories*. Each instalment appeared on textnovel.com, a website dedicated to cell phone stories. Takatsu had read an English translation of Rin's story *If You* and had been impressed by its simple and
40 emotional language. It was a feature he deliberately copied when he started writing *Secondhand Memories*.
⁶__ He now believes that, in English, cell phone novels have a powerful and poetic identity of their own.

Takatsu sees himself, and the other writers who
45 contribute to textnovel.com, as part of a literary movement which blends drama, technology, pop culture and social media. Cell phone novels encourage young people to engage in fiction, even those who would not normally pick up
50 a book. They could be described as teen novels for the 21st century.

Photo description
I can describe a photo and answer questions about it.

A

B

1 SPEAKING Work in pairs. Describe photo A. What do you think has happened? How do you think the woman in the white shirt is feeling? Why?

2 🎧 **3.19** Listen to a student describing the photo. How does her description differ from yours?

3 KEY PHRASES Complete the phrases for speculating with the words below.

clear   could   hard   judging   looks   pretty   sure

Speculating
I can't be ¹_____ , but I'd say that ...
It ²_____ be (that) ...   It's ³_____ to say, but ...
It ⁴_____ as if ...   I'm ⁵_____ certain that ...
It's ⁶_____ that ...
⁷_____ by (his expression), I'd say that ...

4 🎧 **3.19** Listen again. Which phrases from exercise 3 did the student use in her answer?

5 Compare and contrast photos A and B in exercise 1. Follow steps 1–5 and use the words below to help you describe photo B.

ceiling   drip (v)   leak (n, v)   look up
phone book   plumber

1 Describe each scene in general.
2 Say what the people are doing and wearing.
3 Point out similarities.
4 Point out differences.
5 Say how the people might be feeling and how you might feel in a similar situation.

Would you be good at receiving and dealing with emergency calls? Why? / Why not?

6 🎧 **3.20** Listen to a student answering the question above. Complete the sentences with the words below.

appeal   finally   idea   only   reasons   simple   view

1 There are a number of _____ why I say that.
2 In my _____ , you need to stay very calm.
3 Not _____ that, but you have to deal with people who are very upset.
4 The _____ of being on the phone all day doesn't _____ to me.
5 _____ , I really wouldn't be the right person for the job for the _____ reason that I can't stand the sight of blood!

7 SPEAKING Work in pairs. Take turns to answer the question in exercise 6. Use phrases for speculating and phrases from exercise 6 in your answers.

> **Speaking Strategy**
> • Speak in a loud, clear voice.
> • Look at the other person when they are speaking to you and when you are speaking to them.

➡ **Vocabulary Builder** Road accidents: page 125

8 SPEAKING Work in pairs. Read the Speaking Strategy. Look at photos C and D below. Describe one photo each.

9 SPEAKING Work in pairs. Take turns to compare and contrast photos C and D. Follow the steps in exercise 5.

10 SPEAKING Work in pairs. Student A: make notes for question 1. Student B: make notes for question 2.

1 What could you do if your car broke down and you didn't have a mobile phone with you?
2 How can we make our roads safer for cyclists?

11 SPEAKING Present the answer you prepared to the question in exercise 10.

C

D

Writing

A narrative

I can write a story.

1 **SPEAKING** Work in pairs. Have you ever been late for a lesson or an exam? If so, why? How did you feel?

2 Read the task and the story. Which words did the writer's friend misunderstand?

> Write a story about a problem that arose because of a misunderstanding or a lack of communication.

I've always been really keen on swimming. About a year ago, I decided to do an exam to become a lifeguard. My dad agreed to drive me there, and we set off from home in his car.

A few minutes later, we passed a friend of mine from school. He was walking along the pavement and chatting to somebody on his phone. We stopped, and I told him I was on my way to an exam at the sports centre. 'Me too!' he replied. We offered him a lift and he accepted.

After a while, we arrived at the sports centre. At that moment, my friend started to look worried. 'Where are we?' he asked. 'This isn't the music centre!' He told us he had a piano exam at the music centre in ten minutes. Obviously, he hadn't listened properly when we'd offered him a lift!

Fortunately, my dad agreed to drive him to the music centre and they arrived just in time. Afterwards, my friend was really grateful and bought my dad a present.

3 Complete the paragraph plan with the phrases below.

lead up to main event   main event   set the scene
the ending

Paragraph 1: _____
Paragraph 2: _____
Paragraph 3: _____
Paragraph 4: _____

> **Writing Strategy**
>
> 1 You can make your narrative more interesting by using comment adverbs such as *luckily, unfortunately, thank goodness*, etc.
>
> 2 When you are narrating events, use a variety of tenses such as past simple, past continuous, present perfect, past perfect, *used to*, etc.

4 Read point 1 of the Writing Strategy. Circle two comment adverbs in the story in exercise 2.

5 Read point 2 of the Writing Strategy. Find and underline all the different past tenses that the writer used in the story in exercise 2. Which tenses does the writer use to …

1 set the scene?
2 narrate a sequence of events?
3 refer to events that happened before other events in the story?

6 **KEY PHRASES** Add the phrases below to the correct groups. How many of them can you find in the story?

about a year ago   a few minutes later   at last
in the end   later on   one Saturday last month

> **Narrative time expressions**
>
> **Non-specific time expressions for starting a narrative**
> 1 _____   2 _____
>
> one day last week   a while back   about a month or so ago
>
> **Expressions for ordering events**
> 3 _____   4 _____
>
> later   at first   after a while   afterwards
>
> **Expressions for bringing the narrative to an end**
> 5 _____   6 _____
>
> eventually   finally

7 Read the Learn this! box below. Find two examples of a verb with two objects in the story in exercise 2: one with *offer* (in paragraph 2) and one with *buy* (in paragraph 4).

> **LEARN THIS!** Verbs with two objects
>
> Some verbs can be followed by an indirect and a direct object. The indirect object comes first and is usually a person.
> *I showed my friend some photos.*

➡ Grammar Builder 8.3 page 141

8 You are going to do the task in exercise 2. Make notes using the paragraph plan in exercise 3.

9 Write your story using your notes from exercise 8.

> **CHECK YOUR WORK**
>
> Have you …
> • used a variety of narrative tenses?
> • used some comment adverbs?
> • checked your grammar and spelling?

9

Journeys

Unit map

● **Vocabulary**
Forms of transport
Travel: places
Collocations: verb + noun
Units of measurement
Holiday activities
Holiday accommodation

● **Word Skills**
Verb patterns

● **Grammar**
Third conditional
Participle clauses

● **Listening** Travel solutions

● **Reading** Miscalculations

● **Speaking** Guided conversation

● **Writing** A formal letter

● **Culture 9** Victorian explorers

● **Vocabulary Builder** page 125

● **Grammar Builder and Reference** page 141

Travel and transport

I can talk about travel and transport.

1 VOCABULARY Match photos A–F with six of the words below. Which would be the most exciting way to travel? Why?

Forms of transport aircraft cable car coach cruise ship ferry helicopter hot-air balloon hovercraft motorbike scooter tram underground yacht

2 Work in pairs. Check the meaning of all the words in exercise 1. In two minutes, how many more forms of transport can you think of?

boat, van, …

3 Complete the travel facts with forms of transport from exercise 1. Check your answers with your partner.

1 A 'drone' is an unmanned _____ .
2 In 1783, the Montgolfier brothers made the first manned flight in a _____ .
3 The *Titanic* is the famous _____ that sank in the North Atlantic in 1912.
4 The first _____ line was opened beneath the streets of London in 1863.
5 A _____ can travel on land, water, mud, or ice.
6 The first _____ weren't electric. They were pulled by horses and appeared in New York in 1832.
7 The longest _____ in the world is 13.2 km long and carries people between the towns of Örträsk and Mensträsk in Sweden.
8 In 1493, Leonardo da Vinci designed a machine that looked like a _____ , but it was never built.

4 SPEAKING In pairs, discuss the forms of transport in exercise 1 and decide:

1 which would be a) the fastest, b) the cheapest and c) the most spectacular way to travel across a large city.
2 which would be a) the safest, b) the most environmentally friendly and c) the most comfortable way to travel across the sea to another country.

> I think the fastest way to travel across a large city would be by scooter.

> I agree. / I don't agree. I think travelling by underground would be faster.

5 VOCABULARY Check the meaning of the words below. Put them into the correct groups: a) sea travel, b) air travel, c) road travel and d) rail travel. Some can go in more than one group.

Travel: places airport arrivals hall buffet car bus stop cabin car park check-in desk coach bay coach station deck departure gate filling station harbour level crossing lost property office platform port service station sleeper taxi rank ticket barrier ticket office train station waiting room

➡ **Vocabulary Builder** Travel problems: page 125

6 🎧**3.21** Listen to six dialogues. For each one, write:

1 what form(s) of transport is / are involved.
2 where the people are. Choose from the places in exercise 5.

RECYCLE! The passive

1 We form the passive with the verb *be* and the past participle of the verb.
   This cruise ship <u>was built</u> ten years ago by Hyundai.

2 We use a passive infinitive after certain verbs. We use a passive base form (infinitive without *to*) after modal verbs.
   The passengers needed to be rescued by the emergency services.
   All passports must be shown at the departure gate.

3 When we want to say who or what performed the action in a passive sentence, we use *by*.

7 Read the **Recycle!** box. Complete the questions using the passive and the verb in brackets.

1 On which ferries _____ the return tickets _____ ? (can / use)
   On which ferries can the return tickets … ?

2 Why _____ the train _____ ? (past simple / *delay*)

3 Where _____ the jacket _____ ? (past simple / *leave*)

4 Where does the passenger want _____ ? (passive infinitive / *drop off*)

5 Why _____ the motorway _____ ? (present perfect / *close*)

6 Why _____ the passenger _____ to wait? (past simple / *ask*)

8 🎧**3.21** Listen again and answer the questions in exercise 7. Write the answers.

9 SPEAKING Work in pairs. Choose one of the sets of instructions below and plan a role-play for it.

1
Student A: You want to travel to London by coach, coming back in two days. You need to find out about ticket prices, times and which bay the coach leaves from. Have a conversation with a clerk at the ticket office.
Student B: You are the clerk. Help the passenger.

2
Student A: You are at the airport, meeting a friend from a foreign country. Welcome him / her and ask about the journey. Offer to help with the luggage and say how you will take the visitor to your home.
Student B: You are visiting a friend abroad, and have arrived at the airport. Greet your friend, tell him / her about the journey and respond to his / her questions.

3
Student A: You have left something on a train. Go to the lost property office and describe the lost item, and say when and where you left it.
Student B: You are the clerk at the lost property office. Ask questions about the lost item and explain what you will do.

10 SPEAKING Act out your dialogue to the class.

9B Grammar

Third conditional

I can talk about imaginary events in the past.

1 SPEAKING Describe the photo. What are the people discussing, do you think?

Sally   We were supposed to be there by five and it's 5.15 already. If you'd remembered the satnav, we wouldn't have got lost.

Ben   We aren't lost. I know where we are on the map. We're nearly there.

Sally   If we'd left home on time, we'd have arrived by now.

Ben   Well, that isn't my fault, is it? We'd have left on time if your mum hadn't phoned just as we were leaving.

Sally   Don't blame my mum! And we wasted so much time at the services. If we'd made sandwiches (like I suggested), we wouldn't have had to stop for lunch.

Ben   Look, we're here now, and only fifteen minutes late. That isn't so bad.

2 🎧**3.22** Read and listen to the dialogue. Look at the highlighted sentences and answer the questions. Then find one more third conditional sentence in the dialogue.

1 Did Ben remember the satnav?
2 Did they leave home on time?
3 Did they make sandwiches for the journey?

3 Look at the highlighted sentences in the dialogue and answer the questions below. Then read the Learn this! box and complete the examples.

1 What tense is used in the *if* clause?
2 What form is used in the main clause?
3 How is *have* pronounced?

> **LEARN THIS!**   Third conditional
>
> **a** We form the third conditional with *if* + past perfect, *would have* + past participle.
> *If I had seen her, I would have offered her a lift.*
>
> **b** As in all conditional sentences, the *if* clause can come before or after the main clause.
> *I would have come to meet you if you* ¹_____ *(phone).*
>
> **c** We use the third conditional to talk about imaginary situations and to say how things could have been different in the past.
> *If you hadn't gone by taxi, you* ²_____ *(not arrive) on time.*
>
> **d** We often use it to express regret or criticism.
> *If you* ³_____ *(leave) earlier, you* ⁴_____ *(not be) late!*

➥ **Grammar Builder 9.1** page 141

4 Write sentences and questions in the third conditional.

1 Tom / take / a taxi // if / he / have / some cash on him
   Tom would have taken a taxi if he'd had some cash on him.
2 if / you / find / 80€ / on the way to school this morning // you / keep / it ?
3 if / I / know / it / be / your birthday // I / buy / you / a present
4 if / we / walk / all the way home // we / be / exhausted
5 if / I / not want / to work on this journey // I / not take / the train
6 Jim / pass / his maths exam // if / he / work / harder ?
7 if / we / have / more time // we / can / change / some money at the airport
8 what / you / do // you / oversleep / this morning ?

> **! LOOK OUT!**
>
> In written English we do not usually contract the verb *have* in third conditional sentences. But in spoken English, we do, pronouncing it as /əv/.
>
> Written form: *would have*   *I'd have*   *wouldn't have*
> Pronounced as: *'would've'*   *'I'd've'*   *'wouldn't've'*

5 🎧**3.23** Read the Look out! box. Then read out the sentences in exercise 4 using contractions where appropriate. Listen and check.

6 Read the sentences about what actually happened. Then write sentences about how things might have been different. Use the third conditional.

1 We turned left and we got lost.
   If we hadn't turned left, we wouldn't have got lost.
2 I didn't go by train because the ticket was so expensive.
3 I didn't meet you at the airport because I didn't know when you were arriving.
4 We stopped at the service station because we were nearly out of petrol.
5 I wasn't late for the meeting because I took a taxi.
6 I bought the tickets on the train because there wasn't a ticket office at the station.
7 You missed your train because you didn't check the timetable.

7 Complete the sentences with true information. Use the third conditional.

1 If I'd felt ill this morning, _____ .
2 If there hadn't been school last Friday, _____ .
3 If I'd felt hungry on the way home from school yesterday, _____ .
4 If I'd forgotten to do my homework at the weekend, _____ .
5 If I hadn't studied English in primary school, _____ .
6 If I'd been late for school this morning, _____ .

8 SPEAKING Work in pairs. Ask and answer about the sentences in exercise 7.

> What would you have done if you'd felt ill this morning?

> I'd have … / I wouldn't have …

Listening

Travel solutions

I can identify the context of a conversation and its register.

1 Read the text. Find the name of the inventor and the invention.

As air travel becomes more and more popular, simply getting to the airport can be a challenging and unpleasant experience. You pay a fortune to park your car, then you have to walk for hours with heavy suitcases to arrive at the terminal. Well, a farmer from China called He Liang has come up with an idea which solves both problems: a suitcase that you can ride like a motorbike. He has called it the City Cab. It is powered by a battery and can travel up to 60 km at a speed of 20 km/h. And, of course, you don't need to find a car park for the City Cab – you just drive into the airport terminal and check it in!

Listening Strategy 1

It is sometimes difficult to catch names and proper nouns when you listen. However, you can use the words around them (including collocations) to work out what they are (a person, a place, etc.). For example, if you hear '*We stayed four nights at the Grand Plaza*', the underlined words tell you that the Grand Plaza is a hotel.

2 VOCABULARY Read Listening Strategy 1. Match the verbs and nouns below to make travel-related collocations. Some verbs can go with more than one noun.

Collocations: verb + noun

Verbs board book check in check into hail hire miss reach stay at

Nouns a cab / taxi a car a destination a holiday a hotel luggage / bags a plane / flight a room a ship a train

to board a plane / a flight / a ship / a train

3 🎧 **3.24** Listen to six short extracts and answer the questions. Listen for verbs and nouns from exercise 2 to help you.

Who or what is …
1 the *Princess Ariadne*?
2 a *tuk tuk*?
3 Ely?
4 Martins & Cole?
5 Damian Fairchild?
6 Bellagio?

Listening Strategy 2

Being aware of formal register can help you identify the context. Formal terms used in announcements include:

adjacent to (next to) due to (because of) prior to (before)
beverages (drinks) to commence (to begin)
to depart (to leave) to proceed to (to go to)
to purchase (to buy) refreshments (food and drink)
to terminate (to end)

4 🎧 **3.24** Read Listening Strategy 2. Then listen again. Which extracts (1–6) are formal? Which words from the strategy do they include?

5 🎧 **3.25** Listen to four extracts. For each question, circle the correct answers (a–c).

1 What is the speaker's main purpose?
  a to offer the passengers a drink or snack
  b to warn the passengers against standing up
  c to inform the passengers that they will take off late
2 It is the speaker's opinion, not a fact, that
  a nobody told him about the delay at check-in.
  b staff in the airport knew the reason for the delay.
  c a number of passengers got cross when they saw how long they'd have to wait for the flight.
3 What happened to the woman at the airport?
  a She caused her plane to take off late.
  b Her plane took off late because a fellow traveller wasn't on board.
  c She was asleep when they called her flight.
4 Where is this announcement made?
  a on a train   b in an airport   c in an aeroplane

6 Make the phrases more formal by replacing the underlined words with words from the list below.

ahead of schedule   appreciate   approaching
approximately   complimentary   in due course
inform   refreshments   regret   remain   request

1 I <u>am sorry</u> to <u>tell</u> you that … _____ _____
2 I would <u>ask</u> that passengers <u>stay</u> seated … _____ _____
3 … give you an update <u>later</u>. _____
4 … pass through the cabin with <u>free</u> <u>food and drink</u>. _____ _____
5 … we are <u>getting near</u> our destination. _____
6 … we should be there <u>about</u> ten minutes <u>early</u>. _____ _____
7 We <u>understand</u> that this is inconvenient … _____

7 🎧 **3.26** Listen to the formal extracts from exercise 3 again. Check your answers to exercise 6.

8 SPEAKING Work in pairs. Tell your partner about a journey on which you experienced travel problems, for example a delay. What was the problem? How did it affect your journey?

9D Grammar
Participle clauses
I can use participle clauses correctly.

1 SPEAKING Work in pairs. Do you think space programmes, which cost millions, are a good way for governments to spend money? Give reasons.

2 SPEAKING Read part 1 of the article. How would you have felt if you had been one of the Apollo 13 astronauts?

> **LEARN THIS!** Participle clauses
>
> **a** We use participle clauses to give more information about a noun. You can think of them as shortened relative clauses (defining or non-defining).
> *There were two men sitting on the bench.* (= who were sitting on the bench)
>
> **b** Participle clauses can begin with a present participle (*-ing* form). The participle replaces an active verb of any tense, including state verbs.
> *I saw a man wearing* (= who was wearing) *a space suit.*
> *Students needing* (= who need) *a lift should wait here.*
>
> **c** Participle clauses can also begin with a past participle. The participle replaces a passive verb of any tense.
> *We lived in a large house, built* (= which had been built) *in the 17th century.*

3 Read the Learn this! box. Do the participle clauses in the examples replace defining or non-defining relative clauses?

4 Rewrite the underlined participle clauses in part 1 of the article as relative clauses (defining or non-defining).
… which was launched from Florida on 11 April 1970.

➡ **Grammar Builder 9.2** page 142

5 Read part 2 of the article. The Apollo 13 mission has been described as a 'successful failure'. Why?

6 Rewrite the underlined clauses in part 2 as participle clauses.
   1 *… fitted with its own oxygen tank …*

7 Identify the relative clauses in these sentences. (Some contain more than one.) Rewrite them as participle clauses.
   1 The word *astronaut*, which is formed from two Greek words, means 'star sailor'.
   2 Only flights which reach an altitude of 100 km or more are considered space flights.
   3 People who are chosen to become NASA astronauts have to complete a difficult training programme which lasts twenty months.
   4 Astronauts who spend long periods in space do exercises which have been designed to keep them strong.
   5 Spacecraft which intend to escape from Earth's gravity need to reach a speed of about 40,000 km/h.
   6 People who watched the Apollo 13 mission on TV or who listened on the radio were very relieved when the astronauts returned safely.
   7 James Lovell received the Exceptional Service Medal, which was awarded by NASA.
   8 The film *Apollo 13*, which was made in 1995 and starred Tom Hanks, was nominated for many awards, which included nine Oscars.

PART 1
Apollo 13, launched from Florida on 11 April 1970, was the third Apollo mission designed to land on the moon. The three astronauts chosen for the mission were James Lovell, Fred Haise and John Swigert. The launch, watched by millions on TV, went smoothly and for the first two days in space, everything went well. The crew gave a 49-minute TV interview explaining how they lived and worked in zero gravity. However, nine minutes after the interview finished, a tank containing oxygen exploded and John Swigert, noticing a red warning light, said the famous words: 'Houston, we've had a problem here.' They checked all their equipment and realised that they were running out of water, power and oxygen – and fast. They were in a damaged spaceship floating 320,000 kilometres from Earth.

PART 2
The astronauts left the main part of the spaceship and went inside the lunar module, ¹which had been fitted with its own oxygen tank. But inside the smaller module, ²which was designed to hold only two people, carbon dioxide levels started rising. The astronauts, ³who had been following instructions from the ground crew, made special filters out of plastic bags and cardboard. Then they waited in the cold and dark while the ground crew, ⁴who were working 24 hours a day, tried to work out a way to bring them home. If some people in America were losing interest in the Space Program, the Apollo 13 crisis, ⁵which was discussed on all the TV news programmes, changed all that. The astronauts ⁶who were risking their lives and the people ⁷who were trying to save them all became national heroes – especially when Apollo 13 returned safely to Earth with all three astronauts alive.

8 SPEAKING Discuss the questions with your partner. Use the nouns and adjectives below to help you.

Nouns adventure danger discomfort excitement fear loneliness

Adjectives brave calm fit hard-working intelligent logical serious

   1 What personal qualities do astronauts need?
   2 What would the best thing about the job be?
   3 What would the hardest thing about the job be?

Word Skills
Verb patterns
I can identify and use verb patterns.

1 SPEAKING Describe the photo in pairs. What would be the best and worst things about going on a long trip on a boat like this? Talk about the topics below or your own ideas.

accommodation   boredom   food   freedom
pirates   relaxation   safety   sightseeing   weather

2 Read the text. If you had been on a trip like this, would you have enjoyed it? Why? / Why not?

When Jane and Clive Green stopped working, they decided to go on a trip to Spain in their yacht. They expected to be away for about a week – but in the end, they continued travelling for sixteen years! After they reached Spain in their ten-metre yacht, they did not fancy returning home, so they kept sailing. After crossing the Atlantic, they stopped to explore the islands of the Caribbean for a while. Then they continued to sail west around the world. They ended up visiting 56 countries and sharing some amazing experiences. They particularly enjoyed swimming with seals near the Galápagos Islands. However, they remember feeling very anxious near Somalia because a boat would not stop following them and they had heard about pirates in that area. It was actually a fishing boat with an injured man on board, so Jane offered to help him before they continued on their way. They managed to pay for their trip by selling their house back in the UK. Most of the time, they could afford to buy food, but they ran out of money on an island near Fiji. Fortunately, a local woman agreed to give them a box of fruit and vegetables in exchange for some underwear!

LEARN THIS! Verb patterns

a Some verbs are followed by the infinitive of another verb.
Do you want to go out? She hopes to be a teacher.

b Some verbs are followed by the *-ing* form of another verb.
She always avoids paying. I spend a lot of time texting.

c Some verbs are followed by either an infinitive or an *-ing* form without any change in meaning.

d Some verbs change their meaning depending on whether they are followed by an *-ing* form or an infinitive.
I didn't remember speaking to Jo. (I forgot that I had spoken to her.)
I didn't remember to speak to Jo. (I didn't speak to her.)

e The verbs *let* and *make* are followed by an infinitive without *to*.
She let me drive. I made her laugh.

3 Read the Learn this! box. Then look at the highlighted verbs in the text above. Which verb pattern (a–e) does not have an example in the text?

4 Add the verbs from the text to the table. Can you add any more verbs?

verb + infinitive	verb + -ing form	infinitive or -ing (same meaning)	infinitive or -ing (different meaning)
choose	not mind	like	remember
want	spend (time)	start	try
hope		prefer	

5 Compare sentences a and b. How is the meaning of the underlined verb different when followed by an *-ing* form or an infinitive?

1 a I <u>tried</u> buying a present for her, but she was still angry with me.
   b I <u>tried</u> to buy a present for her, but everything was too expensive.
2 a I <u>stopped</u> talking to my friend when the film started.
   b I <u>stopped</u> to talk to my friend when I met him in town.
3 a After the film, they <u>went on</u> eating popcorn.
   b After the film, they <u>went on</u> to eat pizza.
4 a I won't <u>forget</u> visiting the Taj Mahal – it was amazing.
   b I won't <u>forget</u> to visit the Taj Mahal – I've heard it's amazing.

6 Complete the text with the infinitive (with or without *to*) or *-ing* form of the verbs in brackets.

In the UK, people who are travelling long distances by road often stop **1**_____ (spend) the night at a roadside hotel. But David and Jean Davidson have spent 22 years **2**_____ (live) in one. The couple own a flat in Sheffield, in the north of England, but choose **3**_____ (stay) at a Travelodge hotel about 65 km away.

The Davidsons first tried **4**_____ (visit) Travelodge hotels in 1985. They enjoyed **5**_____ (be) there so much that gradually they stopped **6**_____ (go) back to their own home. When a new Travelodge opened 65 km from Sheffield, they decided **7**_____ (become) permanent guests. They like **8**_____ (live) there because it is safe and convenient, they say, and they don't mind **9**_____ (hear) the noise from all the cars and lorries in the car park outside. The staff look after them well and let them **10**_____ (have) family get-togethers at the hotel.

The retired couple can afford **11**_____ (pay) for their room because they book it weeks in advance and get a good rate. In fact, last year, they managed **12**_____ (save) enough money for a three-week holiday abroad in the USA. And where did they end up **13**_____ (stay)? In an American Travelodge hotel, of course!

7 SPEAKING Work in pairs. Tell your partner about something that you:

1 loved doing.
2 once made somebody do.
3 often forget to do.
4 will never forget doing.
5 fancy doing after school.
6 will try doing one day.

Miscalculations

I can understand texts about mistakes.

mm

1 SPEAKING Read the saying below. What does it mean? Why is it good advice?

Measure twice, cut once.

2 Read texts A–D quickly. Match them with photos a–d and titles 1–4 below.

1 Can't slow down! ___ , ___   3 Meet you in the middle? ___ , ___
2 Too fat to fit! ___ , ___   4 Top heavy! ___ , ___

> **Reading Strategy**
> When a statement can match more than one text, you need to make sure you have matched all of the possible texts to each statement. First decide which text matches with a particular statement. Then check that none of the other texts match the statement.

3 Read the Reading Strategy. Then carefully read text A and the two statements below. Does the text match with one or both of the statements? Find evidence in the text for your answer.

1 The mistake could only be rectified by altering something else.
2 One company failed to pass on all the information that it had to another company.

4 Match the texts (A–D) with statements 1–6 below. Two texts match with two statements.

This mishap:
1 had two distinct causes.
2 was caused because somebody failed to measure something.
3 involved engineers from two countries.
4 was the result of a mistake made in a country outside Europe.
5 resulted in a loss of life.
6 will need even more money to rectify.

5 Complete the third conditional sentences using information from the text.

1 The trains would have been the right width if _____
_____ .

2 If the NASA engineers had all used metric measurements,
_____ .

3 If the German and Swiss engineers had calculated sea level in the same way, _____ .
4 The *Vasa* would not have sunk if _____
and if _____ .

6 VOCABULARY What units of length do these abbreviations represent? Which are metric? All the units are in the texts.

> **Units of measurement**
> 1 cm   3 m   5 in
> 2 mm   4 km   6 ft

> ➤ **Vocabulary Builder** Size and dimensions: page 125

7 In the text, underline the units of length and distance listed in exercise 6, and say what they refer to.

1 – centimetres. The French trains were three centimetres too wide for the stations.

8 SPEAKING Work in pairs. Discuss these questions. In your opinion, which was a) the most serious mistake and b) the least serious mistake? Why?

9 INTERNET RESEARCH Research other famous mistakes made by engineers. Use these questions to help you and present your findings to the class.

1 What was the mistake?
2 Why was it made?
3 What were the consequences?

Disastrous MISTAKES!

🎧 3.27

A There were red faces at the headquarters of French train company SNCF in 2014 when they discovered that 2,000 new trains they had ordered were three centimetres too wide for many station platforms. The error appears to have happened because RFF, the company that runs the rail network, gave SNCF the wrong measurements. Instead of measuring all the platforms on
5 the rail network, they only measured platforms that were less than thirty years old. They didn't realise that the gap between platforms built more than fifty years ago is narrower, because trains in those days were a bit slimmer. The new trains cost €15 billion, so there is no question of rebuilding them. It will be cheaper to alter the width of the platforms. But that has so far cost €50 million and the job is not yet finished: there are still 1,000 platforms that need adjusting.

B
10 In September 1999, after a trouble-free 286-day journey from Earth, the *Mars Climate Orbiter* fired its engines in order to slow down and put itself into orbit around Mars. Its mission was to collect information about the Martian climate and try to discover whether there was water on the surface of the red planet. The engines fired successfully, but that was when the problems started. The spacecraft was only sixty kilometres from the planet's surface, instead of 160 kilometres. According
15 to NASA scientists in Florida, the engine quickly overheated, stopped working and was unable to prevent the spacecraft from continuing straight past the planet. It is now probably orbiting the sun. The accident happened because two sets of engineers, one working in metric (millimetres) and the other working with the imperial system (inches), failed to communicate while they were building the spacecraft. It turned out to be an expensive mistake – the *Mars Climate Orbiter* cost £125 million!

C
20 What is sea level? Surely it is the same everywhere on Earth? Well, in fact, it isn't, and that is what led to a problem with a bridge being built across a river between Germany and Switzerland in 2004. In Germany, people measure height in relation to the North Sea, while Switzerland chooses to use the Mediterranean, which is 27 centimetres lower. The engineers were fully aware of this difference between the two versions of sea level. However, as the two
25 sides of the bridge came closer to each other, it became clear that they would not meet exactly, as there was a height difference of over half a metre: 54 centimetres, to be precise. Instead of subtracting 27 centimetres, the German engineers had added 27 centimetres. The German side therefore had to be lowered before the bridge could be completed.

D
30 In 1628, the *Vasa* was the most powerfully armed warship in the world, with 64 enormous cannons. Her Swedish makers were justifiably proud of her. But twenty minutes into her first journey, she was hit by strong winds. She tipped over to the side, water rushed into the ship and she quickly sank, only a mile from the port. Thirty people died. Over the centuries, scientists have tried to explain why the ship was unstable. Most agreed that the top of the ship was far too heavy, but that was not enough to explain why the ship sank. Now, however, scientists at the Vasa Museum, where the ship is displayed,
35 believe they have the answer. They measured every piece of wood in the ship and found that the vessel is asymmetrical and one side of the ship is much heavier than the other. How did this happen? The scientists discovered four rulers that the workman had used. But the rulers used different scales. Two used 'Swedish feet', which were divided into twelve inches, while the others used 'Amsterdam feet', which had eleven inches in each foot. So different carpenters were using different systems of
40 measurement and this led to the wood on one side being thicker than on the other.

Guided conversation

I can have a conversation about holiday plans.

Reply questions and question tags

a In reply questions and question tags, we use auxiliary verbs (*do, have, would,* etc.) or the verb *be.*

b We can use reply questions to respond to a statement. They express interest or surprise.
'We're nearly at the hotel.' 'Are we?'
'You didn't tell me.' 'Didn't I?'

c We can use a question tag when we want somebody to confirm what we are saying.
You booked the hotel, didn't you?
We aren't lost, are we?

1 Describe the photo and answer the questions below.

1 **VOCABULARY** Which of these activities are likely to be on offer at or near this location? Where could you do the others?

Holiday activities fishing hiking horse riding kayaking mountain biking scuba diving shopping sightseeing skiing swimming

2 Would you prefer to be on holiday here or in an expensive hotel in a city? Give reasons.

> **Speaking Strategy 1**
>
> Use your preparation time to read the task carefully. Make sure that you understand each of the points that you need to discuss. If you have time, think of two or three key pieces of information or vocabulary connected with each topic.

2 Read Speaking Strategy 1. Then read the task below. Under which of the four points in the task are you most likely to mention these?

1 a job
2 a month of the year
3 a popular tourist area
4 buses and trains
5 a week / a fortnight
6 borrowing / lending
7 youth hostels
8 beaches and the sea

> You are planning to go on holiday with friends this summer. Discuss the holiday with one of the friends. Make a decision about each of these four points:
> - when you want to go and for how long
> - choice of destination
> - transport
> - paying for the holiday

3 🎧 **3.28** Read Speaking Strategy 2. Then listen to a student doing the task above. Do you think he reacts appropriately during the conversation?

> **Speaking Strategy 2**
>
> In a guided conversation, it is important to interact appropriately with the other person. Do not just give your opinions and ignore what the other person is saying.

4 Read the Learn this! box. Write reply questions for statements 1, 3 and 5 and add question tags to statements 2, 4 and 6.

1 That's a long time!
2 The Baltic coast is lovely.
3 There's more to do there.
4 We need quite a lot of money.
5 My parents will give me some money too.
6 That's kind of them.

5 🎧 **3.28** Listen again and check your answers to exercise 4.

➡ **Grammar Builder 9.3 & 9.4** pages 142 and 143

6 **VOCABULARY** In pairs, check the meaning of the words below. Then discuss which types of accommodation you prefer.

Holiday accommodation B&B (bed and breakfast) campsite caravan site holiday camp hostel hotel self-catering apartment villa

> I prefer caravan sites to campsites.

> Do you? I prefer campsites.

7 Read the task below. Think about what ideas and vocabulary you will need for each point. Use notes 1–4 below to help you.

> You are planning to go away for a few days with your penfriend while he or she is visiting you this summer. Discuss your ideas with your penfriend. Make a decision about each of these four points:
> - choice of destination
> - accommodation
> - holiday activities
> - what you need to take with you

1 Think about destinations you know well and can talk about.
2 Use the list of words in exercise 1.
3 Use the list of words in exercise 6.
4 Think about clothing, equipment (for activities) and entertainment (books, gadgets, etc.).

8 **SPEAKING** Work in pairs. Do the task in exercise 7. Decide who is playing which role. Make sure you both respond appropriately to what the other person says.

9H Writing

A formal letter

I can write a formal letter of enquiry.

1 SPEAKING Describe the photo. Have you ever stayed in a youth hostel? How are they different from hotels?

2 Read the writing task and the letter. Has the writer covered all four points in the task?

> You are planning to visit Bristol in the UK this summer with a small group of friends and have been given a recommendation for a youth hostel. Write a letter to the youth hostel in which you:
> - give information about your group.
> - inform them of the dates you want to stay and ask about availability.
> - ask about food and drink.
> - ask for suggestions about places to visit in Bristol.

3 KEY PHRASES Look at the beginning and the end of the letter. Complete the rules in Writing Strategy 1. Use the phrases below.

Dear Miss / Mrs / Ms / Mr ... ,   Dear Sir or Madam,
Yours faithfully,   Yours sincerely,

Writing Strategy 1

- If you know the name of the person you are writing to, start with ¹_____ and finish with ²_____ followed by your signature and your full name.

- If you don't know the name of the person, start with ³_____ and finish with ⁴_____ followed by your signature and your full name.

Writing Strategy 2

1 Divide your letter into paragraphs.

2 In the first paragraph, which can be a single sentence, say why you are writing.

3 Each paragraph should have its own topic. It is usually best to deal with each point in the task in a separate paragraph.

4 In the final paragraph, which can be a single sentence, say that you expect a reply.

5 Avoid colloquial language and short forms.

---

4 Read Writing Strategy 2 and do the tasks below.

1 Divide the letter into six paragraphs.

2 Find three examples of short forms. Correct them.

3 Find words and phrases in the letter which would be better expressed with these more formal words and phrases:
   friends   I would be grateful if you could inform me
   I would certainly be interested   receiving a reply
   recommendations

4 Find words and phrases in the letter which express these things in a more formal way:
   ask about   soon   sort out   tell me about

Dear Sir or Madam,

I am writing to enquire about a visit to your youth hostel in Bristol next month. I'll be travelling to Bristol with three mates from school. All four of us are female and aged seventeen or eighteen. We're planning to stay for seven nights between 10 and 17 August. Please tell me whether you have beds available for those dates. I'd also like to know whether your youth hostel has a café or restaurant. If not, would it be possible to recommend any places to eat near the hostel which are not too expensive? This will be our first visit to Bristol. Although I have read about the city on the internet, I'd love to hear any tips for places to visit in the city. I look forward to getting an answer from you in due course so that we can finalise the details of our visit.

Yours faithfully,

Hazel Jones

Hazel Jones

> You are planning to visit York in the UK this summer with a friend from school and have been given a recommendation for a small hotel. Write a letter to the hotel in which you:
> - give information about who will be travelling and when.
> - enquire about prices and availability.
> - ask about the best way to get to the hotel using public transport.
> - ask about suggested activities in the surrounding area.

5 Read the task above. Make a paragraph plan and include brief notes for each of the four points in the task.

Paragraph 1: giving reason for writing
Paragraph 2: first point in task
Paragraph 3: second point in task
Paragraph 4: third point in task
Paragraph 5: fourth point in task
Paragraph 6: requesting a reply

6 Write your letter using your notes from exercise 5. Remember to follow the advice in the two strategies.

CHECK YOUR WORK

Have you ...
- covered all four points in the task?
- avoided contractions and informal language?
- divided the letter into paragraphs?
- opened and closed the letter correctly?

---

5 Exam Skills Trainer

Reading

Exam Strategy

In a four-option multiple-choice task, the questions always follow the order of the text. Read the whole text once, then go through the questions and eliminate any obviously incorrect options. Finally, go back and check the part of the text which relates to each question, and make your final choices.

1 Read the strategy above. Then quickly read the text. Now look at the questions and try to eliminate any obviously incorrect options.

2 Read the article about a 17th-century travel writer. Choose the best answer (A–D).

Thomas Coryat was not one of those famous explorers who found new trade routes or mapped unexplored territory. But in his time, he was an extremely well-known traveller and writer. In fact, his writings about his extensive tours of Europe and parts of Asia opened the eyes of many readers to the geography and customs of other countries.

Born in England in 1577, Coryat was educated at Winchester College and Oxford. Not long after he finished his education, he was employed by Prince Henry, the eldest son of King James I, as a royal entertainer. This is evidence of his intelligence and sense of humour, which later became more widely known through his travel writing.

In 1608, Coryat began a long tour of Europe, partly on foot. The book that he published about the tour in 1611 gives a lively picture of European life at the time. His book was extremely popular, partly because people were very curious about life in other countries. They also preferred reading about someone else's adventures to travelling, since travel was difficult and dangerous at the time. Later the same year, Coryat published a second book giving more details about his journey.

Unable to settle down for long, in 1612 Coryat started on another tour. This time he decided to go beyond Europe, and eventually travelled to the eastern Mediterranean, Persia and India. He sent home detailed letters describing his experiences and observations. These were published while he was still abroad. If he had lived longer, he would certainly have published a book about this trip, but his life was cut short by illness in 1617.

Not only were Coryat's writings entertaining and very popular, but they also influenced society in unexpected ways. People say that he brought the table fork to the attention of English society, and that he introduced the word 'umbrella' into the English language. His work is also important to music historians – a lot of their knowledge of Venetian musicians and composers of the time depends on his accounts. At about this time, rich people began to send their sons to Europe to see great monuments and works of art. Today, historians call this journey 'the Grand Tour', and they think that the tradition partly began because of Coryat's books.

1 The writer says that Coryat
  A was like some of the great explorers.
  B taught people a lot with his writing.
  C discovered new places.
  D started out making maps.
2 The fact that Prince Henry hired Coryat shows us that
  A Coryat was a well-known writer.
  B the prince was very clever.
  C Coryat was amusing.
  D Coryat was a talented actor.
3 What is true about Coryat's first book?
  A It described places that many people were interested in.
  B It encouraged people to travel.
  C It convinced readers that travel was safe.
  D It made walking tours popular.
4 Why did Coryat not publish a book about his 1612–1617 trip?
  A He decided to only write letters.
  B Nobody was interested in publishing his writing.
  C There wasn't very much to write about the trip.
  D He died before he could write it.
5 Which is the best title for the article?
  A The discoverer of new worlds
  B A travelling entertainer
  C A writer who changed our ideas about travel
  D The first man to write about travel

Listening

Exam Strategy

When completing a summary of a listening, first read through the summary to get an idea of what the listening text will be about. Think of possible answers to fill the gaps.

3 Read the strategy above. Then read the summary in exercise 4 and try to think of possible answers.

4 🎧 3.29 You will hear a dialogue between two friends about teenagers and mobile phones. Complete the information in the summary. Use no more than three words in each gap.

Erin was reading a magazine article about mobile phones. The article reported that some ¹_____ had to sign a contract with their parents about how much they could use their mobiles. Erin agreed that the contract was ²_____ . However, Carl said that he ³_____ if he was asked to sign a document. He insisted that his parents ⁴_____ him to keep his promises. He also said that he wasn't ⁵_____ phones and he complained that it was ⁶_____ that Erin spent so much time on her phone.

Use of English

5 Read the strategy above. Complete the text with words formed from the words in brackets.

A hovercraft is a unique kind of vehicle which has the ¹_____ (able) to travel over any kind of terrain: land, water, mud, or ice. It has special engines that blow air below the vehicle. The pressure of this air is ²_____ (high) than the pressure in the atmosphere and the ³_____ (different) in the pressure lifts the hovercraft above the surface so that it can travel over small obstacles quite ⁴_____ (easy), making it one of the most ⁵_____ (environment) friendly vehicles in the world.

The hovercraft was first designed in Britain in the 1950s. Today, these vehicles are used all over the world. They are particularly ⁶_____ (use) during disasters, because they can get to places that a boat or a helicopter can't reach. The ⁷_____ (manufacture) have created hovercraft in various sizes. The smaller models are easy to drive and their designers always have ⁸_____ (safe) in mind.

Speaking

6 Read the strategy above. Then read the situation below. Write notes for each question.

Describe a situation when you used a mobile phone to solve a problem.
- When and where did it happen?
- Who used the phone?
- What problem did you solve?
- How did you feel?

7 These photos (A and B) show people using their mobile phones to solve a problem. Compare and contrast the photos. Include the following points:

- Where are the people and what are they doing?
- What problems can they solve using a mobile phone?
- What other means of communication could they use?

8 In pairs, discuss questions 1 and 2 below. Use evidence from the photos in your discussion, if possible.

1. Is it important to carry a mobile phone with you at all times?
2. What dangers may be connected to using a mobile phone in certain situations?

Writing

9 Read the strategy above. Then read the student's letter. Find eight grammar, vocabulary and spelling mistakes and correct them.

Dear Sir / Madam,

I'm writing complain about a bus journey that I made on one of your coaches on 28th January. I took the 14.20 coach from Ostrava to Prague.

First of all, the coach delayed for over two hours, but the passengers were not told when it would be leaving and they were left waiting on the bus stop in freezing weather. Secondly, I had bought my ticket online, but when I'm showing it to the driver, I was told that I could not use it for that particular travel and I had to buy another one. When we finaly set off, the heating on the coach was not working and it was really cold!

I believe that you should improve your service. If a coach is late, you should make sure that the passengers inform about this and that they are told what time the coach will leave. I would also suggest that you explain the conditions clearly on your website. Lastly, there should be heating on your coaches in January.

I hope my sugestions are useful and I look forward to your reply.

Yours faithfully,

Alex

10 Read the task below and write a letter of complaint to the airline operator.

You recently travelled by plane and you were very dissatisfied with the airline's service. Write a letter of complaint in which you describe what went wrong and suggest how the airline company could improve their service.

Reading

1 Read the strategy above. Then match the best summary statement (1–3) to with the extracts from three texts (A–C).

A Art and personality

The author makes the case for how even the smallest life events can have an influence on an artist's work.

B Barbara Hepworth: A life of forms

This biography of Hepworth shows the impact of her passion for sculpture on her private life.

C Picture this: How pictures work

How do different lines, colours and shapes affect the emotions? This book explores this theme in depth.

The author of the book

1 analyses the effect of art and design on the viewer.
2 links its subject's personal and professional life.
3 argues that each life experience affects artists' work.

2 Read the book reviews. Match the book reviews (A–C) with the sentences (1–6). Each book review matches two sentences.

A Paul Gauguin: A complete life

This new biography, based on original research and extensive travel by the author, tries to find the truth about the eccentric painter and sculptor Paul Gauguin. Many myths have grown up around Gauguin's life story, and the writer of this book attempts to clear them up. He examines the artist's unusual childhood, which was spent partly in France and partly in Peru. He also closely examines the unhappy time that Gauguin spent as a businessman, and why he left France for a new life on the Pacific islands. The writer paints a colourful picture of this complicated man, who created some of the most famous works of 19th century art.

B Images from the underworld

While the cave paintings found in Europe are very well-known to the general public through books and articles, the cave paintings of Guatemala are hardly known at all. This book tries to correct that by taking us inside the deep caves where the ancient Mayan people recorded their lives, traditions and beliefs. The book helps us understand these ancient people, and also illustrates and analyses many unique works, some of which have since been destroyed by vandals. Not many of us can travel to see these amazing paintings, but reading this book gives us a good idea of what they are like.

C Artful collage from found objects

Many craft books today are published to promote products that you can buy from a shop and put together with little effort or creativity. This book goes back to the basics, guiding the reader through the process of creating art by using objects that you can find in your home, on your travels or in the natural environment. The book covers all the basic techniques of collage – the art of sticking things onto a picture surface. It then goes on to suggests themes, the best materials to use, and how to preserve and display your finished projects.

In this book, the author

1 discusses works of art that can no longer be seen. ___
2 tries to correct some untrue ideas about its subject. ___
3 enables readers to develop their own creativity. ___
4 gives information about less well-known works of art. ___
5 suggests unusual places to find things for use in art. ___
6 creates an interesting picture of an artist. ___

Listening

3 🎧 **4.02** You will hear an interview with a business expert twice. Choose the correct answers, A, B, C or D.

1 The interviewer thinks young people
   A usually set up part-time businesses.
   B never achieve international success.
   C are starting new businesses at a lower age than previously.
   D should only set up small businesses.

2 The interviewer doesn't understand
   A how young people can create successful businesses.
   B how most new businesses actually work.
   C where the money for new businesses comes from.
   D why young people would want to start businesses.

3 Lisa says that very young people
   A are unlikely to create successful businesses.
   B do not achieve business success very often.
   C do not understand what they need to do to start a business.
   D have the right qualities for creating businesses.

4 What does Lisa say about knowledge and experience?
   A They are very necessary.
   B They take a lot of time to develop.
   C They can sometimes be a disadvantage.
   D They are the best tools for solving problems.

5 Why does Lisa believe young people 'think outside the box'?
   A They've learned what the 'right' answers are.
   B They don't feel there's only one way to do things.
   C Education is more creative than it was in the past.
   D They've grown up with digital technology.

6 Lisa thinks young people use digital technology
  A to be more positive.
  B to avoid making mistakes.
  C to feel more confident about success.
  D to connect with customers in new ways.

7 What is Lisa talking about when she says 'no one likes to hear this'?
  A the fact that rules must be followed
  B the idea that troublemakers may be good at business
  C the idea that listening to others is important
  D the fact that few people succeed in business

8 In general, how does Lisa feel about young people in business?
  A She's very positive about their qualities.
  B She doubts their skills.
  C She admires their ambition.
  D She's not optimistic about their chance of success.

Use of English

> **Strategy**
> Word formation tasks test you on vocabulary as well as grammar. Learn common endings for nouns (e.g. *or, er, ance, ity, ion, ness*), adjectives (e.g. *able, y, ful, less*) and adverbs (*ly, ily*).

4 Complete the text with words formed from the words in brackets.

Bonsai

Bonsai, one of many art forms for which Japan is famous, involves ¹_____ (GROW) trees in shallow ²_____ (CONTAIN) so that they never grow taller than two metres. Bonsai trees that are bigger than 152 cm are called Imperial bonsai and they are usually grown outdoors. Most bonsai trees are between 20 and 60 cm, however, and these smaller trees can be kept indoors. The ³_____ (SMALL) kind of bonsai is called *Keshitsubo*, which only grows up to 2.5 cm. Although bonsai is now strongly associated with Japanese culture, the tradition first started in China about 1,500 years ago. There, it was known as *penzai*. Pictures of *penzai* can be seen ⁴_____ (CLEAR) on ancient Chinese drawings. Some people think it is ⁵_____ (HARM) to trees to grow them as bonsai, but bonsai trees aren't damaged or genetically modified in any way. Bonsai growers take great care when looking after their trees and use their artistic ⁶_____ (IMAGINE) to decide how to shape them. Many different species of trees are ⁷_____ (SUIT) for growing as bonsai trees. Sometimes one kind of tree is shaped so that it takes on the ⁸_____ (APPEAR) of a different species.

Speaking

> **Strategy**
> If you have to talk about one picture, imagine you are describing it to someone who can't see it. This will help you focus on the details. Don't forget to include information about all the points you're given.

5 Talk about the photo for one minute. Include information about the points below.

the activity   the relationship between the people
what they are talking about   how they are feeling

6 'It's better to work alone because people in groups spend too much time talking.' Do you agree? Why? Why not? Give reasons for your answers.

Writing

> **Strategy**
> An essay may require you to express an opinion on a topic. As well as giving your own opinion, you need to consider and write about different points of view.

7 Read the essay title and answer the questions below.

In some countries, CCTV cameras are installed in classrooms. Is it a good idea? Write an essay in which you present your opinion and arguments for it.
1 What is your experience of the topic?
2 What are your first thoughts about the topic?

8 Look at the arguments for and against CCTV cameras in classrooms. Divide the arguments into two categories: a) effects on security and b) effects on privacy.

stopping bad behaviour   less theft at break times
more stressed teachers and students   students have rights
fewer problems for school authorities
nobody likes people watching them

9 Read the task below and write the essay.

More and more people listen to music for free on websites rather paying to download music or buying CDs. Is this a good thing? Write an essay in which you present your opinion and discuss it from the point of view of musicians and music fans.

B2 Exam Skills Trainer 2

Reading

> **Strategy**
> When doing a missing sentences task, look for reference words like *it*, *him*, *this*, *that*, *here* and *there*. Reference words are used to avoid repetition, and they usually relate to words or phrases which come before them.

1 Read the strategy above. Complete the sentences with the reference words below.

that them there those

1 There are some people over there. Let's ask _____ .
2 He was hungry. Maybe _____ is why he got so angry.
3 The Fig Tree was a small shop near my school. You could buy all kinds of sweets _____ .
4 Some people stayed and some people went home. _____ who left early missed a great night!

2 Now read the text and match sentences A–G with gaps 1–6. There is one extra sentence .

It was getting dark, and Marcus was becoming desperate for a little rest, some kind of a meal and a long cold drink. The sound of insects was getting louder as evening fell. Now and then, a bird called out above them, somewhere up in the trees. The warm rainforest smell of damp vegetation and soil filled his nostrils, like the scent of a well-kept greenhouse. **¹___** Now, though, he was starting to feel that he wanted to be free of it. The air seemed even warmer, stickier and heavier than usual and he wished for a cool breeze.

They had been walking through the jungle for four days now, and their supplies were running low. **²___** All they saw as they walked was trees and more trees.

This was not what Marcus had signed up for. The purpose of the trip had been to find samples of rare plants that were only found in this part of the Amazon rainforest. **³___** The organiser of the trip had told them that it should take no more than a couple of days to reach the area, collect their samples and return to the village where the research station was located.

What he had failed to tell them, though, was that the jeep was in a terrible state, and could break down at any moment. **⁴___** The engine had caught fire, and they had no way to repair the damage. Their satellite phones – which were their lifeline in an emergency – failed to work at all. The whole trip had been a total disaster!

Marcus stopped for a second and leaned forward to catch his breath. His shirt was sticking uncomfortably to his skin and his backpack felt heavy. He called out to the two men ahead of him, 'Are we thinking of stopping any time soon? I'm nearly ready to collapse!'

Eric stopped and turned. There was a wide smile on his face. 'Good news!' he said. 'I think we're going to have a much better rest than in last night's camp.' 'What do you mean? You don't …' Marcus began. He ran forward to join the others. **⁵___** And now he could smell cooking too: vegetables and meat or maybe fish. He had no idea of where they were, but at least they were *somewhere*, and the happiness that he felt was

almost too much for him. He grabbed Eric's arm to keep from falling over, and felt a tear run down his face.

Marcus hadn't been able to tell the others how frightened he had been – how sure he had felt that they would never find their way out of the jungle. And if they hadn't found this village, how long would they have survived? **⁶___** They were going to be able to eat and sleep, and that was all Marcus needed to think about right now.

A They had prepared themselves thoroughly for it, bringing maps, scientific equipment and satellite phones with them.
B There, just visible through the trees, was a group of small huts.
C That was why they had brought satellite phones with them.
D They would never know, but it didn't matter now.
E Marcus had loved it at the beginning.
F But they seemed no closer to civilisation than they had been when their jeep had broken down.
G Well, it had done exactly that – and in spectacular fashion!

Listening

> **Strategy**
> In multiple matching tasks, one or more options may summarise the function of what a speaker is saying (e.g. *claim*, *predict*, *remember*, *insist on*). Listening to the speaker's tone of voice and the phrases they use to express their feeling will help you choose the correct answers.

3 Read the strategy above. Paraphrase the sentences using the verbs below. Start each sentence with 'The speaker …'

regret doubt want be pleased be convinced

1 'I'm sure James will win.'
2 'I wish it would rain.'
3 'I'm so glad everyone came.'
4 'If only I hadn't dropped Sam's phone!'
5 'I'm pretty sure the radio won't work.'

4 🎧 4.03 You will hear four speakers talking about forms of writing twice. Match statements A–E with speakers 1–4. There is one statement that you do not need.

The speaker
A thinks that a change is bad for young people.
B regrets never having learned a form of writing.
C was thrilled to learn about an old form of writing.
D regrets not learning a form of writing earlier.
E believes a form of writing is simpler than it appears.

Speaker 1		Speaker 2		Speaker 3		Speaker 4	

Use of English

5 Choose the correct words to complete the text.

You probably think of paper banknotes **¹___** you hear the words 'printed money'. In the past, however, materials like wood, leather, clay, or thin metal were **²___** and used as money. And nowadays, many banknotes are made of a kind of plastic that looks like paper, but **³___** is far stronger.

Paper money was first used in China over a thousand years ago. At that time, it took the form of notes that had a handwritten promise of payment on them, **⁴___** the machine-printed banknotes that we use today. The first printed banknotes **⁵___** in Europe in 1661.

The first ATM, or cash machine, was **⁶___** in London in June 1967. Plastic bank cards didn't exist at that time. **⁷___** get money out of the machines, people had to put cheques into them and enter a four-digit PIN.

Some people predict that we won't be paying for things with cash much longer. They think people will just use their mobile phones to **⁸___** a purchase. However, there are still billions of banknotes in circulation around the world today, and it looks **⁹___** though we will be using them for many more years to come.

1	A supposing	B when	C unless	D while
2	A bruised	B impressed	C represented	D stamped
3	A what	B which	C this	D so
4	A whereas	B unlike	C similar	D alike
5	A appeared	B occurred	C presented	D developed
6	A installed	B planted	C fixed	D placed
7	A For	B They	C So	D To
8	A make	B take	C do	D get
9	A if	B as	C that	D like

Speaking

6 Read the strategy above. Then answer the questions below.

1 Do you usually wear smart or casual clothes? Why? Has your style been different in the past? If so, how?

2 Think of someone who wears very different clothes from you. Do you like their style? Why? / Why not?

3 Do you think it's a good idea for children to wear school uniform? Why? / Why not?

4 What sort of judgements do people make about other people based on their clothes and personal appearance?

5 Do you think society puts too much pressure on young people to follow fashions? Why? /Why not?

6 In what ways do you think people can use body language and the way they dress to convey a positive impression?

Writing

7 Read the Strategy. Then decide if the sentences below are recommendations or opinions. Write *R* or *O*.

1 Some of the double rooms are rather small, so it's advisable to ask for a large room. ___

2 The hotel benefits from a large garden, which is full of beautiful trees and flowers. ___

3 One drawback is that the hotel has no parking. ___

4 The third-floor restaurant is worth visiting, as it offers many local specialities. ___

5 I suggest booking a room at least three weeks ahead. ___

6 The location is a huge advantage, as the hotel is situated between the sea and the train station. ___

8 Read the task below and write the report.

A local magazine is interested to know which local cafés and restaurants are most popular with families and young people.

We are putting together a list of cafés and restaurants which are popular with families and young people in your area.

Please send us a short report about a café or restaurant which you like visiting with your friends or family. Give:
- a brief description of the place and the food.
- your views.
- any recommendations.

Ethnic minorities in the UK

1 **SPEAKING** Describe the photo opposite. Does it match your idea of typical British children? Why? / Why not?

2 Read the text. Where did immigrants to Britain mostly come from …

1 in the 1950s?
2 in the 1960s and 1970s?
3 in the first decade of the 21st century?

3 Read the text again. Are these sentences true or false? Write T or F.

1 In the 20th century, immigrants to Britain mainly came from countries that used to be part of the British Empire. ___
2 People from the Caribbean were invited to come and work in Britain. ___
3 Britain has generally refused to adopt any traditions of immigrant cultures. ___
4 Many Asian immigrants came from other British colonies. ___
5 The majority of immigrants to Britain in the 21st century do not settle permanently. ___

4 🎧 **4.05** Listen to five people whose families emigrated to Britain talking about their lives. What is the ethnic origin of each speaker?

5 🎧 **4.05** Listen again. Match sentences A–F below with the speakers (1–5). Some sentences match with more than one speaker.

Which speaker(s) …
A have experienced racism in the UK? ___
B make a negative comment about the weather? ___
C did not personally emigrate to Britain? ___
D consider themselves British? ___
E mention good British friends? ___
F mention problems finding a job? ___

6 **SPEAKING** Discuss questions 1 and 2 in pairs. You can use the phrases below to help you.

I think people might …   In my view …
I'm not certain, but …   It could be that …
It's probably true to say that …

1 What are some of the reasons why people emigrate to another country?
2 Do you know any immigrants to your country? Where are they from? Why are they there?

🎧 **4.04**

BRITAIN – a mix of cultures

Britain has always been a mixture of different nationalities and cultures. The country itself is made up of four nations – England, Scotland, Wales and Northern Ireland – each with its own cultural heritage. Back in the 17th century, Britain became a global power and gained an enormous empire. By the 1920s, the empire was home to 458 million people – a fifth of the world's population! But forty years later, most of the colonies had gained their independence, and immigrants from Britain's former colonies had begun to arrive in the UK and contribute to its multicultural society.

The longest-established ethnic minority in Britain is the black Caribbean population. After the Second World War, there was a labour shortage in the UK and people from Jamaica and Trinidad, former British colonies, were encouraged to come and work in Britain. In 1948, five hundred came over on the steamship *Empire Windrush*, and throughout the following decade, thousands more arrived. Many immigrants experienced some form of racism at that time. However, Caribbean culture – especially food and musical styles such as ska and reggae – gradually became part of British life. The Notting Hill Carnival – the biggest street festival in Europe – was started by Caribbean immigrants.

Another wave of immigration to the UK occurred in the 1960s and 1970s. India and Pakistan were formerly part of the British Empire, and many people arrived from those countries. In previous decades, Indians and Pakistanis had also gone to work in British colonies in Africa. But after those African countries gained independence, Asians were forced to leave and came to the UK. Asians in Britain formed a close community and on the whole retained their own customs and languages. However, Indian food is now part of British culture, with Indian restaurants found all over the country. Curry is one of Britain's most popular meals.

Since the expansion of the European Union in 2004, the UK has seen more immigrants from continental Europe. Most come to work in Britain and then return home after a few years, but others have chosen to settle in their new homeland.

Tinseltown

1 SPEAKING Discuss these questions in pairs.

1 What were the last three films you saw?
2 Where did you see them?
3 How many of the films were made in America? Do you like American films? Why? / Why not?

2 Read the text. Match paragraphs A–D with the correct headings (1–4).

1 'Talkies' take over ___
2 Moving west ___
3 Fewer but bigger ___
4 The Golden Age ___

3 Answer the questions in your own words.

1 Why did early film studios want to move away from New York?
2 Why did cinema audiences in the 1920s often hear piano music during films?
3 Why were Hollywood films particularly popular during hard times?
4 Why were cinema audiences smaller from the 1960s onwards?

4 🎧**4.07** Listen to an interview about some of the biggest failures in cinema history. Which film does the guest think was the best of the three?

When Time Ran Out   Sahara   Hulk

5 🎧**4.07** Listen again and circle the correct answers (a–c).

1 Why is it not surprising that the interviewer doesn't know the films they discuss?
   a They are all from the 1970s or earlier.
   b They were not made by well-known directors.
   c They were not seen by many people.
2 Which part of *When Time Ran Out* is most likely to make you laugh, according to the guest?
   a The special effects.
   b The ending.
   c The acting.
3 Why did *Sahara* lose so much money?
   a The stars of the film demanded big salaries.
   b The film was extremely expensive to make.
   c Audiences for the film were small.
4 Why was *Hulk* not a commercial success?
   a It had to compete with other more successful movies based on comic book characters.
   b It did not appeal to people who usually like this genre.
   c It was visually very appealing, but boring in other ways.

🎧**4.06**

A The first American films were made in the very early years of the 20th century. At that time, the centre of the film industry was New York, where the inventor Thomas Edison had huge power because he had patented a lot of the film-making equipment. Around 1910, film studios began to move to the west coast, as far away from New York – and from Edison – as possible. Hollywood was born.

B For most of the 1920s, Hollywood produced 'silent movies' with no speaking or soundtrack. When these movies were shown in cinemas, a pianist or organist played music while the audience watched. By the late 1920s, the technology existed to add sound – but not everybody liked the idea. 'Who wants to hear actors talk?' said Harry Warner, the owner of one of the largest studios. But he was wrong, and silent movies soon became a thing of the past.

C Between the 1930s and the 1950s, the big Hollywood studios, like MGM and Paramount, were making hundreds of films a year. Cinema tickets cost only a few cents, and millions went to see the latest films, even in times of war or recession – in fact, especially during those times, because movies offered a form of escapism. But by the 1950s, cinema had a rival: television. And as the famous Polish-born film producer Samuel Goldwyn said, 'Why should people go out and pay money to see bad films when they can stay at home and see bad television for nothing?'

D By the 1960s, cinema audiences had declined, mainly because of the popularity of TV, and Hollywood had to change. They began to make fewer films each year, concentrating on a small number of expensive blockbusters. This is basically still their approach today. A box office hit can make a lot of money for the studio and the investors, but a failure can be a major disaster.

6 SPEAKING Discuss these questions in pairs.

1 What is the worst film you've ever seen, in your opinion? What was so bad about it?
2 Did you watch the film with other people? If so, what did they think of it?
3 Are there certain types of film that you often dislike? What are they?

7 SPEAKING Share your ideas from exercise 6 with the class. Did anybody else choose the same film? Are there certain types of film which are generally unpopular?

British sporting events

1 SPEAKING Answer the quiz questions (1–6) in pairs. Choose from the sports below.

cricket football golf horse racing
motor racing rowing rugby tennis

1 The Open and the Ryder Cup are both famous events in which sport?
2 In which sport does a British team compete against teams from other countries in the Davis Cup?
3 In which sport do England, Wales, Scotland, Ireland, France and Italy compete in a competition called the Six Nations?
4 In which sport do Oxford and Cambridge compete on the River Thames each year?
5 If England is playing Australia at Lords in an Ashes match, what sport is it?
6 The Grand National and the Derby are both famous events for which sport?

2 🎧 **4.08** Listen and check your answers to the quiz in exercise 1. Which contestant wins: John or Milly?

3 Read the fact files. Which of these pieces of information (a–f) are in all three fact files?

a when the event was first held
b prize money
c where the event is held
d frequent winners
e when the event is held
f size of the audience

4 SPEAKING Work in pairs. Decide on the advantages and disadvantages of seeing a major sporting event a) live at the event and b) on television. Use the words below and your own ideas.

action replay atmosphere close-ups
commentators / commentary convenience
cost crowds excitement memories

5 INTERNET RESEARCH Find out about a sporting event in your own country. Use the list in exercise 3 to help you. Present the information as a fact file.

ROYAL ASCOT

♛ Ascot Racecourse in the south of England is less than 10 km from Windsor Castle, a royal residence, and has been a horse racing venue for more than three hundred years.

♛ Royal Ascot takes place every June and lasts for five days. Each day begins with the arrival of the royal party.

♛ Spectators who enter the Royal Enclosure at Ascot must be dressed formally, including top hats for men.

♛ The Queen is a fan of horse racing and has owned 22 winners at Ascot. Owners can receive up to £350,000 if their horse wins a race.

THE FA CUP FINAL

⚽ The FA Cup is a competition for football clubs from all divisions of the English league and has been held every year since 1872, except during the two World Wars.

⚽ The clubs which have won the trophy most often are Manchester United and Arsenal (both twelve times) and Tottenham Hotspur (eight times). The winning team receives £1.8 million.

⚽ Since 1923, the final has been played at Wembley Stadium in London. About 200,000 spectators watched the first Wembley final, far more than the official capacity of the stadium.

⚽ During the 1956 final, Manchester City goalkeeper Bert Trautmann broke his neck. However, he kept playing for the remaining seventeen minutes and made several important saves, helping his team to victory.

THE WIMBLEDON CHAMPIONSHIPS

🎾 The Championships are held for two weeks every summer at the All England Lawn Tennis Club in London.

🎾 About half a million spectators come to watch the tennis matches live, while TV coverage is seen by roughly 380 million people in nearly 200 countries.

🎾 In 1968, the prize money was £2,000 for the men's singles champion and £750 for the women's singles champion. Between 1877, when the event started, and 1968, the winners received nothing.

🎾 These days, men and women receive equal prize money – nearly £2 million for a singles title.

4 Culture

Royal palaces

1 SPEAKING Work in pairs. Discuss the questions.

1 Have you visited any castles or palaces in your country? Which are the most famous ones? Why?
2 Do you recognise the palace in the photo? What do you know about it?

2 Cover the fact file. Discuss and try to guess the answers to the quiz about Buckingham Palace.

How many ...

1 ... rooms are there?
   a 263   b 542   c 775
2 ... people work there?
   a over 600   b over 800   c over 1,000
3 ... clocks are there?
   a 150   b 250   c 350
4 ... guests are entertained there every year?
   a over 10,000 b over 50,000 c over 100,000
5 ... people can have dinner together?
   a 150   b 370   c 600
6 ... times has the Palace been broken into?
   a none   b 6   c 12

3 Read the fact file and check your answers to exercises 1 and 2. What do you think is the most interesting or surprising fact?

4 🎧4.09 Listen to a radio programme. Complete the information about the Queen's residences. Use the places below in the first column.

Belfast, Northern Ireland   Edinburgh, Scotland
the Highlands, Scotland   London, England
near London, England   Norfolk, England

Royal Residence	Location	Private or state-owned?
Buckingham Palace		
Windsor Castle		
Sandringham House		
Balmoral Castle		
Holyrood Palace		
Hillsborough Castle		

5 🎧4.09 Listen again and complete each sentence with up to three words.

1 When the Queen is in this country, she has quite a strict _____ .
2 Once a week she has a meeting with with the British _____ .
3 The Queen usually spends _____ at Windsor Castle.
4 Windsor Castle has been a royal home since _____ .
5 The Royal Family spend _____ at Sandringham House.
6 Sandringham House was damaged in the First _____ .
7 The Queen spends the _____ in Scotland.
8 Queen Victoria bought Balmoral because she really liked _____ .
9 Buckingham Palace receives lots of _____ when it is open during the summer.

Buckingham Palace

* Buckingham Palace is the Queen's official London residence, but she doesn't own it. It belongs to the state.

* The first monarch to use Buckingham Palace as her official residence was Queen Victoria, who moved there in 1837.

* Buckingham Palace is like a small town – it has a chapel, post office, swimming pool, staff cafeteria, doctor's surgery, cinema and police station.

* It has seven hundred and seventy-five rooms. Fifty-two are Royal and guest bedrooms and seventy-eight are bathrooms. There are one hundred and eighty-eight bedrooms for the staff.

* There are secret tunnels under the streets of London, connecting the Palace to the Houses of Parliament.

* The gardens are huge – sixteen hectares – and include tennis courts, a lake and a helicopter landing area. There are thirty species of birds and three hundred and fifty species of wild flowers; some of them are very rare indeed.

* Over eight hundred people work at the palace, including two people who work full-time to look after the palace's three hundred and fifty clocks!

* The Queen has over fifty thousand guests each year at lunches, dinners, receptions and parties. The kitchens are able to serve a sit-down dinner for six hundred people at one time.

* Hundreds of famous people have visited the palace, including Mozart, J. F. Kennedy, Nelson Mandela, Pope John Paul II, and Mahatma Gandhi – in his loincloth and sandals!

* The palace has been broken into on at least six occasions. Teenager Edward Jones broke in three times between 1838 and 1841 and stole some of Queen Victoria's underwear! Michael Fagin broke in in 1992 and went to Queen Elizabeth's bedroom, where he woke her up before he was arrested.

6 SPEAKING Discuss these questions in pairs. Give reasons for your opinions.

1 What do you think about Queen Elizabeth's way of life? Would you enjoy being king or queen? Why? / Why not?
2 Do you think it is right that one family should have so many places to live?
3 What would your ideal house be like?

Benjamin Franklin

1 SPEAKING Can you think of any famous people from your own country's history who were famous for more than one reason? Use the words below to help you.

actor composer explorer inventor musician
politician / statesman scientist soldier
sportsman / sportswoman writer

2 🎧 4.10 Read the introductory paragraph. Then listen. Complete the missing dates in the timeline of Benjamin Franklin's life.

Benjamin Franklin is a giant of American history, partly because he was successful in so many different areas. Today, he is perhaps remembered mostly as a scientist and inventor, but he was also a publisher, a musician, a newspaper owner, a politician and a philosopher. And he was able to do all of this despite quite a poor background.

1706	Born in Boston, USA, the eighth of ten children.
1____	Leaves school after only two years because his parents cannot afford to pay.
1718	Starts working for his brother James, a printer.
1728	Starts his own printing company in Philadelphia.
2____	Becomes owner of a newspaper, the *Pennsylvania Gazette*.
1731	Founds America's first lending library.
3____	Begins to publish the first in a series of almanacs, yearly books containing interesting facts, stories and puzzles. Their success makes Franklin rich.
1748	Retires from printing to spend more time on science and experiments.
1750	Publishes important work on electricity.
4____	Carries out his famous experiment with a kite in a storm.
1776	Becomes the first American Ambassador to France, and works to improve the relationship between the two countries.
1785	Retires from politics.
5____	Dies at the age of 84. Funeral is attended by 20,000 people.

3 🎧 4.10 Listen again and complete the collocations with the verbs below.

attend build carry out found publish
retire start write

1 _____ your own business
2 _____ an article for a newspaper
3 _____ a book
4 _____ a hospital
5 _____ a scientific experiment
6 _____ strong relations between two countries
7 _____ from a job
8 _____ a funeral

4 SPEAKING Describe the picture using the words below. Have you heard of this experiment? What do you think Franklin was trying to discover?

cord electricity key kite
lightning spark storm clouds

5 🎧 4.11 Listen to a news report about Franklin's famous kite experiment. Are the sentences true or false? Write T or F.

1 Franklin's experiment became well known in America and other countries too. ___
2 According to the traditional story, Franklin bought a kite and attached a piece of metal to it. ___
3 According to the story, Franklin put his hand near the piece of metal and felt an electrical spark. ___
4 Dr Tom Tucker began investigating the experiment while working at a university. ___
5 Dr Tucker first became suspicious after reading Franklin's own reports of the experiment. ___
6 Dr Tucker successfully recreated Franklin's experiment when he used a modern kite. ___
7 Dr Tucker thinks that Franklin's theories about electricity were correct, even if his report of the experiment was invented. ___

6 SPEAKING In pairs, discuss these quotations by Benjamin Franklin. Decide what they mean and whether you agree or disagree with them.

'Hard work is the mother of good luck.'

'Some people die at 25 and aren't buried until 75.'

'Having been poor is no shame, but being ashamed of it, is.'

British public schools

🎧 **4.12**

In the UK, 93% of children go to state schools, which are funded by the government. The remaining 7% go to private schools, which the government does not fund or control. The students pay fees to attend these schools. A small group of very old private schools are, confusingly, known as 'public schools'. These include Eton College, which has educated nineteen British Prime Ministers over the past three centuries – as well as many other famous people from around the world, including Prince William and Prince Harry, actor Hugh Laurie and the former king of Nepal.

To many people, these public schools seem very odd and old-fashioned, with their strange uniforms and confusing traditions. For example, all of the public schools divide the academic year into three terms. At Eton College, these are called 'halves', but at Charterhouse they're called 'quarters' (and the shortest of the three is known as the 'long quarter').

Although private schools seem irrelevant to most British people, the influence they have on society is very real. That is because a very large number of people in important positions attended these schools, including 71% of senior judges and 62% of senior officers in the armed forces. Some people even argue that the UK parliament does not represent the country because 32% of MPs are privately educated.

1 SPEAKING Describe the photo, which shows children having breakfast at a 'public school' in England. How is it different from the canteen at your school? Would you like to eat here? Why? / Why not?

2 Read the text. Which of these sentences is true about schools in the UK?

a All 'public schools' are private schools.
b All private schools are 'public schools'.
c All state schools are 'public schools'.

3 VOCABULARY Match a–f with 1–6 to make compounds. They are all in the text.

1 state   a year
2 private   b minister
3 prime   c forces
4 academic   d school
5 senior   e officer
6 armed   f school

4 Read the text again. Complete labels 1–5 in the charts with the correct words.

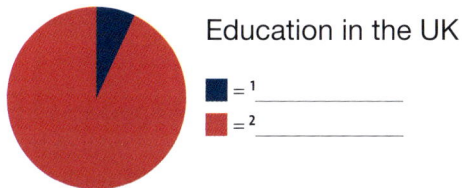

Education in the UK

■ = ¹ _____
■ = ² _____

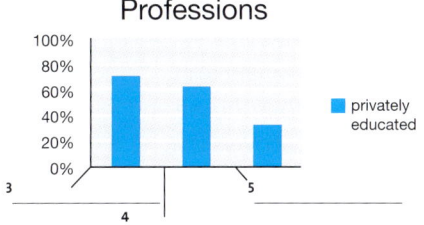

Professions

5 🎧 **4.13** Listen to a radio interview about public schools. How many public schools do they mention?

6 🎧 **4.13** Listen again and circle the correct answers (a–d).

1 David Brown decided to write a book about public school traditions because
  a they reminded him of his own school days.
  b he's always had an interest in public schools.
  c he works in a public school.
  d somebody else asked him to write it.
2 'The Wall Game' is a game which
  a is only played at a small number of public schools.
  b has been played since 1909.
  c involves kicking a ball over a wall to score.
  d has very few goals.
3 The sport of rugby was invented
  a by a schoolboy called Rugby in 1823.
  b by a schoolboy called Ellis at a school called Rugby College.
  c in various different countries around the same time.
  d at Eton College.
4 What does the game called 'the Greaze' involve?
  a Students throw books at a cook.
  b Students make a pancake.
  c Students try to get a piece of a pancake.
  d Students throw a pancake as high as possible.

7 SPEAKING What traditions are there in schools in your country? Use the ideas below to help you.

ceremonies   clothes   first / last day at school
food   graduation   public holidays
shows and performances   songs

Charles Dickens

1 SPEAKING Work in pairs. Have you heard of the writer Dickens? Can you name anything he wrote? Have you ever seen a film or TV version of something he wrote?

2 🎧4.14 In pairs, do the quiz about the life and works of Dickens. Circle the correct answers (a–c). Then listen and check your answers.

1 Where was Dickens born?
   a west coast of England
   b east coast of England
   c south coast of England
2 In which century did Dickens live?
   a 18th   b 19th   c 20th
3 What genre of writing is Dickens most famous for?
   a novels   b plays   c poetry
4 Which city did Dickens often write about?
   a London   b Liverpool   c New York
5 What is Scrooge, the Dickens character in the picture, famous for?
   a his kindness
   b his pessimism
   c his meanness

3 🎧4.14 Listen again. Complete the titles of works by Dickens with the words below.

Christmas   David   Friend   Great   House   ~~Papers~~   Twist

1 *The Pickwick Papers*
2 *Oliver* _____
3 *A _____ Carol*
4 *Bleak _____*
5 *_____ Expectations*
6 *Our Mutual _____*
7 *_____ Copperfield*

4 Read part 1 of a summary of *Oliver Twist*. Does Oliver have an easy or difficult start in life? Why do you imagine Dickens often writes about people like this?

PART 1

At the start of the novel, Oliver is born in a workhouse (a place where very poor and homeless people go to live). His mother dies immediately after he is born, without telling anyone her name or the name of Oliver's father. Oliver is brought up as an orphan at the workhouse, where he is shown no kindness. After a famous scene in which he asks for more food, he is treated even more unkindly, so he runs away to London. There, he meets a boy called Jack Dawkins, whose nickname is the Artful Dodger. The Dodger introduces Oliver to a 'gentleman' called Fagin.

5 🎧4.15 Listen to two extracts from *Oliver Twist*. Which events from the summary in exercise 4 do they show?

6 🎧4.15 Listen again and answer the questions about each extract. For some questions, you need to speculate or give your own opinion.

Extract 1
1 Why did the boys' food bowls never need washing?
2 What did one boy threaten to do to the boy who slept in the next bed?
3 When Dickens describes the master as 'fat and healthy', what contrast is he making?
4 What two punishments does Oliver receive for asking for more food?

Extract 2
5 What evidence is there in the extract that the room is a kitchen, a bedroom and a dining room?
6 How do you think Oliver feels when the Dodger calls him 'my friend' and Fagin calls him 'my dear'? Why might he feel that way?
7 If you were Oliver, where would you prefer to be: in the workhouse or with Fagin and the boys? Why?
8 What do Fagin and the boys do to earn money? Are there any clues in the extract?

7 Read part 2 of the summary and complete it with appropriate words. Check your answer to question 8 in exercise 6.

8 SPEAKING In your opinion, who is your country's most important writer? What kind of works does he / she write? How many of them have you read?

PART 2

Fagin is the leader of a gang of young pickpockets who he sends out onto the streets of London ¹_____ steal money, watches and handkerchiefs. Oliver is part of the gang until one of their attempts goes wrong. Oliver is caught, but instead ²_____ being punished, he is looked after ³_____ a kind gentleman called Mr Brownlow. However, Fagin and his gang are worried that Oliver knows ⁴_____ much, so they force him to leave Mr Brownlow's house and join their gang again. In ⁵_____ end, Oliver discovers that he is from a rich family. Fagin is caught and punished ⁶_____ his crimes, while Oliver inherits a lot of money.

Helen Keller

1 SPEAKING Work in pairs. Discuss the quotation. What was Helen Keller talking about, do you think? Do you agree with her?

'The best and most beautiful things in the world cannot be seen or even touched – they must be felt with the heart.' Helen Keller

2 Read the first part of the story of Helen Keller's life. Are the sentences true or false? Write T or F and correct the false sentences.

1 As a baby, Helen had normal sight and hearing. ___
2 A relation of one of the family servants gradually taught Helen sign language. ___
3 Helen's mother was very unhappy and frequently got cross with her. ___
4 Anne Sullivan was partially blind. ___
5 The first word that Helen understood through finger-spelling was 'doll'. ___

3 🎧**4.17** Listen to the second part of the story of Helen Keller's life. What is the significance of these numbers and dates?

a ten years   c 1904   e 81
b 1900   d 1936   f 1968

4 🎧**4.17** Listen again. Answer the questions.

1 What took Helen 25 years of hard work to master?
2 Why didn't she study at Harvard?
3 What else did she do while she was at university?
4 What political and social causes did she support?
5 How old was Helen when she died?

5 Write some short messages or sentences in English for your partner. Do not show him / her.

Hello. How are you?

6 Work in pairs. Take turns to close your eyes while your partner spells out their messages on your palm using their finger. Can you understand?

7 SPEAKING Imagine you were deaf-blind. What practical and emotional problems would you face? Use the phrases below to help you.

One problem would be that …
It would be difficult / impossible to …
You'd have to …
I would hate not being able to …

8 INTERNET RESEARCH Find out about the life of another inspirational person who overcame disability or other difficulties. Make notes about:

• their name, nationality and background
• the disability or difficulties they overcame
• their achievements
• why you admire them

Silent darkness

🎧**4.16**

Helen Keller was born in 1880 in Alabama, with the ability to both see and hear, like any normal child. She began to speak when she was six months old and to walk at the age of one. But six months later, she contracted a serious illness, possibly meningitis. After she had recovered, her mother noticed that Helen didn't react to sounds, or when she waved her hand in front of Helen's face. The illness had left her both deaf and blind.

As she grew up, she learned to communicate with the daughter of the family cook using sign language that they invented together. But Helen was an unhappy child and often flew into a rage. Her mother was very patient with her and tried to help her. She had read about the successful education of another deaf-blind child, and when Helen was seven she contacted a special school for blind children in Boston. The director of the school suggested that Helen work with Anne Sullivan, who was herself visually impaired and a recent graduate of the school. It was the beginning of a 49-year relationship between pupil and teacher.

Anne travelled to Helen's home and immediately began teaching her 'finger-spelling': spelling out words on the palm of Helen's hand. The first word she tried to teach her was 'doll' – Anne had brought Helen a doll as a present. But Helen could not make the connection between the letters and the objects and became very frustrated. After about a month, however, there was a breakthrough. Helen realised that the movements of Anne's fingers on her palm, while she poured water over her other hand, signified 'water'. By the end of the day Helen had learned thirty new words.

Victorian explorers

1 SPEAKING Work in pairs. What were the explorers below famous for?

Roald Amundsen   Christopher Columbus
Captain James Cook   Marco Polo

2 Complete the text about the explorer Mary Kingsley. Write one appropriate word for each gap.

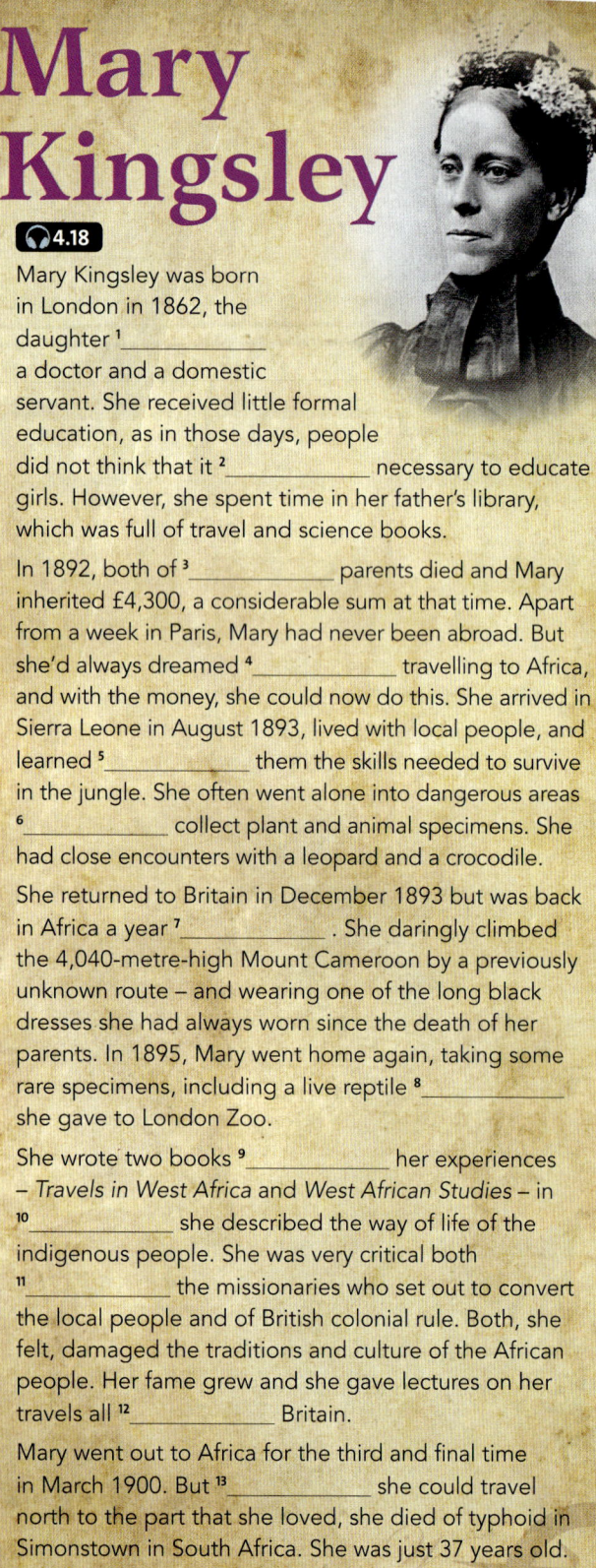

Mary Kingsley

🎧 4.18

Mary Kingsley was born in London in 1862, the daughter ¹_____ a doctor and a domestic servant. She received little formal education, as in those days, people did not think that it ²_____ necessary to educate girls. However, she spent time in her father's library, which was full of travel and science books.

In 1892, both of ³_____ parents died and Mary inherited £4,300, a considerable sum at that time. Apart from a week in Paris, Mary had never been abroad. But she'd always dreamed ⁴_____ travelling to Africa, and with the money, she could now do this. She arrived in Sierra Leone in August 1893, lived with local people, and learned ⁵_____ them the skills needed to survive in the jungle. She often went alone into dangerous areas ⁶_____ collect plant and animal specimens. She had close encounters with a leopard and a crocodile.

She returned to Britain in December 1893 but was back in Africa a year ⁷_____ . She daringly climbed the 4,040-metre-high Mount Cameroon by a previously unknown route – and wearing one of the long black dresses she had always worn since the death of her parents. In 1895, Mary went home again, taking some rare specimens, including a live reptile ⁸_____ she gave to London Zoo.

She wrote two books ⁹_____ her experiences – *Travels in West Africa* and *West African Studies* – in ¹⁰_____ she described the way of life of the indigenous people. She was very critical both ¹¹_____ the missionaries who set out to convert the local people and of British colonial rule. Both, she felt, damaged the traditions and culture of the African people. Her fame grew and she gave lectures on her travels all ¹²_____ Britain.

Mary went out to Africa for the third and final time in March 1900. But ¹³_____ she could travel north to the part that she loved, she died of typhoid in Simonstown in South Africa. She was just 37 years old.

3 Read the text again. Answer the questions.

1 Why was Mary not sent to school?
2 How could she afford to travel to Africa?
3 What did she wear to climb Mount Cameroon?
4 What was her opinion of missionaries and of British colonial rule?
5 How many expeditions to Africa did she go on?
6 What did she die of?

4 🎧 **4.19** Listen to an account of David Livingstone's expeditions and:

1 match the routes on the map with his first, second and third expeditions.
2 say what happened at the four places marked with crosses and dates.

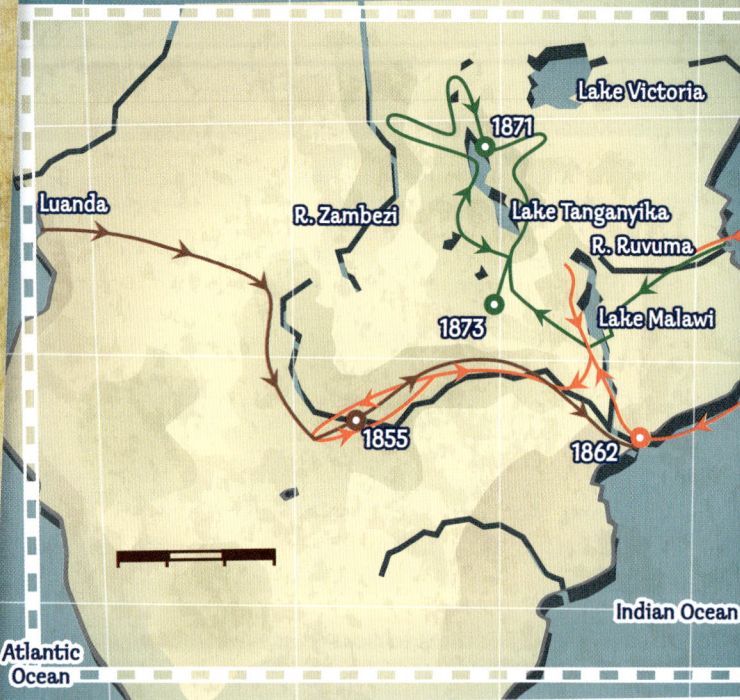

5 🎧 **4.19** Listen again. Number the events of Livingstone's life (A–E) in the correct order.

___ **A** He returned to Africa to search for the source of the Nile.
___ **B** He studied medicine and theology.
___ **C** He attempted to sail up the Zambezi and Rovuma rivers.
___ **D** He became the first European to cross southern Africa.
___ **E** He worked in a cotton mill.

6 SPEAKING Work in pairs. Kingsley and Livingstone thought they were doing good in Africa. What do you think? Give reasons.

7 INTERNET RESEARCH Use the internet to write about another famous explorer or expedition. Find out:

- nationality, date of birth and death.
- what were they looking for and why.
- whether they were successful.
- other interesting facts and information about them.

Vocabulary Builder

Introduction

IA Describing visitor attractions

1 Complete the adjectives with the missing vowels, *a, e, i, o* and *u.*

1 _ tm _ sph _ r _ c	9 h _ st _ r _ c
2 b _ _ _ t _ f _ l	10 _ mpr _ ss _ v _
3 b _ r _ ng	11 p _ _ c _ f _ l
4 b _ sy	12 r _ m _ t _
5 ch _ _ p	13 r _ m _ nt _ c
6 cr _ wd _ d	14 sp _ ct _ c _ l _ r
7 d _ s _ pp _ _ nt _ ng	15 t _ _ r _ sty
8 _ xp _ ns _ v _	

2 Answer the questions.

1 Which two adjectives in exercise 1 describe cost and price?
2 Which three adjectives imply that there will be a lot of visitors there?
3 Which five adjectives usually have negative connotations?

3 Describe a visitor attraction that you know, using at least three of the adjectives in exercise 1.

Old Town Square in Prague is very impressive. There are lots of historic buildings, but it's a bit touristy.

IC Adjective endings

4 Read the Learn this! box and complete the examples. Can you add any more adjectives to each group?

> **LEARN THIS!** Adjective endings
>
> Some adjective endings have a particular meaning.
> **a** noun + *-ful* = giving or full of *hopeful* ¹*meaning_____*
> **b** noun + *-less* = without ²*hope_____* ³*meaning_____*
> **c** noun + *-ly* or *-y* = like, with the quality of *friendly* ⁴*snow_____*
> **d** verb + *-able* = possible to ⁵*drink_____* ⁶*afford_____*
> Other adjective endings have no particular meaning but usually go with either a noun or a verb.
> **e** noun + *-ous* ⁷*adventur_____* ⁸*mountain_____*
> **f** verb + *-ive* ⁹*impress_____* ¹⁰*support_____*

5 Complete each gap with an adjective formed from the noun or verb in brackets. Use a dictionary if necessary.

1 It was a _____ (courage) decision, and fortunately his friends were very _____ (support).
2 Parts of the route were very _____ (mountain) and quite _____ (danger).
3 He's popular because of his _____ (friend) and _____ (like) personality.
4 The film wasn't _____ (wonder) but it was quite _____ (watch).
5 It was a _____ (snow) day and the drive home was _____ (hazard).
6 She was trying to be _____ (help), I know, but it was _____ (care) of her to drop my laptop bag.

Unit 1

1A Noun plural forms

1 Study the plural forms below. Then complete rules a–f in the Learn this! box with the correct endings. Then match each spelling variation (g–i) with one of the nouns below.

ancestors   boxes   buses   lunches   clothes
countries   kisses   men   potatoes   sheep   toys
videos   wishes   wives

> **LEARN THIS!** Noun plural forms
>
> To make a noun plural:
> **a** We add ¹_____ to most nouns.
> **b** We add ²_____ to nouns ending in *-ch, -sh, -ss, -s* and *-x.*
> **c** We add ³_____ to most nouns ending in *-o.*
> **d** We add ⁴_____ to nouns ending in a vowel + *-y.*
> **e** With nouns ending in a consonant + *-y*, the spelling changes to ⁵_____ .
> **f** With nouns ending in *-f* or *-fe*, the spelling changes to ⁶_____ .
> **g** Some nouns have irregular plural forms.
> **h** Some nouns have the same singular and plural forms.
> **i** Some nouns are plural and have no singular form.

2 How many more nouns can you add to each group?

1E Phrasal verbs

> **LEARN THIS!** Phrasal verbs
>
> Many common phrasal verbs have meanings which you cannot guess or work out from the main verb. Instead, you need to learn them as separate vocabulary items.

3 Read the Learn this! box. Then read the sentences and circle the correct meaning, a or b. Use a dictionary to help you.

1 She gave up halfway through the London Marathon.
   a went faster
   b stopped trying
2 The film turned into a comedy towards the end.
   a stopped being a comedy
   b became a comedy
3 We set off just as it was getting dark.
   a started our journey
   b finished our journey
4 The rocket blew up as it entered the Earth's atmosphere.
   a exploded
   b changed direction
5 A woman in the front row of the audience passed out.
   a left the room
   b became unconscious / asleep
6 At the age of 65, my grandfather took up ice skating.
   a stopped doing it
   b started doing it

V Vocabulary Builder

Unit 2

2C Diets

1 Circle the correct answers: a, b or c.

1 If you're on a low-salt diet, you should avoid … .
   a bacon   **b** tomatoes   **c** eggs
2 A vegetarian would not eat … .
   a pasta   **b** mushrooms   **c** tuna
3 There are lots of vitamins and minerals in … .
   a vegetables   **b** crisps   **c** butter
4 A good source of iron is … .
   a peanuts   **b** steak   **c** cheese
5 Brown rice and wholemeal bread contain more … than white rice and white bread.
   a fibre   **b** calcium   **c** fat
6 Which of these is not a source of carbohydrate?
   a chicken   **b** rice   **c** cereal
7 Organic food does not usually contain … .
   a nutrients   **b** protein   **c** additives

2F Prepositions of place

2 Study the Learn this! box. Then complete the examples with the correct prepositions.

> **LEARN THIS! Prepositions of place**
>
> **a** We use *on* with surfaces. We use *in* with three-dimensional spaces.
> **1**_____ a box **2**_____ the floor **3**_____ the cupboard
> **4**_____ the wall
>
> **b** We often use *in* with large areas or spaces. We often use *at* to talk about a place where something happens.
> Turn right **5**_____ the crossroads. Kate lives **6**_____ London.
> I met Joe **7**_____ a party. Sam's playing **8**_____ the park.
>
> **c** *Between* means 'in the space that separates two or more things'. *Among* means 'in the middle of' or 'surrounded by'.
> She got lost **9**_____ the crowds of people.
> Andorra lies **10**_____ France and Spain.
>
> **d** *Opposite* means 'facing something but on the other side'. *In front of* means 'near to the front of'.
> The teacher stood **11**_____ the class.
> The bank is **12**_____ the chemist's.

3 Underline the correct prepositions.

1 The shop is on the left hand side of the road, **opposite** / **in front of** our house.
2 The plates are **on** / **in** the shelf and the knives are **on** / **in** the drawer.
3 We stopped for lunch **at** / **in** the motorway service station.
4 Didcot lies **among** / **between** Reading and Oxford.
5 Janet lives **at** / **in** the north of England.
6 The cottage is hidden **among** / **between** the trees.
7 I missed my train because there were so many people **opposite** / **in front of** me in the queue for tickets.

Unit 3

3F Homonyms

1 Complete the sentences with the homonyms, using each word below twice. Use a dictionary to help you.

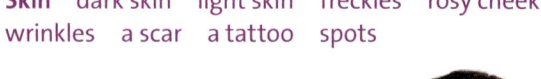

arms   chest   foot   hand   head   nail

1 I need to cut the _____ on my right thumb.
2 His _____ rose and fell as he breathed in and out.
3 It's getting late. Let's _____ for home.
4 The big _____ on the clock is pointing to twelve.
5 He shook his _____ and said 'no'.
6 I need a _____ to hang the picture on the wall.
7 Jason can kick a ball with either _____ .
8 She held the baby in her _____ as it went to sleep.
9 'Put your _____ up if you know the answer,' said the teacher.
10 Cathy is five _____ six inches tall.
11 We keep all the towels in a _____ in the bathroom.
12 British police don't usually carry _____ .

3G Describing appearance

2 Describe the people in photos A–C using as many of the words and phrases below as possible.

Hair styles a bob a fringe highlights a parting a ponytail dreadlocks plaits spiky hair bald balding receding

Facial hair a beard a goatee a moustache sideburns stubble clean-shaven

Skin dark skin light skin freckles rosy cheeks wrinkles a scar a tattoo spots

3 Write five sentences describing yourself and your friends or family. Use words and phrases from exercise 2.

V Vocabulary Builder

Unit 4

4E Collocations: *do* or *make*?

1 Underline the correct verb: *do* or *make*.

1 Can I **do** / **make** a suggestion?
2 We need to **do** / **make** more research before we buy a car.
3 I helped my parents to **do** / **make** the housework.
4 We didn't **do** / **make** a sound as we entered the house.
5 Let's try not to **do** / **make** a mess in the living room.
6 A car drove into our wall, but it didn't **do** / **make** much damage.
7 Before we start eating, I'd like to **do** / **make** an announcement.
8 I often **do** / **make** the cooking at weekends.

2 Complete the sentences with the correct form of *do* or *make*.

1 I didn't enjoy the exercise class, but it probably _____ me good.
2 He finds exams difficult, but he always _____ his best.
3 It wasn't my birthday yesterday – you _____ a mistake.
4 Both hotels look great, but we have to _____ a choice.
5 I like your new haircut. It _____ a big difference to your appearance.
6 Did you see that motorbike? It was _____ about 200 km/h!

4G In the house

3 Match the pictures (1–6) with six words from the list below.

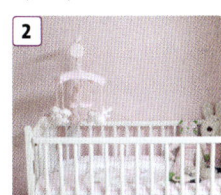

armchair   basin   blinds   bucket   bunk bed   carpet
chandelier   cot   curtains   desk lamp   dishwasher
doormat   duvet   fireplace   freezer   fridge
hairdryer   kettle   mattress   pillow   radiator
rug   sink   sofa   shutters   stool   toaster
tumble dryer   wall light   wardrobe   washing machine

4 In the list of words in exercise 3, find:

1 three things you sit on.
2 four things you can fill with water.
3 at least nine things powered by electricity.
4 six things you usually find only in a bedroom.
5 three things that cover windows.
6 three forms of lighting.
7 two things which can make a house warmer.
8 three things which you use to cover the floor, or part of it.

Unit 5

5F Verb–noun collocations

1 Cross out the one verb which <u>cannot</u> be used to complete each sentence grammatically. The sentences may have different meanings with each correct verb.

1 Today is not the best time to **fail** / **set** / **make** / **complete** the test.
2 Our class **took part in** / **held** / **organised** / **opened** a history competition.
3 I hate **informing** / **receiving** / **delivering** / **passing on** messages that are upsetting.
4 John **got into** / **overheard** / **joined in** / **took up** an interesting conversation about robots in the canteen.
5 I'm sure some of us might **guess** / **speculate** / **offer** / **expect** some kind of an answer.
6 The team **gained** / **deserved** / **claimed** / **were awarded** a prize for their entry.
7 We regularly **log onto** / **update** / **set up** / **post** promotional websites for marketing.
8 Do you think we'll ever be able to **crack** / **decipher** / **smash** / **unlock** the secret codes?

5H Describing computer equipment

2 Match a–f with 1–6 and g–l with 7–12.

1 operating	**a** desktop	7 flash	**g** engine
2 all-in-one	**b** drive	8 graphics	**h** filter
3 wireless	**c** life	9 anti-virus	**i** horse
4 widescreen	**d** mouse	10 spam	**j** card
5 battery	**e** display	11 Trojan	**k** protection
6 hard	**f** system	12 search	**l** drive

3 Complete the sentences with compounds from exercise 2.

1 'What type of computer have you got?' 'It's an _____.'
2 The _____ on my laptop isn't great so I have to keep recharging it.
3 I'll copy lots of songs onto a _____ so you can load them onto your computer.
4 You can stop most unwanted emails if you install a _____.
5 You use a _____ by entering a keyword in the box and pressing enter.
6 You need a really good _____ in your computer if you want to play games with fast-moving and detailed images.
7 _____ helps to protect the data on your computer from hackers.
8 Occasionally a _____ is attached to something you download from the internet. This might allow someone to gain access to your computer.

Vocabulary Builder

Unit 6

6F Verb plus preposition

1 Complete the sentences with the prepositions and verbs below.

about   apply   apologise   believe   congratulate
experiment   for   from   like   object   on   to

1 If you want to visit China, you'll have to _____ for a visa.
2 I feel _____ an ice cream. We can get one at the corner shop.
3 Do you _____ in the existence of UFOs?
4 Can you please turn off the music? I'm trying to concentrate _____ my homework.
5 I must _____ Sam on passing his driving test.
6 I completely forgot _____ the invitation to Tom's party.
7 Do you think it's always unacceptable for scientists to _____ on animals?
8 We're having a barbecue at the weekend so we're hoping _____ some fine weather.
9 Jack should _____ to you for his rudeness.
10 I hope that your grandma recovers quickly _____ her operation.
11 A lot of people _____ to plans for a new airport near London.
12 I've subscribed _____ lots of YouTube channels.

6G Working and employment conditions

2 Complete the sentences with the words and phrases below.

bonus   overtime   paid holiday   paperwork   pay rise
salary   shifts   sick pay   training course   workload

1 When she changed jobs, she took a large cut in _____ .
2 If he meets his sales targets, he receives a £5,000 _____ .
3 Some weeks, she has to work three eight-hour _____ in two days.
4 As a teacher, she gets thirteen weeks' _____ a year, including six weeks in the summer.
5 He's been off work since the accident, but he'll receive _____ until he's well enough to go back.
6 He's been doing a lot of _____ recently to earn some extra money for his holiday.
7 I used to earn more than you, but I haven't had a _____ for three years.
8 The company is sending all its employees on a _____ to improve their customer service skills.
9 He enjoys the practical aspects of his job, but he hates sitting at his desk doing the _____ .
10 It's an interesting job, but he's finding it exhausting because of the huge _____ .

Unit 7

7G Cultural events and venues

1 Complete the sentences with the words below.

arena   art gallery   circus   comedy club   concert hall
library   opera house   museum   theatre

1 We saw an amazing collection of Ancient Egyptian jewellery at the _____ .
2 I enjoy watching acrobats at the _____ , but I don't think they should use animals.
3 On Thursday evenings at my local _____ , anyone can have a go at being a comedian.
4 I went to see Mozart's *The Magic Flute* at the Met, a world-famous _____ in New York.
5 Some of these Impressionist paintings are privately owned and have never been seen in any _____ .
6 The Globe is a _____ in London where Shakespeare's plays are performed.
7 While we were in Vienna, we went to a _____ to hear a Beethoven piano recital.
8 At the O2 _____ in London, up to twenty thousand people can watch some of the biggest acts in music.
9 The British _____ holds around 170 million books and other items for students and researchers to access.

7H Describing stories

2 Complete the sentences with the words below.

based   characters   identify   made   main
story   what

1 The _____ character is Bilbo Baggins.
2 I couldn't _____ with Bella Swan.
3 It's been _____ into a film called *The Golden Compass*.
4 It's the _____ of a group of boys who get stranded on a desert island.
5 _____ I liked about the book was the way it described teenage alienation and disillusionment.
6 It's _____ on the author's experience of the unjust treatment of African Americans in 1930s America.
7 I found the _____ of Harry, Ron and Hermione rather unconvincing.

3 Match the sentences in exercise 2 with the books below that they refer to. Which ones have you read?

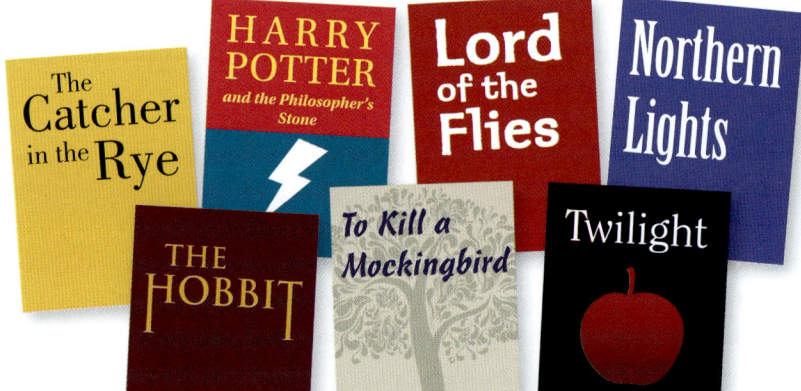

Vocabulary Builder

Unit 8

8F Publications

1 Which of the publications below are non-fiction? Which are fiction?

atlas autobiography biography comic cookbook dictionary encyclopaedia grammar book guidebook magazine short story manual newspaper novel play textbook thesaurus

2 Which publication from exercise 1 would you use to …

1 find interesting places to visit while on holiday?
2 read a long story?
3 read an account of someone's life, written by that person?
4 find where a country was?
5 find out how to operate a gadget?
6 discover new recipes?
7 find lots of different words with similar meanings?
8 find the meaning of a word that you don't understand?
9 read a story that is written for the theatre?
10 revise for your school exams?

8G Road accidents

3 Complete the newspaper report of a road accident with the correct form of the words and phrases below.

be damaged be injured be killed breathalyse collide crash lose control knock down skid suffer whiplash swerve

A pedestrian was seriously ¹_____ when she was ²_____ by a car in the town centre last night. The driver of the car ³_____ to avoid a dog that had run onto the road, ⁴_____ on the wet surface and ⁵_____ of the vehicle. The car ran onto the pavement and ⁶_____ with the woman, who was waiting at a bus stop. After knocking the woman down, the car ⁷_____ into the bus stop, which was badly ⁸_____ . The driver was ⁹_____ by police at the scene of the accident but was not over the legal alcohol limit. The woman is being cared for in St Mary's Hospital and is expected to make a full recovery. The driver of the car ¹⁰_____ , but was otherwise unhurt. A police spokesman said that it was lucky that nobody had been ¹¹_____ .

Unit 9

9A Travel problems

1 Add the words below to the table.

choppy congestion diverted dirty roadworks

The flight was	cancelled. delayed. ¹_____ (to another airport). bumpy.
The train / bus was	overcrowded. ²_____ . slow.
The car journey was slow because of	³_____ . slow-moving traffic. ⁴_____ / traffic jams. a diversion. an accident.
The sea crossing was	⁵_____ . rough.

2 Write a paragraph describing the worst journey you can remember. Include phrases from exercise 1.

9F Size and dimensions

3 Read the Learn this! box. Then complete the information with the correct adjectives.

LEARN THIS!

Noun	width	length	depth	height
Adjective	¹_____	²_____	³_____	⁴_____ and ⁵_____

a We usually use *high* for mountains and waterfalls, and ⁶_____ for people, buildings and trees.

b We can ask about size with *How* + adjective: *How wide / long / far / big / deep etc. is … ?* or *What's the* + noun: *What's the length / width / size etc. of … ?*

4 Make seven pairs of opposites from the words below.

deep high long low narrow shallow short small tall thick thin wide

5 Complete the sentences with the correct adjectives.

1 Mount Everest is 8,848 m _____ .
2 The Mariana Trench in the Pacific Ocean is 10,911 m _____ .
3 The Empire State Building is 443 m _____ .
4 The Amazon River is 6,992 km _____ .
5 The country Chile is 4,300 km _____ but less than 350 km _____ .

6 Write as many questions as you can that you could ask about the size and dimensions of:

1 a lake. 2 a box. 3 a person. 4 a building.

1 *How deep is it? How …*

G Grammar Builder and Reference

Introduction

I.1 Past simple

We form the past simple (affirmative) form of regular verbs by adding -ed.

> + -ed   work → worked   play → played

If the verb ends in -e, we add -d.

> + -d   dance → danced   die → died

If the verb ends in a consonant + -y, we change -y to -i and add -ed.

> -y → -ied   study → studied   cry → cried

If the verb ends in a short stressed vowel + a consonant, we double the consonant and add -ed.

> -p → -pped   drop → dropped

Some verbs have irregular past simple (affirmative) forms. There are no spelling rules for these forms; you need to learn them by heart. See the irregular verb list in the Workbook.

For the negative, we use *didn't* + the infinitive without *to*. For the interrogative, we use *did* + subject + infinitive without *to*.

We didn't arrive on time.

Did you bring any food?

The past simple of *be* is *I / he / she / it was* or *you / we / they were*. The past simple of *can* is *could*. For the negative and interrogative forms of *be* and *can*, we do not use *did / didn't*.

They weren't at school. Were they ill?

I couldn't see the stage. Could you see it?

1 Complete the sentences with the verbs in brackets. Use the past simple affirmative.

1 I _____ Turkey in August. (visit)
2 The weather _____ great in July. (be)
3 The sea was warm, so we _____ swim. (can)
4 I _____ you a postcard. (send)
5 I _____ English at a school in Brighton. (study)
6 We _____ every day. (sunbathe)
7 I _____ kayaking in June. (go)

2 Make the sentences in exercise 1 negative.

3 **SPEAKING** Ask and answer using the prompts below. Use the past simple. Give extra information in your answer.

buy anything last weekend   do any sport during the week
go out last night   have a big breakfast
phone anybody yesterday   send any texts

> Did you go out last night?

> No, I didn't. I stayed in and watched TV.

I.2 Contrast: present simple and present continuous

We use the present simple:

- for something that always happens or happened regularly (e.g. *every week, often, sometimes*).
  Laura cycles to school every day.
- for facts.
  Cows eat grass.

We use the present continuous:

- for something happening at this exact moment or around this time.
  Luke is wearing a T-shirt. (at this moment)
  Luke is working hard this term. (around this time)
- for future arrangements.
  We're playing volleyball tomorrow.

We can use dynamic verbs in simple and continuous forms.

I work in London.

Dad's working in the garden.

Verbs describing a state or situation (state verbs) are not usually used in continuous tenses.

I understand. (state of mind)

NOT ~~I'm understanding.~~ ✗

Who does this watch belong to? (possession)

NOT ~~Who is this watch belonging to?~~ ✗

Common state verbs:

- *hate, like, love, need, prefer, want, wish;*
- *believe, know, mean, realise, recognise, remember, suppose, understand;*
- *belong, contain, depend, matter, owe, possess.*

There is a group of verbs that can be used as either state or dynamic verbs. These are some of them:

- *appear, consider, feel, look, see, smell, taste, think.*
  What are you <u>thinking</u> about? (dynamic – to think)
  What do you <u>think</u> of my new tie? (state – to have an opinion)
  We're <u>seeing</u> John next week. (dynamic – to meet with somebody)
  I <u>see</u> what you mean. (state – to understand)

1 Complete the sentences with the verbs in brackets. Use the present simple or the present continuous.

1 'Where _____ you _____ (go)?'
  'To the shops. I _____ (need) to get some bread.'
2 _____ you usually _____ (wear) jeans to school?
3 I _____ (not understand) this question.
4 Why _____ you _____ (smile)? It isn't funny!
5 '_____ you _____ (come) bowling with Jan and me tonight?'
  'No, thanks. I _____ (not like) bowling.'
6 Hurry up! The bus _____ (leave) in three minutes.

2 Complete the sentences with the present simple and present continuous form of the verb given.

1 work
   a Dad _____ in a factory.
   b Mum _____ at home today for a change.
2 have
   a We _____ fish for dinner tonight.
   b We usually _____ fish on Fridays.
3 take
   a I _____ a coat today because it's a bit cold.
   b I _____ a few weeks off work over the summer.
4 arrive
   a I'll phone you as soon as I _____ .
   b Come on! The train _____ . We mustn't miss it.
5 listen
   a 'What _____ you _____ to?' 'It's Adele's latest album.'
   b Liam _____ to music while he's doing his homework.

3 Choose the correct tense to complete the sentences. Then decide if the verb is state or dynamic.

1 This pizza **tastes** / **is tasting** good.
2 What **do you look at** / **are you looking at**?
3 Mandy **has** / **is having** brown hair.
4 Look. The sun **appears** / **is appearing** from behind those clouds.
5 **I think** / **I'm thinking** that we should go.
6 **I don't see** / **I'm not seeing** what the problem is.

I.3 Articles

We use *a* when we talk about something for the first time. We use *the* if we mention it again.

I've got a cat and a dog. The cat is black and white.

We use *the* when it is clear what we are talking about, perhaps because there is only one of them.

Let's go to the park. (There's only one park near here.)
Pass me the cup. (I'm pointing to it.)
Look at the moon!
She's the tallest person in her class.

We use *a* to say what someone's job is.

My uncle is a taxi driver.

We don't use an article when we are making a generalisation.

I don't like spicy food.
NOT ~~I don't like the spicy food.~~ ✗

We use *a* to mean 'per' or 'in each'.

She earns £10 an hour.
There are only two buses a day into town.

Some set expressions include *the*:

at the weekend, in the morning / afternoon / evening, listen to the radio, go to the cinema, play the guitar

Some set expressions don't have an article:

on Monday, at night, watch TV, listen to music, go to bed, go to school / work, be at home / at work / in hospital / at university, have breakfast / lunch / dinner

1 Find eight more mistakes with articles in this paragraph.

It was my mum's birthday last night, so we had ~~the~~ dinner in a restaurant near the station. Restaurant was quite expensive – water was about £5 the bottle – but it was worth it because food was fantastic! For me, a best part of the meal was the main course. My dad and I both had salmon with potatoes and a delicious sauce. My dad said it was very well cooked, and he's chef so he knows about cooking. My brother ordered steak because he hates the fish. My dad had ordered a birthday cake for pudding. We had a great time and didn't leave the restaurant until 11.30 at the night.

I.4 *will* and *going to*

We use *will*:

- to make factual statements about the future.
  There will be a solar eclipse in 2026.
- to make predictions, especially when they are based on what we know or when they are just a guess. We often use *I think / don't think* … to make these predictions.
  I think you'll do well in your exams.
  I don't think England will win the next World Cup.
  NOT ~~I think England won't~~ … ✗
- to make offers.
  I'll carry your bags.
  I'll lend you my phone.
- to make promises.
  I'll always love you.
  I won't forget.
- to make instant decisions (decisions that we make while we are speaking).
  Look! There's Tommy. I'll go and say hello.

We use *going to*:

- to make predictions, especially when they are based on what we can see or hear.
  Look at that man! He's going to jump in the river!
  Listen to the thunder. There's going to be a storm.
- to talk about our plans and intentions.
  I'm going to invite her to my party.

Grammar Builder and Reference

1 Complete the dialogue with the correct form of *will* or *going to* and the verbs in brackets.

Laura Hi, Harry. What are you doing here? Are you meeting somebody?

Harry No, I just came in for a drink.

Laura I **1**_____ (buy) you a drink. I owe you one from last weekend.

Harry Thanks! I **2**_____ (have) a coffee.

Laura Would you like a cake too?

Harry No, thanks. I **3**_____ (have) dinner soon.

Laura OK. What are your plans for the weekend?

Harry I **4**_____ (do) some preparation for our exam on Monday. What about you? **5**_____ you _____ (revise) tomorrow?

Laura Yes. But in the evening, I **6**_____ (go) to a gig at the town hall.

Harry Really? Who's playing?

Laura They're called The Wave. I **7**_____ (meet) Poppy there.

Harry It sounds like a good night out.

Laura I **8**_____ (get) a ticket for you too, then. OK?

Harry Thanks! I **9**_____ (give) you the money for it now. How much is it?

Laura I'm not sure. But it **10**_____ (not be) expensive. They aren't a well-known band.

Unit 1

1.1 Past tense contrast

We use past tenses to talk about past events. We use the past continuous to describe a scene in the past. The events were in progress at the same time.

The sun was shining. A man was standing at the bus stop waiting for a bus.

We use the past simple for actions or events that happened one after the other.

Tom got up, had a shower and got dressed.

We use the past continuous to describe a longer background event, and the past simple to describe an action or event that interrupted it.

The phone rang while we were having dinner.

We use the past perfect to talk about an event that happened before another event in the past.

I didn't have any money because I'd lost my wallet.

Notice that with regular verbs the past simple and the past participle form of the past perfect are the same.

She arrived yesterday night.
She had arrived before we served the dinner.

However, with irregular verbs the past simple and the past participle form of the past perfect are often different.

I ate an apple.   *I'd already eaten.*

1 Complete the sentences. Use the past simple or the past continuous form of the verbs in brackets.

1 I _____ (have) a crash while I _____ (learn) to drive.

2 Sam _____ (get) his first job while he _____ (live) in London.

3 It _____ (rain), so we _____ (decide) to cancel the barbecue.

4 What _____ you _____ (do) when I _____ (see) you in town?

5 Emma _____ (not hear) the phone ringing because she _____ (listen) to music in her bedroom.

6 Ryan _____ (break) his arm while he _____ (ski) in France.

7 Harry _____ (work) as a chef when he _____ (meet) Sally.

8 You obviously _____ (not listen) when I _____ (ask) you to turn down the music.

2 Complete the sentences. Use the past simple or the past perfect form of the verbs in brackets.

1 My uncle and aunt _____ (already / get engaged) before they _____ (emigrate) to Australia.

2 I _____ (not / can) buy anything because I _____ (forget) my wallet.

3 Robert _____ (be) upset because he _____ (split up) with his girlfriend.

4 Kelly _____ (start) her first business before she _____ (leave) university.

5 As soon as Sara _____ (inherit) the money from her grandmother, she _____ (buy) a car.

6 By the time Joe _____ (retire), he _____ (become) a grandfather.

7 After Fred _____ (settle down) in London, he _____ (decide) to have a change of career.

8 We _____ (spend) the weekend moving house, so we _____ (go) to bed very early on Sunday.

3 Choose the best ending (a or b) for the sentences.

1 We couldn't open the front door because
   a it had snowed all night. **b** it snowed all night.

2 It was a lovely spring day and the birds
   a sang.   **b** were singing.

3 I looked out of the window and noticed that
   a it had stopped raining.   **b** it was stopping raining.

4 The plants died because we
   a were forgetting to water them.
   b forgot to water them.

5 Before I left the house, I
   a locked all the windows. **b** was locking all the windows.

6 I wasn't particularly hungry because
   a I'd already had lunch.   **b** I already had lunch.

Grammar Builder and Reference

1.2 *used to*

We use *used to* plus the infinitive without *to* to describe past situations or habits that are different now.

I used to go ice skating. (I don't go now.)

She didn't use to be confident. (She's confident now.)

Affirmative	Negative	Interrogative
We used to live in the city.	We didn't use to go hiking.	Did you use to live near the sea?

1 Complete the dialogue with the correct form of *used to* and the verbs in brackets.

Maria Let me see that photo. Hey, you **1**_____ _____ (have) long hair! I didn't know that.

Sam I know. I was about fourteen then. I **2**_____ _____ (be) a fan of heavy metal.

Maria My brother **3**_____ (like) heavy metal. He often went to concerts with friends. But he **4**_____ (not invite) me.

Sam I **5**_____ (not go) to concerts. The tickets were too expensive. But I **6**_____ _____ (listen) to CDs a lot. What about you? What kind of music **7**_____ (you / listen) to when you were younger?

Maria I **8**_____ (enjoy) listening to pop music and dancing with my friends.

Sam **9**_____ (you / go) to discos?

Maria Not really. We were too young. But my dad **10**_____ (take) me to pop concerts sometimes. I loved those.

2 Complete the sentences with *used to / didn't use to* and the verbs below.

cook cost drink go live play sell win

1 They _____ in Canada. Then they moved to the USA.
2 You can buy a laptop quite cheaply now. They _____ a lot more.
3 I _____ the guitar. I started learning it last month.
4 That shop _____ computers. It was a bookshop.
5 My sister _____ skiing every winter, but now she prefers snowboarding.
6 I _____ milk with every meal, but now I always have water.
7 My dad _____ dinner every evening, but now my sister and I usually do it.
8 I really enjoyed chess when I was younger, but I _____ very often.

Unit 2

2.1 Present perfect and past simple contrast

We use the past simple to talk about a specific occasion in the past.

I went rollerblading last Saturday.

We use the present perfect to talk about an event during a period of time that is still continuing.

I've lived in Cornwall all my life.

We use the present perfect to say how long a situation has existed, often with *for*, *since* and *how long*.

I've been at this school for six years.

'How long have you had that jacket?' 'Since last spring.'

We use the present perfect to talk about an event that has a strong connection with the present, often with *just*, *already* and *yet*.

Look! The sun has come out.

Has it stopped raining yet?

I've lost my maths textbook. Have you seen it?

We use the present perfect to talk about an experience at an unspecified time in the past, often with *ever* or *never*.

I've never been to France.

Have you ever eaten Japanese food?

My cousin has met Orlando Bloom.

We often use the present perfect to ask or talk about an experience and then the past simple to give specific information about it.

'Have you been to Italy?' 'Yes, I have. I went there last summer.'

We often use finished past time expressions with the past simple (*yesterday*, *three months ago*, *last week*, *in 1999*), but unfinished past time expressions with the present perfect (*for*, *since*, *already*, *just*, *yet*).

I started school in 2006.

I haven't done my homework yet.

I've had a cold for four or five days.

already, *yet* and *just*

We use *already* with the present perfect in affirmative sentences. We put it before the past participle or at the end of the sentence.

Kate has already left. / Kate has left already.

We use *yet* with the present perfect in negative sentences and questions. We usually put it at the end of the sentence.

Kate hasn't left yet. Has Kate left yet?

We use *just* with the present perfect in affirmative sentences and questions to mean 'a very short time ago'.

I've just finished my homework.

Have you just eaten?

been and *gone*

We use both *been* and *gone* as the past participle of the verb *go*.

We use *been* when somebody has returned.

Henry has been to town. (He went to town, but he's here now.)

We use *gone* when somebody has not returned.

Henry has gone to town. (He is still in town.)

We form the present perfect with *have* / *has* + the past participle.

Grammar Builder and Reference

1 Write the past participles of the verbs below.

1	see	5	ride
2	have	6	dance
3	speak	7	stop
4	break	8	hurry

2 Write questions with *yet* and answers with *already* or *yet*.

1 Jake / finish his homework? ✓
Has Jake finished his homework yet?
Yes, he's already finished it.
2 Sam / eat? ✗
Has Sam eaten yet?
No, he hasn't eaten yet.
3 Alice and David's plane / land? ✓
4 Jim / read *The Hobbit*? ✗
5 Fran / tidy her bedroom? ✓
6 Simon and Clare / arrive at school? ✗
7 Terry / see / the latest Batman film? ✓

3 Write *been* or *gone*.

1 Hannah isn't at school. She's _____ home.
2 You're late. Where have you _____?
3 'Is Jackie coming to the party this evening?' 'No, she's _____ to London.'
4 Jack's _____ shopping, but he'll be back soon.
5 Nice suntan! Have you _____ on holiday?

4 Complete the sentences. Use the past simple or present perfect form of the verbs in brackets.

1 Joe _____ (live) in London between 2009 and 2012.
2 'Emeli Sandé _____ (just / bring out) a new record. _____ (you / hear) it yet?'
'Yes, I _____ (download) it last night.'
3 'Sorry I'm late! _____ (you / be) here long?'
'No, I _____ (just / arrive).'
4 '_____ (you / ever / visit) the USA?' 'Yes, I _____ (go) there last summer.'
5 '_____ (you / eat) before you _____ (leave) home?'
'Yes, I _____.'
6 I _____ (have) this MP3 player for a year.

2.2 Present perfect simple and continuous

We form the present perfect continuous like this:
have / has been + -ing form
We've been doing housework.

We use the present perfect continuous:
• for an action that began in the past and is still in progress. We often use *for* or *since* to say how long the action has been in progress.
I've been learning the saxophone since 2010.
• for an action that has recently been in progress and which explains the current situation.
I've been tidying my room. It looks a lot better now!

• for an action that has happened repeatedly during a recent period (rather than continuously).
I've been getting a lot of junk emails recently.

We form the present perfect simple like this:
have / has been + past participle

We use the present perfect simple:
• for an action that began in the past and is still in progress. We often use *for* or *since* to say how long the action has been in progress, particularly when it is a long time.
I've lived in this house since I was a child.
• for an action that has recently been in progress, when we want to make clear that it is now completed.
I've done my homework. Let's go out!
• with verbs not used in continuous tenses.
She's had that car for years.
NOT She's been having that car for years. ✗

1 Complete the sentences with the verbs below. Use the correct affirmative, negative or interrogative form of the present perfect continuous.

answer   cook   make   play   save   use   watch   worry

1 My eyes are sore. I _____ computer games for too long!
2 We _____ for weeks so that we can pay for our next holiday.
3 I'm so happy you phoned. I _____ about you all day.
4 I love the new sitcom on BBC1. _____ you _____ it?
5 She recently bought a new bike, but she _____ it much.
6 Maybe her phone is broken. She _____ my calls.
7 My hands are cold because we _____ a snowman.
8 I hope they enjoy the food. I _____ for hours!

2 Complete the second sentence in each pair to mean the same as the first. Use the correct affirmative or negative form of the present perfect continuous.

1 It started snowing just a short time ago.
It _____ for very long.
2 I put these jeans on yesterday afternoon, and I haven't taken them off yet!
I _____ these jeans since yesterday afternoon!
3 I started feeling unwell two days ago.
I _____ well for two days.
4 She sat down in the sun three hours ago, and she hasn't moved.
She _____ in the sun for three hours now.
5 I began this book nearly a year ago, and I haven't finished it yet.
I _____ this book for nearly a year.
6 We moved to Scotland three years ago.
We _____ in Scotland for three years now.

Grammar Builder and Reference

3 Choose the best tense in these sentences.

1 I love that film. **I've seen / I've been seeing** it three times!
2 She's got some great ideas for her book, but she **hasn't written / hasn't been writing** it yet.
3 Sorry I'm late. How long **have you waited / have you been waiting**?
4 My mum often works abroad. This week, **she's worked / she's been working** in Paris.
5 Don't take my plate away. I **haven't finished / haven't been finishing** my lunch!
6 **We've got / We've been getting** ready for the party. We still need to decorate the room.
7 Can you speak more slowly? I **haven't understood / haven't been understanding** everything.

4 Complete the email. Use the present perfect continuous form where possible. If not, use the present perfect simple.

Hi Joel,

How are you? **1**_____ you _____ (enjoy) the holiday? This is our last week, isn't it? And I **2**_____ (not finish) that science project. In fact, to be honest, I **3**_____ (not start) it. I **4**_____ (spend) a lot of time with my neighbour, Seth. You **5**_____ (not meet) him, but he's really nice – and a great guitarist. We **6**_____ (play) the guitar a lot, and he **7**_____ (teach) me some new songs. **8**_____ you _____ (buy) a bass guitar yet? You **9**_____ (talk) about it for months. Let's start a band!

See you back at school!

Maxwell

Unit 3

3.1 Speculating and predicting

We use *will / won't* to make predictions.
We'll send people to Mars in the near future.
Liverpool won't win the Champions League this year.

We can use phrases with *will / won't* to make the predictions stronger or weaker.

- *I think / I don't think / I doubt / I'm not sure* + *will* (but not *won't*)
  I don't think she'll come to the party.
  NOT ~~I think she won't ….~~ ✗
  I doubt she'll come to the party.
  NOT ~~I doubt she won't ….~~ ✗
- *I'm certain / I'm sure* + *will / won't*
  I'm certain she'll come to the party.
  I'm sure she won't come to the party.

We can also use adverbs such as *probably* and *definitely* with *will* and *won't*.
She'll definitely come to the party.
She probably won't come to the party.

We use *may / might / could* + the infinitive without *to* to talk about future possibilities.
My phone may / might / could be in my bedroom.

We use *may not / might not* for the negative, to say that it is possible that something will not happen. We don't use *could not*.
My phone may not / might not be in my bedroom.
NOT ~~My phone could not be in my bedroom.~~ ✗

1 **USE OF ENGLISH** Complete the second sentence so that it has the same meaning as the first. Use the words in brackets.

1 Wendy probably won't eat with us.
  I don't think Wendy will eat with us. (don't think)
2 I'm certain you'll pass all your exams.
  You _____ . (definitely)
3 I don't think it'll rain tomorrow.
  I _____ . (doubt)
4 You'll definitely enjoy the film.
  I _____ . (sure)
5 It's possible that Ben will come round later.
  Ben _____ . (might)
6 I might not go to school tomorrow.
  I _____ . (may)
7 George will probably know the answer.
  I _____ . (think)
8 I doubt we'll go away this summer.
  We _____ . (probably)

3.2 First conditional

We use the first conditional to make predictions about the future.
If I'm late for school, my teacher will tell me off.

We form the first conditional with the present simple in the conditional clause and *will* + infinitive in the result clause.

Conditional clause	Result clause
If I'm late for school, (present simple)	my teacher will tell me off. (*will* + infinitive)

The conditional *if* clause usually comes first, but it can come after the result clause.
My teacher will tell me off if I'm late for school.

The modal verbs *may*, *might* and *could* can be used instead of *will* or *won't* in the result clause in order to make the prediction less certain.
Scientists may find a cure for cancer if governments invest more money in medical research.

1 Complete the first conditional sentences. Use the verbs in brackets.

1 If I _____ (not phone) my parents, they _____ (be) upset.
2 If I _____ (tell) you a secret, _____ (you / promise) not to tell anybody?
3 We _____ (have) a barbecue tomorrow if it _____ (not rain).
4 My mum _____ (not buy) me a new phone if I _____ (lose) this one.
5 What _____ (you / do) if you _____ (feel) unwell tomorrow morning?
6 If you _____ (give) me your number, I _____ (be able to) text you.
7 Joe _____ (make) Sally very happy if he _____ (send) her some chocolates.
8 If you _____ (not shout) at me, I _____ (not get) angry.

3.3 Future continuous and future perfect

We form the future perfect with *will have* + past participle.
She'll have finished that book soon.

We form the future continuous with *will be* + *-ing* form.
I'll be waiting for you at the bus stop.

We use the future perfect to talk about a completed action in the future. We use the future continuous to talk about an action in progress in the future. Look at the calendar and sentences below.

Now	Mon	Tue	Wed	Thu	Fri

✈ Amy is travelling to Japan

On Monday, Amy will be travelling to Japan. (The journey will be in progress.)
By Friday, Amy will have arrived in Japan. (The journey will be finished.)

1 Complete the sentences with the future continuous form of the verbs below.

have pack shine stay study visit

1 When I'm twenty, I _____ medicine at university.
2 Don't call me at 8 p.m. because we _____ dinner.
3 When I step off the plane in Jamaica, the sun _____ .
4 My cousin's in New York this week. Next week, she _____ San Francisco.
5 Tomorrow, my parents _____ their bags to go on holiday.
6 Come and see me in London. I _____ at the Savoy Hotel.

2 Complete the sentences. Use the future perfect form of the verbs in brackets.

1 Harry and Luke are going travelling for a month, but they _____ (return) before September.
2 They're building a new football stadium, but they _____ (not finish) it in time for next season.
3 I've sent grandad a postcard, but he _____ (not receive) it by the time we get home.
4 By this time next year, we _____ (do) all our exams.
5 Don't call for me before 7 p.m. because I _____ (not have) time to get changed.
6 When my dad retires next month, he _____ (be) with the same company for 36 years.

Unit 4

4.1 Comparison

The comparative and superlative forms of adjectives and adverbs with one syllable are formed by adding *-er* or *-est*. The same is true of adjectives with two syllables ending in *-y*.

Subject + verb	Comparative form	Object	
Zoe is	young (+ *er*) younger thin (+ n + *er*) thinner lazy (*y* + *ier*) lazier	than	Toby.
Zoe works	fast + (*er*) faster		

Subject + verb	Superlative form
Zoe is	(*the* +) young (+ *est*) the youngest. (*the* +) thin (+ n + *est*) the thinnest. (*the* +) lazy (*y* + *iest*) the laziest.
Zoe works	(*the* +) fast (+ *est*) the fastest.

The comparative and superlative forms of adjectives and adverbs with two syllables or more are formed by putting *more* or *the most* before the adjective or adverb.

Subject + verb	Comparative form	Object	
Zoe is	(*more* +) intelligent more intelligent (*more* +) generous more generous	than	Toby.
Zoe writes	(*more* +) clearly more clearly		

G Grammar Builder and Reference

Subject + verb	Superlative form
Zoe is	(the + most +) generous. the most generous.
Zoe writes	(the + most +) clearly. the most clearly.

We can also form comparatives and superlatives of adjectives and adverbs with *less* and *the least*.

Less is the opposite of *more*. *Least* is the opposite of *most*.

Subject + verb	Comparative form	Object	
Toby is	(less +) thin less thin (less +) intelligent less intelligent	than	Zoe.
Toby writes	(less +) clearly less clearly		

Subject + verb	Superlative form
Toby is	(the + least +) generous. the least generous.
Toby writes	(the + least +) clearly. the least clearly.

We can use *less* and *least* with uncountable nouns.
I've got less spare time than you.
Who's got the least money?

We often use *of* after superlative adjectives.
Jamie is the smallest of the three brothers.

But we use *in*, not *of*, with a group or place (e.g. *the world, the class, London*).
the best café in Oxford
the most intelligent boy in the class
the longest river in Africa

We can make comparisons with clauses as well as with nouns.
Gemma is more intelligent than you think.
The weather is hotter than it was last week.

We often use a superlative with the present perfect and *ever*.
Alex has got the biggest dog I've ever seen!

We can compare two things, using (*not*) *as … as*.
Julie is as tall as Mike. (= They are the same height.)
Leah isn't as tall as Joe. (= Joe is taller.)

We use double comparatives to emphasise that something is changing.
The weather is getting hotter and hotter.

We use *the … the* and comparatives to say that one thing changes with another.
The more carefully you check your work, the fewer mistakes you'll make.

Remember irregular comparative and superlative forms.

Adjective	Comparative	Superlative
good	better	the best
bad	worse	the worst
far	further	the furthest
Adverb	**Comparative**	**Superlative**
well	better	the best
badly	worse	the worst
far	further	the furthest

1 Correct the mistakes in the sentences.

1 I'm busyer today than I was yesterday.
2 He's the shortest boy of the class.
3 Kate's more short than Alice.
4 You're not as clever than me.
5 Today is longest day of the year.

2 Complete the sentences with the comparative form of the adverb in brackets and *than*.

1 Mum drives _____ Dad. (fast)
2 Dad drives _____ Mum. (well)
3 Fred writes _____ Grace. (beautifully)
4 Harry works _____ me. (slowly)
5 Pete usually arrives at school _____ than everyone else. (late)
6 Who speaks French _____ : Dave or Bess? (fluently)

3 Complete the sentences with the superlative form of the adverb in brackets.

1 Who writes _____ ? (neatly)
2 Sarah finished her homework _____ . (fast)
3 Tom plays chess _____ . (badly)
4 Joe speaks _____ . (loud)
5 Ian definitely tries _____ of all of us. (hard)
6 Who gets up _____ in your family? (early)

4 Rewrite the sentences with *less* or *least*.

1 Janet is more confident than Ryan.
   Ryan _____ Janet.
2 Hannah and Ellie are more intelligent than Vicky.
   Vicky _____ of the three girls.
3 Marcus's house and Daniel's house are more spacious than Donna's.
   Donna's house _____ of the three.
4 Harriet's flat is more cramped than Clare's flat.
   Clare's flat _____ Harriet's flat.
5 Jess and Maisy live in a more lively area than Annie.
   Annie lives _____ area.

5 Complete the sentences with *than* or *as* and the phrases below.

> I thought she would be   I was before
> it looks from the outside   ~~it used to be~~
> it was when I first moved into it   there used to be

1 This part of town is much less popular than it used to be.
2 My flat isn't as charming _____ .
3 The house is actually more spacious _____ .
4 Kelly wasn't as late _____ .
5 There are fewer contemporary buildings in the town centre _____ .
6 I'm happier in my new flat _____ .

6 **USE OF ENGLISH** Complete the second sentence so that it means the same as the first. Use the words in brackets.

1 My car is smaller than yours.
  My car _____ . (as)
2 There aren't as many people on the beach now.
  There _____ . (fewer)
3 Flats are usually cheaper than houses.
  Flats _____ . (expensive)
4 The weather is becoming increasingly hot.
  The weather _____ . (hotter)
5 We've never stayed in a less spacious hotel room.
  This is _____ . (least)
6 As you spend more on the flat, it becomes more valuable.
  The _____ . (the)
7 I didn't think the rent would be so high.
  The rent _____ . (than)

4.2 Second conditional

We use the second conditional to talk about an imaginary situation or event and its result.

If I lived in a bigger house, I'd have parties every weekend.

We form the second conditional by using the past simple in the conditional *if* clause and *would* + infinitive in the result clause.

Conditional clause	Result clause
If I lived by the sea, (past simple)	I'd learn to surf. (*would* + infinitive)

Notice that you can use *were* instead of *was* in the conditional clause with *I*, *he* and *she*. Both *was* and *were* are generally acceptable, although using *were* is considered more correct, especially in formal situations.

If I were you, I'd spend more time revising.
If she were older, she'd find her own flat.

We normally use *could* for *would* + *can*.

If we lived nearer to each other, we could meet up more often.

1 Complete the second sentence in each pair to mean the same as the first. Use the second conditional.

1 I can't drive a car; I'm too young.
  If _____ , _____ a car.

2 He won't offer you a job; you aren't reliable enough.
  If _____ , _____ a job.
3 She hasn't got a dog; her flat is really small.
  If her flat _____ , _____ a dog.
4 I can't use my brother's phone; I don't know the password.
  If I _____ , _____ my brother's phone.
5 She isn't a good guitarist; she doesn't practise.
  If _____ , _____ a good guitarist.
6 We can't go to the beach; it isn't sunny today.
  If _____ , _____ to the beach.

2 Complete these second conditional sentences with the correct verb form and your own ideas.

1 If I _____ (live) in the USA, _____ .
2 If I _____ (have) ten brothers and sisters, _____ .
3 If humans _____ (can) fly, _____ .
4 If I _____ (can) travel through time, _____ .
5 If computers _____ (not exist), _____ .
6 If I _____ (find) a diamond ring, _____ .

4.3 I wish … , If only …

We use *I wish* … or *If only* … with the past simple to say that we want a situation to be different from how it really is.

I live in a village. I wish I lived in a big city.

Notice that you can use *were* instead of *was* after *I wish* … or *If only* … .

It's Monday today, but I wish it were Saturday.

We use *I wish* … or *If only* … with *would* + the infinitive without *to* to say that we want somebody (or something) to behave differently.

I wish she wouldn't shout.
If only the phone would stop ringing.

1 Rewrite these critical sentences using *I wish* … or *If only* … + *would*.

1 Jack is always forgetting his sports kit.
  I wish Jack wouldn't forget his sports kit.
2 My dad is always singing in the shower.
3 She's always sending me text messages at night.
4 You're always borrowing my dictionary.
5 Our car is always breaking down on the motorway.
6 You're always telling people my secrets.

2 Complete the sentences with the past simple or *would* + the infinitive without *to* form of the verbs in brackets.

1 I wish I _____ (have) a brother or sister.
2 If only they _____ (stop) talking – I can't hear the film.
3 I wish you _____ (take) a photo of me so I could send it to my friends.
4 If only we _____ (understand) Spanish, we could ask for directions.
5 I wish you _____ (like) Chinese food; I don't want pizza again.
6 I wish you _____ (finish) that burger; I don't like the smell.

4.4 *would rather, had better*

We use *would rather* (*not*) + the infinitive without *to* to express a preference.
I'd rather (not) stay at home.

We use *would rather* + subject + past simple to say we would prefer a situation to be different.
She'd rather her friends were more outgoing.

We use *had better* + the infinitive without *to* to say what we or somebody else should do.
I'd / You'd better ask before I / you borrow that bike.

1 Write a preference using *I'd rather* and the words in brackets. Include any other words that are necessary.

1 My friends all play basketball. (football)
  I'd rather they played football.
2 I live near the sea. (mountains)
3 My sister often gives me books. (CDs)
4 My friend Sally always arrives late. (early)
5 My dad usually cooks pasta for dinner. (burgers)
6 Our neighbours have got a large dog. (a cat)

2 Rewrite the advice using *had better* instead of *should* or *ought to*.

1 I don't think you should phone her now.
  You'd better not phone her now.
2 I think we should save some money for the journey.
3 I don't think you should tell her about that email.
4 We ought to go home – it's late.
5 I think we should work hard for these exams.
6 I don't think you should drink that milk; it smells funny.

Unit 5

5.1 Quantifiers

Each, *every* and *either* are followed by a singular countable noun. *Each* and *every* have the same meaning. However, we often use *each* when all the people or things it refers to are seen individually. *Every* is used to refer to all the people or things.
I go to school every day except Sunday.
Each day is different.

Either is used when we want to refer to one thing or another.
I'll see you on either Saturday or Sunday.
'Tea or coffee?' 'I don't mind. Either is fine.'

Both means 'the two' or 'one and the other'.
'Do you prefer tea or coffee?' 'I like them both.'
I like both tea and coffee.

Few and *a few* are followed by a plural noun. *Few* has a negative meaning. *A few* has a neutral or positive meaning.
Few friends wanted to come to the cinema with me. It was a shame.
I went to the cinema with a few friends.

Little and *a little* are followed by an uncountable noun. *Little* has a negative meaning. *A little* has a neutral or positive meaning.
Sam works very hard and has little time for his friends.
I have a little time this evening. I can help you with your homework then.

Many is followed by a countable noun. *Much* is followed by an uncountable noun.
There aren't many students in the classroom.
I haven't got much money.

All, *most*, *some*, *any* and *no* can be followed by either a countable or an uncountable noun.
Most people here have no free time at the weekend.
Some books are missing, but all the CDs are here.

Most quantifiers can be followed by *of*.
A few of my friends came to the party. (plural noun)
All of the milk has been drunk. (uncountable noun)

When we use *no* and *every* with *of*, they change to *none* and *every one*. We use a plural noun with *every one*.
Every one of the students passed the exam. None of them failed.

In informal style, we use a plural verb with *none*. In formal style, we use a singular verb.
None of my friends were there. (informal)
None of my friends was there. (formal)

1 Put the nouns below into two lists: a) countable and b) uncountable.

document gadget habit health homework information money music software website

2 Choose the correct words to complete the sentences.

1 In our school, not **every** / **each** student studies English.
2 John can kick the ball really well with **either** / **both** foot.
3 The exam was very difficult, so **few** / **a few** managed to finish.
4 This coffee is rather bitter. Can you put **little** / **a little** sugar in it, please?
5 How **much** / **many** pizzas shall we buy?
6 Do **all** / **every** cats like milk?
7 The teacher has marked **every** / **all** piece of homework.
8 **All the** / **Every** student answered the question, but **each** / **every** student gave a different answer.

Grammar Builder and Reference

3 Answer the questions with complete sentences. Use the words in brackets.

1 Did you finish your homework? (most)
  I finished most of it.
2 Which friends are you going to invite to your party? (all)
3 How many wearable gadgets have you got? (any)
4 Do you prefer tablets or laptops? (like / both)
5 How much money have you got left? (a little)
6 How many students got full marks in the exam? (none)
7 Did you win all of your matches? (every)
8 Do you like Adele and Emeli Sandé? (either)

5.2 Modals in the past

We use *may / might / could have* for speculating about past events.

She may / might / could have sent me a message. (= It's possible she sent me a message, but I don't know.)

We use *may / might not have* (but not *could not have*) as the negative.

She might / may not have had her phone with her. (= It's possible she didn't have it, but I don't know.)

We use *must have* and *can't / couldn't have* to make logical deductions about the past.

You can't / couldn't have seen the new Batman film. It isn't out yet. (= It's not possible that you saw it.)
You must have seen an old Batman film. (= That is the only possible explanation.)

We use *should / shouldn't have* to criticise past actions.

You should have taken a taxi. It wasn't safe to walk.
She shouldn't have phoned me so late. I was asleep.

1 Choose the best words (a, b or c) to complete the sentences.

1 You look freezing. You ___ worn a coat.
  a should have **b** might not have **c** could have
2 Ask that question again; the teacher ___ heard you.
  a shouldn't have **b** could have **c** can't have
3 Your brother has been using your email account. You ___ told him your password.
  a must have **b** mustn't have **c** couldn't have
4 Jack is really upset. You ___ laughed at him!
  a may not have **b** can't have **c** shouldn't have
5 I sent you a postcard, but you ___ received it yet.
  a may have **b** should have **c** might not have
6 Your phone is dead. You ___ recharged it this morning.
  a might have **b** shouldn't have **c** can't have
7 I can't remember when I last saw you. Maybe it was last April, or it ___ been in the summer.
  a might have **b** must have **c** can't have
8 You ___ invited Sam to your party. He's a really nice guy.
  a can't have **b** should have **c** might not have
9 Let's run for the bus. It ___ left yet.
  a should have **b** may have **c** might not have

2 Complete the second sentence in each pair to mean the same as the first. Use modals in the past.

1 He can't have been at home.
  He must have been out.
2 I shouldn't have refused the invitation.
  I _____ accepted the invitation.
3 She may not have passed the exam.
  She _____ failed the exam.
4 They must have arrived late.
  They _____ arrived early.
5 You can't have switched the TV off.
  You _____ left the TV on.
6 We should have paid by credit card.
  We _____ paid with cash.
7 They couldn't have stolen the car during the day.
  They _____ stolen the car at night.
8 The pilot might not have died in the accident.
  The pilot _____ survived the accident.

5.3 *even though, in spite of, despite* and *although*

Even though, in spite of, despite and *although* are concession clauses. A concession clause introduces an idea which seems the opposite of the idea in the main clause or makes it more surprising.

Even though he's in his eighties, he still plays football.

We can use *although* or *even though* to introduce a concession clause. The clause can come before or after the main clause.

He smiled even though he felt angry.
Although he felt angry, he smiled.

Despite and *in spite of* also express concession, but are followed by a noun or *-ing* form, not a clause.

Despite / In spite of his anger, he smiled.

1 Complete the sentences with *despite / in spite of* or *although / even though*.

1 _____ exams are important, students also need to continue doing their hobbies.
2 Many young people enjoy extreme sports, _____ the danger.
3 Cooking is an important life skill, _____ many teenagers cannot do it.
4 Most teenagers relax in the evenings, _____ having large amounts of homework.
5 You learn as much from extra-curricular activities as you do in lessons, _____ you don't do exams in them.
6 You can learn a musical instrument at any age, _____ it's easier when you are young.

Unit 6

6.1 Defining relative clauses

Defining relative clauses come immediately after a noun and give vital information about that noun. They tell us which person, thing, or place we are talking about.

She's the nurse. (Which nurse?)
She's the nurse who looked after my father.

They can go in the middle or at the end of sentences.
The nurse who looked after my father is in her fifties.
This is the nurse who looked after my father.

Relative pronouns are different depending on whether they refer to people, places, things, or possessions.

Relative pronouns	
who (that)	people
where	places
which (that)	things
whose	possessions

Who or *which* can replace the subject or object of a sentence. When they replace the object, it is possible to omit *who* or *which*.

That's the boy who helped me. (subject)
That's the girl who I met at Jake's party. (object)
That's the girl I met at Jake's party. (omission)

We often use *that* instead of *which*, and can use *that* instead of *who* in informal English.

Here's the CD that you were asking about.
That's the girl that I met at Jake's party.

In very formal English, we can use *whom* instead of *who* when the pronoun is the object of the clause.

He was a leader whom many people admired.

Prepositions can go at the end of a relative clause or, in very formal style, at the start.

He didn't get the job which he applied for.
He wasn't appointed to the post for which he applied.

1 **USE OF ENGLISH** Choose the correct answer (a–d). Sometimes more than one answer is possible.

1 I met a boy ___ brother is in my class.
   a whose **b** that **c** which **d** no pronoun
2 He's the man ___ I saw on the train.
   a who **b** that **c** which **d** no pronoun
3 Is that the dictionary ___ you bought yesterday?
   a which **b** that **c** where **d** no pronoun
4 Show me the computer ___ you got for your birthday.
   a that **b** which **c** who **d** no pronoun
5 Is that the café ___ you worked last summer?
   a that **b** which **c** where **d** no pronoun
6 New Year's Day is the day ___ comes after New Year's Eve.
   a which **b** who **c** that **d** no pronoun
7 That's the girl ___ phone I borrowed.
   a whose **b** who **c** which **d** no pronoun

2 Join the two sentences together with a relative clause. Use the pronouns *who, which, where* or *whose*.

1 That's the man. / His job is to look after the garden.
   That's the man whose job is to look after the garden.
2 A hostel is a place. / You can stay there quite cheaply.
3 That's the song. / I listened to it at Emma's house.
4 He's the man. / I saw him on TV last night.
5 That's the hotel. / We stayed there last summer.
6 That's the dog. / It barked all night.
7 She's the girl. / I borrowed money from her.
8 That's the boy. / His father owns the shop on the corner.

6.2 Non-defining relative clauses

Non-defining relative clauses come immediately after a noun and give us extra (rather than vital) information about that noun. We often use them to combine information from two simple sentences.

Tom Hanks is a famous actor. He was born in California.
Tom Hanks, who was born in California, is a famous actor.

A non-defining relative clause can go in the middle or at the end of a sentence. It starts with a comma and ends with a comma (if it's the middle of the sentence) or a full stop (if it's the end).

We spent a week in Berlin, where my aunt lives.
Berlin, where my aunt lives, is a great place to visit.

In a non-defining relative clause, we can never omit the relative pronoun, nor can we replace *who* or *which* with *that*.

1 Complete the text with the clauses below (a–f). Add the correct relative pronoun to the start of each clause.

We walked up the steps and knocked on the door, **1**___ . For a minute or two, we heard nothing. Then Alex, **2**___ , knocked again. Almost immediately the door opened. There stood a man in a formal, black suit **3**___ . He smiled and invited us into the hall, **4**___ . 'Lord Bingley will be here shortly,' said the man in the suit, and left. I took out my phone, **5**___ , but the battery was completely dead. 'You should have recharged it,' said Alex, **6**___ . 'I did,' I said. 'Something strange is happening.'

a _____ I always carried in my pocket
b _____ was probably in fashion a hundred years ago
c _____ we stood and looked at the paintings on the wall
d _____ was heavy, dark and wooden
e _____ footsteps echoed loudly as he explored the impressive room
f _____ had insisted on coming with me

2 Combine each pair of sentences to make a single sentence with a non-defining relative clause.

1 The Grand Hotel has closed. We spent three weeks there one summer.
2 My neighbour is learning the guitar. He used to be a singer.
3 Our cousins often come to stay with us. Their parents travel a lot for work.
4 My new laptop has stopped working. It cost over £500.
5 The next bus goes directly to Heathrow Airport. It leaves in ten minutes.
6 There's a party this Friday at the Beat Café. We often go there at weekends.

6.3 Indirect questions

We make indirect questions with phrases like *Can you tell me … ?* and *Do you know … ?* We use them to sound more polite in formal situations.

Excuse me. Do you know where the bank is, please?

To make a *yes / no* question into an indirect question, we use *if* or *whether*.

Could you tell me if the film has started yet?
May I ask whether this seat is free?

To make a *wh-* question into an indirect question, we use the question word.

Would you mind telling me what time it is?

The word order and verb forms in an indirect question are the same as in an affirmative statement.

Could you tell me if there is a train to London after ten this evening?

1 Rewrite the questions as indirect questions. Use the phrases in brackets.

1 Where is the post office? (Could you tell me)
2 Do you have any mayonnaise? (I was wondering)
3 What time does the film finish? (I'd like to know)
4 What is your name? (May I ask)
5 What is the salary for this job? (I'd be interested to know)
6 Should I apply for the job online? (I'd like to know)
7 Did you receive my application? (I'd be interested to know)
8 When does the train leave? (Could you tell me)
9 Do you have a table for four? (I was wondering)
10 When will the interviews take place? (May I ask)

6.4 Preparatory *it*

In English, it sounds very formal and often unnatural to begin a sentence with an infinitive, an *-ing* form or a clause.

~~That she failed her driving test was surprising.~~ ✗
~~To wash your hands before eating is important.~~ ✗

It is far more common to begin this kind of sentence with a preparatory *it*.

It was surprising that she failed her driving test.
It is important to wash your hands before eating.

We use preparatory *it* with the verb *take* followed by an infinitive to talk about duration.

It takes half an hour to walk to school.

We use preparatory *it* followed by an *-ing* form in the following expressions.

It's no use / little use / not much use knocking – nobody's at home.
It's (not) worth asking for a refund if you don't like the food.

1 Rewrite these sentences in a more informal style. Begin each sentence with *It … .*

1 The fact that she once played football for England is true.
   It's true that she once played football for England.
2 To walk along a beach is very relaxing.
3 The fact that we arrived on time is amazing.
4 Asking for a pay rise is no use – you won't get it!
5 To go rock climbing on your own was dangerous.
6 The fact that the restaurant was closed was very disappointing.
7 To fish in this river is illegal.
8 Trying to push the car up the hill was no use.

Unit 7
7.1 The passive

We form the passive with the verb *be* + the past participle.

Tense	Passive form
present simple	Tyres are made of rubber.
present continuous	A new school is being built.
past simple	The CD was invented in 1982.
past continuous	I felt that I was being watched.
present perfect	My watch has been stolen.
past perfect	The money had been lost earlier.
future with *will*	The exam results will be announced tomorrow.

In passive constructions, we use *by* when we want to say who (or what) performed the action.

The TV was invented by John Logie Baird.

After modal verbs, we use a passive infinitive.

Homework must be handed in on time.
We're winning 2–0 with only a minute to go. We can't be beaten now.

1 Complete the passive sentences with the correct form of the verb *be*. One sentence has more than one correct answer.

1 Your homework _____ returned to you tomorrow afternoon.
2 As I was walking home last night, I thought that I _____ followed.
3 The road into town _____ closed for three days last week.
4 'Where _____ parmesan cheese made?' 'In Italy.'
5 Right now the match _____ watched by millions of people round the world.

6 My dress _____ cleaned, so I can wear it tonight.

7 I rang the station, and they told me that the train _____ cancelled.

2 Complete the sentences with the passive form of the verbs below. Use an appropriate tense.

destroy   film   perform   sell   steal   upload   use

1 Six paintings _____ from the museum last night.

2 We had to have our choir rehearsal outside yesterday because the school hall _____ for a meeting.

3 This play _____ only _____ two or three times in the last fifty years.

4 By the time they put the fire out, most of the opera house _____.

5 Millions of photos _____ to social networking sites every day.

6 When the new art gallery opens next year, the old art gallery _____ to property developers.

7 They're halfway through making the film. It _____ in the Middle East.

3 Complete the sentences with a modal verb followed by a passive infinitive. Use the words in brackets.

1 If it rains, the match _____ . (might / cancel)

2 During lessons, your mobile phone _____ in your bag. (must / leave)

3 Meat _____ right through. (should / cook)

4 Books _____ out of the library. (must not / take)

5 School uniforms _____ on the school trip. (needn't / wear)

7.2 *have something done*

You can use the structure *have* + object + past participle to say that you arranged for somebody to do something for you. (You didn't do it yourself.)

He had his car repaired.

I haven't had my hair cut for a year.

You can also use the structure for unpleasant things that have happened to you.

He had his phone stolen on holiday.

1 Complete the second sentence in each pair to mean the same as the first. Use the structure *have something done*.

1 Somebody vandalised our car at the weekend.
We _____ at the weekend.

2 They dyed Grace's hair at the hairdresser's.
Grace _____ at the hairdresser's.

3 They're going to repair my laptop by Monday.
I _____ by Monday.

4 They chose Seth's photo for the front cover of the magazine.
Seth _____ for the front cover of the magazine.

5 My uncle's nose was broken in a boxing match.
My uncle _____ in a boxing match.

6 Somebody designed a new website for my dad's business.
My dad _____ for his business.

2 Write true sentences about your own experiences using *have something done* and the words below.

1 hearing / test
I've never had my hearing tested. / I had my hearing tested when I was very young.

2 some money / steal

3 eyes / test

4 nails / paint

5 bike / repair

7.3 Reflexive pronouns

We use reflexive pronouns when the object of a verb is the same as the subject. We can't use an ordinary object pronoun.

I told myself to be brave.

NOT *I told me to be brave.* ✗

Subject pronoun	Reflexive pronoun
I	myself
you	yourself
he	himself
she	herself
it	itself
we	ourselves
you	yourselves
they	themselves

We can also use reflexive pronouns to add emphasis. The sentence makes sense without it.

They built that house (themselves).

1 Complete the sentences with the correct reflexive pronouns.

1 My sister injured _____ during a basketball match.

2 We must give _____ plenty of time to get to the cinema.

3 Calm down, Tom! You're making _____ anxious for no reason.

4 We saw a dog that had cut _____ on an old drinks can.

5 Can you and your friends find _____ something to eat?

6 My dad taught _____ the guitar last year.

7 I can't see _____ as a school teacher when I'm older.

8 She forced _____ not to think about her exams during the holiday.

2 Complete the sentences with the correct reflexive pronoun.

1 We couldn't find a good plumber, so we fitted the shower _____ .
2 Taste this soup – I made it _____ .
3 You must be able to read this note – you wrote it _____ !
4 My dad doesn't mind when I listen to loud music – he often does it _____ .
5 The drivers weren't hurt in the accident, but the car _____ was completely destroyed.
6 It's a beautiful hotel. You and your family should stay there _____ one day.

Unit 8

8.1 Reported speech

We use reported speech to report what someone has said without using the exact words.

When we change direct speech to reported speech, we often make the verb form go one tense back.
'Fred works in London,' said Ben.
Ben said that Fred worked in London.

Direct speech	Reported speech
Present simple	**Past simple**
'I like chips.'	He said he liked chips.
Present continuous	**Past continuous**
'She's working.'	He said she was working.
Past simple	**Past perfect**
'He went out.'	He said he had gone out.
Present perfect	**Past perfect**
'They've just arrived.'	He said they had just arrived.
Past perfect	**Past perfect**
'I hadn't noticed.'	She said she hadn't noticed.
can	**could**
'She can't swim.'	He said she couldn't swim.
will	**would**
'They will be here soon.'	He said they would be here soon.

These modal verbs don't usually change in reported speech:
might, should, could, would, must, would like.
'I might go to the concert.'
He said he might go to the concert.
'I'd like a coffee.'
She said she'd like a coffee.

The past perfect doesn't change in reported speech.
'I'd never eaten Chinese food.'
She said she'd never eaten Chinese food.

Verbs in subordinate clauses in the reported sentence usually change in the same way.
'I don't think I'll go out this evening.'
He said he didn't think he would go out that evening.

We always use a personal object with *tell*. With *say* we don't need a personal object.
I told you that I'd be late. / I said (to you) that I'd be late.

We often omit *that* in reported speech.
She said she was hungry.

The pronouns and possessive adjectives often change in reported speech.

'I'm cold,' she said.	(I → he / she)
She said she was cold.	
'We're tired,' they said.	(we → they)
They said they were tired.	
'I've borrowed your phone,' he said.	(your → my)
He said he had borrowed my phone.	

Time expressions often change.
'I saw Tom yesterday.'
He said he had seen Tom the day before.

Direct speech	Reported speech
now	then / at that moment
today	that day
tonight	that night
tomorrow	the following day
next week / month / year	the following week / month / year
an hour ago	an hour earlier
yesterday	the day before
last week / month / year	the week / month / year before

References to place can also change.
'I like it here,' said Mel.
Mel said she liked it there.

1 Complete the reported speech with the correct verb forms.

1 'Sue is sleeping,' said Toby.
  Toby said that Sue _____ .
2 'I can't find any clean socks,' said Barney.
  Barney said that he _____ any clean socks.
3 'I'll help Mum,' said William.
  William said that he _____ Mum.
4 'I hadn't thought of that,' said Max.
  Max said that he _____ of that.
5 'I've never been to Portugal,' said Joseph.
  Joseph said that he _____ to Portugal.
6 'Gemma might be at home,' said Fred.
  Fred said that Gemma _____ at home.
7 'Kate's going to the zoo,' said Mike.
  Mike said that Kate _____ to the zoo.
8 'We arrived ten minutes ago,' said Chris.
  Chris said that they _____ ten minutes before.

2 Complete the sentences with the correct form of *said* or *told*.

1 He _____ me that he was thirsty.
2 Sarah _____ to me that she would arrive at six.
3 Martin _____ Toby that he'd like to go to the cinema.
4 They _____ they would be here at four.
5 Did you _____ that you were thinking of becoming a doctor?
6 Kate _____ Madison would be angry with me.
7 Your brother _____ something to me, but I didn't hear it.
8 Juliet _____ it was difficult to hear what the actors were saying.

3 Report the sentences. Take care to change the pronouns and expressions of time correctly.

1 'I'll call you tomorrow,' said Tom to Ryan.
2 'We went to Paris last month,' Geoff told Gerard.
3 'I can't come to your house today,' said Julia to Miranda.
4 'I texted Joanna an hour ago,' Quentin told Leah.
5 'We're all going out tonight,' said Emma to Amy.
6 'I want you to be here at two o'clock this afternoon,' said Maisie to Sarah.

8.2 Reported questions

We use the reporting verb *ask* when reporting questions.
'Is it raining?' I asked.
I asked if it was raining.

When we change direct questions to reported questions, the verb form often goes one tense back, pronouns change and time expressions often change. These changes are the same as for other reported speech (see 8.1).
'What do you want to do tomorrow?' she asked me.
She asked me what I wanted to do the following day.

Notice that in a reported question the subject comes before the verb, and auxiliary verbs like *do* or *did* are not used.
'Where does your friend live?'
She asked me where my friend lived.

With *wh-* questions, we use the same question word in the reported question.
'What did you have for lunch?'
She asked me what I had had for lunch.

With *yes / no* questions, which have no question word, we use *if* or *whether* in the reported question.
'Are you ready?'
He asked her if / whether she was ready.

1 Complete the reported questions with a question word (*who, which, what, how* or *why*) or *if*.

1 I asked my brother _____ he was looking so sad.
2 She asked _____ my best friend's name was.
3 They asked her _____ her favourite subject was maths.
4 I asked my friends _____ they had felt about their exam results.

5 We asked the driver _____ the bus would arrive early or late.
6 He asked me _____ my birthday was.
7 She asked him _____ he could play the piano.
8 I asked her _____ she had ever been to China.

2 Write the direct questions that are reported in exercise 1.

1 '_____?' I asked my brother.
2 '_____?' she asked.
3 '_____?' they asked her.
4 '_____?' I asked my friends.
5 '_____?' we asked the driver.
6 '_____?' he asked me.
7 '_____?' she asked him.
8 '_____?' I asked her.

3 Write these questions as reported questions.

1 'Where's my dictionary?' my sister asked me.
   My sister asked me where . . .
2 'What did you do this morning?' I asked Anna.
3 'Are you going to Jake's party?' Lucy asked me.
4 'Why are you laughing at me?' Adam asked his mother.
5 'Will you be here all day?' I asked my uncle.
6 'Who told you about my idea?' my brother asked me.

8.3 Verbs with two objects

Some verbs can be followed by an indirect and a direct object. The indirect object comes first and is usually a person.
I gave my aunt a present.

If the direct object comes first, we usually have to put a preposition (*to* or *for*) in front of the indirect object.
She reads her children a story every evening.
BUT *She reads a story to her children every evening.*

Verbs which can be followed by two objects include:
bring buy cook find give lend make offer pass promise read sell send show tell

1 Rewrite the sentences without a preposition. (Put the indirect object first.)

1 I gave some amazing presents to my family this Christmas.
2 I didn't tell your secret to anybody.
3 We cooked a special meal for my parents last night.
4 My mum made a wonderful dinner for us.
5 We sold our old car to our next-door neighbours.
6 Have you offered a sweet to everybody in the class?
7 Please can you pass these books to Ben?
8 The estate agent found a much bigger flat for us.

Unit 9
9.1 Third conditional

We form the third conditional with *if* + past perfect, *would have* + past participle.
If you'd gone to bed earlier, you wouldn't have fallen asleep in class.

Grammar Builder and Reference

We use the third conditional to talk about imaginary situations and to say how things could have been different in the past.
If we'd left earlier, we wouldn't have missed the train.

We often use *if* to express regret or criticism.
If you'd been more careful, you wouldn't have dropped those plates.
You would have passed your exams if you'd worked a bit harder.

We can also put the *if* clause at the end of the sentence.
I'd have invited you if I'd known you liked fancy-dress parties.

Notice the short forms used in third conditional sentences. The short form of both *had* and *would* is *'d*.
If I'd had more money, I'd have paid for you.

In spoken English, we often shorten both *would* and *have* in the main clause. However, in written English, we don't usually shorten both forms.

Spoken:

> If I hadn't run out of petrol, I'd've come by car.

Written:
If I hadn't run out of petrol, I'd have come by car.

1 **Write third conditional sentences. Use the verbs in brackets.**

1 If I _____ (drive) faster, we _____ (arrive) before six.
2 If Mary _____ (get) to the cinema earlier, she _____ (see) the start of the film.
3 You _____ (know) what to do if you _____ (listen) to the instructions.
4 You _____ (not cut) yourself if you _____ (not be) so careless with the knife.
5 If I _____ (have) the time, I _____ (call) you.
6 I _____ (not get) angry if you _____ (not be) so rude!
7 Do you think you _____ (pass) your exams if you _____ (work) harder?

2 **Rewrite the two sentences as one. Use the third conditional.**

1 You didn't go to bed early. You were tired the following morning.
   If you'd gone to bed early, you wouldn't have been tired the following morning.
2 Emma didn't catch the bus. She had to walk to school.
3 The tickets were expensive. I didn't travel by plane.
4 I ate too much. I felt ill.
5 I spent all my money. I was broke.
6 I took a painkiller. My headache went away.
7 We didn't save a lot of money. We weren't able to buy a new car.

9.2 Participle clauses

We use participle clauses to give more information about a noun. They can be described as shortened relative clauses (defining or non-defining).
Defining:
A woman wearing a yellow T-shirt ran out of the shop. (= who was wearing a yellow T-shirt)

Non-defining:
Her uncle, looking anxious, was standing on the pavement. (= who was looking anxious)

Participle clauses can begin with either a present participle (*-ing* form) or past participle. Clauses with a present participle (*-ing* form) replace an active verb. The verb they replace can be in any tense.
Outside the café, there was a man selling postcards. (= who was selling postcards)
She gave me a box containing some old letters. (= which contained some old letters)

Clauses with a past participle replace a passive verb. The verb they replace can be in any tense.
A Roman vase found in France last year is being sold. (= which was found in France last year)

1 **Rewrite the sentences using participle clauses to replace the relative clauses.**

1 I saw three men who were arguing about a taxi.
   I saw three men arguing about a taxi.
2 We talked to a young man who wanted to study in England.
3 A suspected burglar, who had been arrested by the police, has escaped.
4 My uncle bought a pen that was made of gold.
5 She was wearing a necklace that belonged to her grandmother.
6 Three men, who were coming out of the restaurant late at night, saw the robbery.

9.3 Reply questions

We use a reply question to respond to a statement. They express interest or surprise.
'I've bought a new bike.'
'Have you? How could you afford it?'

We use the verb *be*, auxiliary verbs (*do, have*), or modal verbs (*will, would*, etc.), depending on the tense and verb form in the statement.
'He hasn't seen that film.'
'Hasn't he? Well, let's rent it, then.'
'I hate cats.'
'Do you? I thought you liked them.'

Tense	Statement	Reply question
Present simple	I like dogs.	Do you?
Present continuous	He's eating.	Is he?
Past simple	She broke her arm.	Did she?
Present perfect	It's finished.	Has it?
Past perfect	They hadn't met.	Hadn't they?

can	She can't swim.	Can't she?
will	She won't forget.	Won't she?
would	He'd enjoy skiing.	Would he?

Notice these special cases:

'I'm not hungry.' 'Aren't you?' NOT ~~Amn't you?~~ ✗

'You never invite me to your house.' 'Don't I?'

'Nothing bad happened.' 'Didn't it?'

'Nobody wants to sit next to me.' 'Don't they?'

1 Match the reply questions (a–e) with the statements (1–5).

1	Yesterday was Monday.	**a** Didn't it?
2	Nothing exciting happened on holiday.	**b** Did it?
3	Our dog had never run away before.	**c** Was it?
4	The train had to stop suddenly.	**d** Has it?
5	My laptop has broken again.	**e** Hadn't it?

2 Write reply questions for these statements.

1 I want to go somewhere different for my holiday this year.
2 Nobody told me about your accident.
3 I'm not ready to go out yet.
4 Our friends hardly ever go out during the week.
5 It costs a lot to send texts abroad.
6 Gorillas can't swim.
7 I'd rather spend this weekend at home.
8 My parents wouldn't enjoy skiing.

9.4 Question tags

We use question tags when we want somebody to confirm something that we are saying. A statement with a question tag often sounds more polite than a direct question or a plain statement.

You live in Madrid, don't you?

When the main verb is affirmative, the question tag is negative, and vice versa.

She was late, wasn't she?
She wasn't late, was she?

We use the verb be, auxiliary verbs (do, have), or modal verbs (will, would, etc.), depending on the tense of the verb in the statement.

Tense	Statement	Question tag
Present simple	She likes dogs,	doesn't she?
Present continuous	He's eating,	isn't he?
Past simple	She broke her arm,	didn't she?
Present perfect	It's finished,	hasn't it?
Past perfect	They hadn't met,	had they?
can	She can't swim,	can she?
will	She won't forget,	will she?
would	He'd enjoy skiing,	wouldn't he?
let's	Let's go to the park,	shall we?

Notice these special cases:

I'm the winner, aren't I?

It hardly ever rains here, does it?

Let's go to the park, shall we?

Nothing's wrong, is it?

Nobody minds if I eat the last piece, do they?

1 Match the question tags below with statements 1–8.

aren't I? didn't you? had you? shall we? were they?
weren't they? will we? wouldn't you?

1 You hadn't seen your friends for years, _____
2 Let's go away for a few days, _____
3 You'd rather be alone this evening, _____
4 Nobody was surprised at his decision, _____
5 We won't arrive on time, _____
6 Your parents were teachers, _____
7 I'm the best chess player in the school, _____
8 You had double maths this morning, _____

2 Add a question tag to these statements.

1 Is isn't too late to change my mind, _____?
2 Nobody wants to go home, _____?
3 We hadn't finished that pizza, _____?
4 You can't see my phone, _____?
5 That shop is never open, _____?
6 Your dad wouldn't give us a lift, _____?
7 You're hardly ever at home, _____?
8 Let's buy some popcorn, _____?
9 I'm your best friend, _____?
10 They aren't listening, _____?
11 Calls from abroad cost a lot, _____?
12 I'll see you soon, _____?

9.5 so and such

We can use so and such to intensify the meaning of an adjective or an adverb.

- be + so + adjective
  I'm so tired!
- so + adverb
  You write so quickly!
- such + a / an + adjective + singular noun
  He's such a rude man.
- such + adjective + plural noun / uncountable noun
  They serve such delicious chips / pizza.

1 Complete the sentences with so or such.

1 The guard on the train was _____ impolite to me!
2 This is _____ a dirty seat!
3 The tickets were _____ expensive!
4 We waited _____ a long time for the train.
5 They serve _____ horrible food in buffet cars!
6 The clerk in the ticket office spoke _____ quickly that I couldn't understand her.
7 Why did the tram travel _____ slowly?
8 There are usually _____ long queues at the ticket machines that I buy my tickets online.

Extra Speaking Tasks

Unit 3

1 SPEAKING Work in pairs. Take turns to describe the photo and do the task below.

1 Do you think the people in the photo spend a lot of time at the gym? What makes you think so?
2 Do you think fitness classes are the best way to get fit? Why? / Why not?
3 Tell me about an occasion when you needed to be fit.

Unit 4

1 SPEAKING Work in pairs. Take turns to do the task below.

You are going to study in the UK. You are looking for a flat to rent with a friend. Compare and contrast the photos above and say which flat you would choose and why.

Unit 5

1 SPEAKING Work in pairs. Take turns to describe and compare the photos. Then ask and answer one question each.

1 Do you agree that in the modern world, science is a more important subject than languages? Give reasons.
2 Do you think technology sometimes makes it harder for people to communicate with each other? Why? / Why not?

Unit 7

1 SPEAKING Work in pairs. Do the task below, using phrases from lesson 7G to help you.

Your English penfriend is staying with you. Your parents have offered to buy you and your penfriend tickets to one of the events in the photos below. You and your penfriend should decide which event is most suitable and talk about the details of the outing. Use the ideas below to help you:

- when to go
- how to book tickets
- travelling to the show
- what to eat and drink